P9-BTN-221

THE MODERN LANGUAGE ASSOCIATION
OF AMERICA

Approaches to Teaching
Masterpieces of World Literature

Joseph Gibaldi, Series Editor

Approaches to Teaching Cervantes' *Don Quixote*

Edited by

Richard Bjornson

The Modern Language Association of America   1984

Copyright © 1984 by The Modern Language Association of America

Library of Congress Cataloging in Publication Data

Main entry under title:

Approaches to teaching Cervantes' Don Quixote.

(Approaches to teaching masterpieces of world
literature; 3)
  Bibliography: p.
  Includes index.
  1. Cervantes Saavedra, Miguel de, 1547–1616—Study
and teaching.   2. Cervantes Saavedra, Miguel de,
1547–1616. Don Quixote.   I. Bjornson, Richard.
II. Series.
PQ6344.A66 1984   863′.3   83-23797
ISBN 0-87352-479-9
ISBN 0-87352-480-2 (pbk.)

Cover illustration in paperback edition: title page of the second edition of *Don
Quixote*, Part 1 (1617)

Published by The Modern Language Association of America
62 Fifth Avenue, New York, New York 10011

CONTENTS

Critical Approaches and the Teaching of *Don Quixote*

Background Materials and the Teaching of *Don Quixote*

Teaching Nonmajors

Participants in Survey of *Quixote* Instructors

Works Cited

Index

PREFACE TO THE SERIES

In his thoughtful and sensitive book *The Art of Teaching* (1950), Gilbert Highet wrote, "Bad teaching wastes a great deal of effort, and spoils many lives which might have been full of energy and happiness." All too many teachers have failed in their work, Highet argued, simply "because they have not thought about it." We hope that the Approaches to Teaching Masterpieces of World Literature series, sponsored by the Modern Language Association's Committee on Teaching and Related Professional Activities, will not only improve the craft—as well as the art—of teaching but also encourage serious and continuing discussion of the aims and methods of our teaching.

The principal objective of the series is to collect within each volume a number of points of view on teaching a particular work of world literature that is widely taught at the undergraduate level. The preparation of each volume begins with a survey of instructors who have considerable experience in teaching the work. The survey enables us to include in the volume the philosophies and approaches, thoughts and methods of scores of experienced teachers. The result is a sourcebook of material, information, and ideas on teaching the work to undergraduates.

This series is intended to serve nonspecialists as well as specialists, inexperienced as well as experienced teachers, graduate students who wish to learn effective ways of teaching as well as senior professors who wish to compare their own approaches with the approaches of colleagues in other schools. Of course, no volume in the series can ever substitute for erudition, intelligence, creativity, and sensitivity in teaching. We hope merely that each book will point readers in useful directions; at most each will offer only a first step in the long journey to successful teaching.

In a time that increasingly demands a rededication to undergraduate teaching of the humanities and to the idea of a liberal education, it may well be that our sometimes divided and fragmented profession will rediscover in its concern for and commitment to teaching a sense of purpose, unity, and community that many believe it presently lacks. We hope that the Approaches to Teaching Masterpieces of World Literature series will serve in some small way to refocus attention on the importance of teaching and to improve undergraduate instruction. We may perhaps adopt as keynote for

viii   PREFACE TO THE SERIES

the series Alfred North Whitehead's observation in *The Aims of Education* (1929) that a liberal education "proceeds by imparting a knowledge of the masterpieces of thought, of imaginative literature, and of art."

Joseph Gibaldi
Series Editor

PREFACE TO THE VOLUME

Don Quixote is one of the best-known fictional characters ever created. Young children delight in the image of a gaunt would-be knight jousting at windmills or charging headlong into a flock of sheep. For many older readers, Cervantes' hero embodies the noble quest for a romantic ideal in a corrupt and fallen world, whereas others regard him as a quintessentially comic figure. The masterpiece in which his adventures are recounted has been read and interpreted in many different ways. Indeed, it has provoked commentary by some of the best critical minds in the Western world, frequently serving them as a point of departure for their own speculations about the nature of being human. Don Quixote is unquestionably one of the richest and most complex texts in our literary heritage, but that is one of the reasons why teaching it continues to be such a challenging and rewarding experience for instructors of undergraduate literature courses.

How can one stimulate an intelligent appreciation for the breadth of Cervantes' seventeenth-century genius among students whose tastes, frames of reference, and attitudes toward literature have been formed in the late twentieth century? How can one provide students with the factual and historical background needed to understand the work without reducing the intensity of their first serious encounter with it? Although answers to such questions can often be found only in the actual process of teaching, new instructors of Don Quixote would undoubtedly benefit from knowing what resources are available to them and what approaches have been successfully adopted by others. Unfortunately, information on texts, secondary materials, and audiovisual aids is not always readily accessible, and teachers of literature seldom have the opportunity to discuss alternative modes of teaching with their colleagues. For this reason, the present volume brings together an overview of available materials, a survey of classroom techniques, and a series of essays in which experienced teachers explain how they have taught the novel. Although beginning instructors and nonspecialists might be expected to derive the greatest profit from this collection, even the most seasoned Cervantistas may discover that it contains much that is of interest to them and their students.

The volume itself is divided into two sections. The first, entitled "Materials," contains descriptions of available texts, translations, reference works, secondary sources, and aids to teaching. It was compiled on the basis of responses to several hundred questionnaires sent to Quixote instructors throughout the United States and Canada in early 1981. The survey provides a remarkable composite account of the methods and ancillary materials currently being used to teach Cervantes' novel. The second section, "Approaches," consists of fifteen essays by a representative cross section of instructors who, having participated in the survey, were invited to explain their classroom techniques in greater detail. Although their contributions do not exhaust the range of possible approaches to *Don Quixote*, they do contain numerous interpretive and pedagogical insights that may assist teachers who find themselves confronted by similar situations and problems. The handbook concludes with a list of those who participated in the original survey, a bibliography of works cited, and an index of proper names.

Many individuals have helped in the preparation of this volume. Participants in the survey generously shared their knowledge and experience with me; I learned a great deal from their considered responses and would like to acknowledge my debt to them. I would also like to thank the MLA Committee on Teaching and Related Professional Activities for their endorsement of the project. The series editor Joseph Gibaldi made many valuable suggestions. Carole Slade and James A. Castañeda read the entire manuscript, and their comments were extremely useful in improving the final version. John Jay Allen and Howard Mancing also read parts of the text and offered insightful suggestions. Bill and Colleen Love helped in many ways; Kim Hill, Dorothy Shoemaker, and Paul Grunden typed portions of the manuscript. For encouragement and support as I worked on this project, I am also grateful to Diether Haenicke, Michael Curran, Marilyn Waldman, Ron Rosbottom, and Don Larson.

The preparation of this volume has been a rewarding experience, because it has convinced me that the masterpieces of world literature continue to be taught with ingenuity, integrity, and a deep sense of commitment. Such works can exert a humanizing influence on contemporary readers, and if this book contributes in some small way to the promotion of excellence in teaching *Don Quixote* and works like it, I will be extremely gratified.

RB

Part One

MATERIALS

Richard Bjornson

EDITIONS

The choice of a text for teaching *Don Quixote* depends on a number of factors—whether the book is to be taught in Spanish or in English, to freshmen and sophomores or to advanced undergraduates and graduate students, for an entire semester or as part of a broader survey course. The previous background of students enrolled in the course and the individual instructor's preferences for annotation and critical apparatus also help determine the most appropriate text. One respondent to the preliminary survey of *Don Quixote* instructors expresses a preference for editions with as few notes as possible because she wants her students to focus on the narrative itself; however, most teachers feel that some explanatory materials help students orient themselves in a complex fictional world where many words, gestures, and actions no longer convey the same meanings they did for seventeenth-century Spanish readers. More mundane considerations—such as cost, availability, format, and legibility—can also affect the choice.

No single edition of *Don Quixote* is equally appropriate for all classroom situations, and each teacher will have to evaluate the available texts on the basis of his or her own needs. The purpose of the following discussion is not to make such evaluations but to present an objective overview of editions currently being used and to provide college and university teachers with information they can use in making their own choices.

Specific features of an edition often influence students' impressions of a literary work, and reasons for liking or disliking it can differ considerably from one generation of students to the next. For example, the linguistic ability of students and their capacity to understand literary or cultural allusions may change over the years. Advances in textual scholarship and the growth of critical commentary also render some older editions obsolete. Although one respondent to the survey alternates among three different editions to "have variety" and "break the monotony of repetitious preparation," most teachers express an understandable reluctance to change texts: they became familiar with a particular edition in graduate school, it contains all their marginal notes, their lectures are keyed to it, or it contains supporting material they regard as essential. Nevertheless, new editions in Spanish and English have appeared, and some teachers might find it useful to compare the new editions with the ones they are using.

In the following discussion, available editions are described under three headings: Spanish texts, English translations, and anthologies in both languages. Emphasis is placed on the reliability and completeness of texts, the extensiveness of the scholarly apparatus, and the usefulness of the format; observations and suggestions made by those who have taught *Don*

Quixote in different classroom situations are also included. Full bibliographical references for all works mentioned in this volume are listed at the
end of the book.

Spanish Texts

Most of those who teach *Don Quixote* in Spanish use one of Martín de
Riquer's frequently reprinted editions. In 1944, his compact, single-volume
text was first published by Juventud; six years later, this edition was revised
and reissued with many new annotations and an index of names and
situations. In both editions there was a useful map of Don Quixote's
journey. When a new edition by Riquer was brought out in 1962 by Planeta,
it contained a vastly improved text with many fewer errors. This edition no
longer included the map or the index, but it did contain an excellent
introduction as well as the complete text of Avellaneda's apocryphal
continuation. A revised paperback version of this edition in 1975 retained
the introduction but dropped the false sequel that had influenced
Cervantes' composition of his own *Don Quixote*, part 2. This edition did
not reprint the map that many teachers had found useful in the Juventud
editions, but the index was readopted and the superior text was of course
retained.

Riquer's editions were standard university texts for teaching *Don
Quixote* during the 1950s and 1960s; many graduate students became
familiar with them at that time and continued to use them when they
started to teach. In fact, the same qualities that initially led to the
widespread acceptance of Riquer's texts still recommend them for use in
the classroom. Respondents to the survey describe them (and particularly
the Planeta edition) as accurate, reliable, complete, legibly printed, cheap,
and readily available in college and university bookstores. They find the
annotations helpful and reasonably complete without being excessive,
distracting, or burdensome to students. Others praise the well-informed
introductory materials in the later editions.

The Juventud edition remains in print, but Riquer's Planeta paperback
has probably supplanted it in most American classrooms where *Don
Quixote* is taught in the original Spanish. Although the Planeta edition no
longer has the map printed in the earlier Juventud editions, it does contain
Riquer's seventy-two-page introduction; a brief biography of Cervantes;
and commentaries on the literary background, Quixote's madness, the
composition, the style, and literary types, as well as the index of names and
situations. The presence of these materials prompts one advocate of this
edition to conclude that it "best takes into account the literary context that
informs the work." Others remark that chapter numbers on each odd-

numbered page help readers locate passages quickly, that the compactness of its one-volume format allows students to bring the entire work to class each day, and that it is the cheapest, most readily available edition that is both adequate from a scholarly point of view and appropriate for use in the classroom.

Robert M. Flores' work on the typesetting of the first and second editions of *Don Quixote*, however, calls into question some of Riquer's editorial choices. Three recent paperbacks have responded in varying degrees to this new information—John Jay Allen's two-volume edition (1977), Luis Murillo's three-volume edition (1978), and Juan Bautista Avalle-Arce's two-volume edition (1979). They have all gained some acceptance in American classrooms.

Of the three, Allen most frequently adopts Flores' principles of emendation. He also develops a consistent method for regularizing the spelling, a procedure that he convincingly justifies in his preface and that American students will certainly appreciate. Appropriately addressed to the broad range of students one might encounter in an advanced undergraduate Spanish class, the introduction contains a biographical sketch, an account of literary backgrounds, a critical discussion of various aspects of the book, and a consideration of its reception by subsequent generations of readers. This introduction is followed by an excellent bibliography. The brief annotations are relevant to an understanding of the text; most of them identify the meanings of words or literary, historical, and geographical allusions rather than present lengthy interpretations or philological commentaries, which most students disregard in any case. Although one instructor laments the sparseness of the notes in Allen's edition, another praises it for "not wasting space on long footnotes about trifles." The bibliography is highly selective, but the works included in it are particularly well chosen for students who are reading the book for the first time and who need guidance in approaching the enormous body of available secondary materials. The attractiveness of this book is enhanced by Pilar Coomonte's line drawings, but the lack of chapter numbers at the tops of pages and the absence of an index make it difficult to locate passages quickly. It should also be pointed out that Allen's edition, although less expensive than those of Avalle-Arce and Murillo, is slightly more costly than Riquer's. Some teachers who know and respect the newer texts continue to use the older one because it is cheaper and because it is bound in a single, easily manageable volume; however, Allen's edition was published simultaneously in Spain and in the United States, and the American version has become competitive in price with Riquer's Planeta edition.

Murillo's approach to annotating *Don Quixote* differs from that of Allen, for he clearly addresses more scholarly readers seeking to orient themselves in the complex world of Cervantine commentary. The third volume of his edition consists of an excellent bibliography of over five hundred items; its schematic organization facilitates the location of books and articles on specific topics. Of particular interest to teachers is the final segment, devoted to themes, episodes, and characters in the novel. This arrangement makes it easy to find essays or sections of books on, for example, Cide Hamete Benengeli or the adventure of the lions. The footnotes in Murillo's text, mostly substantive and more numerous than those in Allen's edition, employ a convenient system of reference to the bibliography for readers who want to pursue a given point further in the abundant secondary literature. Murillo's biographical and critical introductions to the two parts of the novel are relatively brief but scholarly and well-informed. There are a dozen illustrations, including reproductions of frontispieces in chivalric romances, engravings by Hogarth and Doré, and the famous painting by Daumier. Nearly every teacher who uses Murillo's edition praises its meticulous text, its comprehensive notes, its cogent introduction, and its "up-to-date, handy bibliography," although some of them complain that the lack of an index and the failure to include chapter numbers at the tops of pages in the text make it difficult to locate passages. A rather large number of instructors express admiration for Murillo's edition but add that it is too expensive for their students.

Avalle-Arce's edition is printed in a more generous format than the others, and it has larger, more legible type. As one respondent to the survey writes, it is "well laid out and extremely readable." It also contains chapter numbers at the tops of pages and an excellent index of proper names, geographical locations, literary works mentioned, and first lines of poems in the text. Written in a lively style, Avalle-Arce's introduction deals first with textual problems, in particular those raised by the work of Flores, and then moves on to consider the novel's structure; its ideas, themes, and characters; and Cervantes' role in the development of the novel as a literary genre. This discussion is followed by a listing of the principal editions of *Don Quixote* and a rather cursory bibliographical notice. There are numerous footnotes in the text, and many of them are interpretive. Those familiar with Avalle-Arce's previous criticism will undoubtedly recognize some of his dominant concerns in the introduction and footnotes to this edition. As with Murillo, several teachers recommend Avalle-Arce's text but continue to use Riquer's because it is less expensive.

Although seriously outdated, Francisco Rodríguez Marín's eight-volume Clásicos Castellanos edition (1911–13) still has adherents among teachers of *Don Quixote*. One instructor characterizes it as the best available version and commends its scholarly notes, and another points out that it is easy to obtain. The numerous footnotes in this edition are mostly philological, and they do not always bear directly on the text, but they do constitute a rich source of information about literary allusions, linguistic conventions, and usage in Golden Age Spain. Nevertheless, most teachers regard this material as expendable and the overall format as bulky and cumbersome. The introduction is not substantive, there is no index, and the individual volumes are poorly bound. In addition, Rodríguez Marín revised his work when he prepared subsequent editions for different publishers, and these revisions were never incorporated into the Clásicos Castellanos edition. With recent increases in book prices, the cost of eight separate volumes has risen more sharply than that of the single-volume Riquer edition. Several teachers who formerly used the Clásicos Castellanos edition have felt obliged to abandon it for this reason. One respondent reports that he has successfully used Rodríguez Marín's ten-volume Atlas edition (1947–49). According to him, its extensive annotation and carefully established text make it the best edition available, although he admits that it is now difficult to find and very expensive. Several other teachers urge their students to consult the Atlas edition for reference and collateral reading.

A few instructors employ the Colección Austral edition (1940) because it is cheap and readily available, but others regard this inexpensive paperback as unreadable, and one person who taught from it once has vowed never to do so again because "it started to fall apart midway through the course." There are few notes and no critical apparatus in this edition, and the text is not always as reliable as the others. An edition published by Porrúa (1966) is also still used, partly because it is so cheap. This version has hard-to-read double columns and no footnotes, but it does contain an important prologue by Américo Castro, who discusses *Don Quixote* within its sociohistorical context; a biographical sketch of Cervantes, also by Castro; and an extremely helpful analytical index prepared by José Bergúa. Organized according to subject headings, the index enables readers to locate passages and references that cannot be found in the more conventional onomastic indices. The De Onís edition (1958) and the Cortázar-Lerner edition (1969) are seldom used, but the latter does contain an introduction by Marcos Morínigo, extensive annotations (which are indexed), and numerous colorful but highly abstract illustrations by Roberto Páez. There is also a Danish edition of part 1 in simplified Spanish, *Don Quijote de la Mancha, edición simplificada para uso escolar y autoestudio* (1972), but it is seldom assigned as a text because teachers regard its version of Cervantes' style as inappropriate. At the present time, R. M. Flores is preparing a modern-spelling version of the novel, which may eventually prove attractive for use in lower-level Spanish classes.

The only edition of Cervantes' complete works currently used for teaching *Don Quixote* in this country is the single-volume *Obras completas*

(1943), edited and with an introduction by Angel Valbuena Prat. The advantage of this Aguilar publication is obvious, for it permits students to consult *La Galatea*, the exemplary novels, *Persiles y Sigismunda*, and Cervantes' lesser-known works. The disadvantage is also obvious. Double columns of closely spaced print on thin paper make the text of this 1,800-page tome rather tiresome to read. The introduction is not particularly useful, and there are no annotations, although there is an index of characters and place names. A committee from the Cervantes Society of America has begun to prepare an edition of the complete works, and it will probably be available for classroom use in several years.

English Translations

The most widely used translation of *Don Quixote* is still the one originally published by Samuel Putnam in 1949, either in the complete Modern Library edition or in abridged versions included in the Viking *Portable Cervantes* and the popular *Norton Anthology of World Masterpieces*. Many teachers feel that this translation captures the tone, texture, structure, style, and spirit of the original more effectively than other available editions. Some choose the Putnam translation because they regard it as standard, least objectionable, or most easily obtainable, but some experts in the field call it unreliable and inaccurate. In his essay "*Traduttori Traditore: Don Quixote* in English," John Jay Allen points out a significant number of mistranslations in the Putnam edition, contending that "one case in four of verbal irony was lost or significantly distorted" (12) and concluding that it is "unacceptable as a text" (5); however, he also observes that a respect for narrative context prevents Putnam from committing some of the errors perpetrated by other modern translators. Allen's opinion is not universally shared among Hispanists: for example, Joseph R. Jones, who recently collaborated on a new translation of *Don Quixote*, expresses "nothing but admiration for [Putnam's] splendid translation."

The Modern Library edition contains a discussion of previous *Don Quixote* translations into English, a survey of the problems that any translator of the novel will encounter, and a brief sketch of Cervantes' life. Several teachers describe the notes in this edition as "very helpful." Others complain that the notes are difficult to consult because they are gathered together after the first and second parts of the novel rather than listed at the foot of each page. This practice might be an advantage for instructors who want students to focus primarily on the narrative, for the uncluttered pages and larger type of the Modern Library text do make for a readable format. A bibliography at the end of this volume lists English, French, German, and

Italian translations; Spanish texts of *Don Quixote;* and other sources Putnam used in compiling his notes.

The abridgment of this translation in the Viking *Portable Cervantes,* commonly used in large survey courses, contains a new introduction in which Putnam discusses the life of Cervantes as well as the reception and overall design of *Don Quixote.* This section is followed by "Suggested Readings in English," now outdated, and an "Editor's Note" that explains Putnam's principles of abridgment. Omissions from the text are not always clearly indicated, but Putnam does supply summaries for the longer excisions. Some instructors regard the loss of "The Curious Impertinent," parts of the Sierra Morena episode, Camacho's wedding, and the meeting with Don Diego as unfortunate, although others see Putnam's abridged version as an essential *Don Quixote* that can be reasonably taught in a survey course. Two exemplary novels ("Rinconete and Cortadillo" and "Man of Glass") and Cervantes' "Farewell to Life" (a short excerpt from *Persiles and Sigismunda*) are also included in this edition. Notes for the entire book are printed at the end of the volume; they represent a highly condensed version of the notes from Putnam's earlier edition. Teachers who use the Viking *Portable Cervantes* generally regard these notes as not very helpful, excessively brief, and in some cases counterproductive.

When students are asked to read a complete English version of *Don Quixote,* they are often assigned J. M. Cohen's Penguin edition (1950). Just as there are strong proponents of Putnam's translation style, there are those who vociferously reject his version and defend the one produced by Cohen. It is "the most reliable and readable translation in recent times," one teacher of the book declares unequivocally, and another contends that it best renders the flavor of the original text. The advocates of Cohen's edition praise his less archaic, more readable style: they claim that it does not sound translated or seem "stuffy and old-fashioned," an important consideration when students are asked to read rapidly. As one Cervantes specialist declares, it is "written in good, clear, supple English without affection; more lively than Putnam, yet more faithful to the original Spanish." Another Cervantes expert, however, accuses Cohen of attempting to "fix" some of Cervantes' supposed mistakes, and one teacher contends that Cohen's translation overemphasizes the farcical, slapstick elements in *Don Quixote* at the expense of its more serious overtones.

Cohen's translation begins with a brief critical and biographical introduction, but it contains no further scholarly apparatus. Footnotes are almost entirely absent, and there is no bibliography. The print is small but quite readable, and chapter numbers appear on all even-numbered pages. Many respondents to the survey remarked that the Cohen edition is fairly priced and readily available in bookstores.

Less frequently used than either the Putnam or the Cohen versions, Walter Starkie's translation (1964) also has proponents who consider it the best, most available, cheapest edition. Others praise it for being more readable than Cohen's, rendered with sensitivity into modern American English, unmannered, and easy for students to read; however, at least one detractor describes Starkie's translations as idiosyncratic. The introduction is largely biographical; the notes, printed at the foot of each page, are not extensive, but they do provide the sort of factual information that is likely to prove most useful for students. The selected bibliography at the end of this Signet Classic edition was updated in 1979, and it now contains a good short reading list of biographies, scholarly works, and critical articles in English. An abridgment of the Starkie translation is also available, but even though one teacher feels that it includes the most important adventures, another regards it as completely unsatisfactory because most of the authorial intrusions are removed from it, and he adds "they are half the fun." In the abridged text, Starkie does not indicate where he has excised from the original, and, unlike Putnam, he provides no summaries of the omitted scenes. He also fails to respect the conventional numbering of the chapters in Cervantes' novel. There is a brief biographical introduction, and some notes are included in this edition, which is undoubtedly the cheapest one available in English.

A new English text has recently been published by Joseph R. Jones and Kenneth Douglas as a Norton Critical Edition (1981). The translation is not actually a new one but rather a revision (begun by Douglas and continued after his death by Jones) of the older John Ormsby translation (1885). Putnam, Cohen, and Starkie were themselves deeply indebted to Ormsby, who was the first translator to offer English-speaking readers an accurate rendering of the original Spanish text. Convinced that the Ormsby version could be made accessible to contemporary American students, Douglas and Jones eliminated its antiquated Victorian locutions and overly literal translations while attempting to reproduce Cervantes' shifts in tone and register. By modulating the syntax and style in this fashion rather than reducing them to a uniform, smoothly flowing, idiomatic narrative, Douglas and Jones succeed in making readers aware of the breadth and diversity of Cervantes' expressive capacity—a crucial dimension of the text that previous translators had failed to convey.

Because their edition specifically addresses American college students, Douglas and Jones occasionally sacrifice rare and obsolete words or proverbs in favor of contemporary equivalents, thereby circumventing the need for esoteric notes and allowing a more immediate comprehension of the text. The few footnotes they do include are mostly explanatory. A guide to the pronunciation of Spanish names appears at the beginning of the volume; supporting sections "Backgrounds and Sources" and "Criticism" are appended at the end and are followed by a cursory "Selected Bibliography" of books in English. The "Backgrounds and Sources" section contains a brief biographical sketch taken from Manuel Durán's *Cervantes*, an anonymous ballad farce that some scholars believe influenced *Don Quixote*, and excerpts from the chivalric romances *Amadis of Gaul* and *Palmerin of England* as well as from Ariosto's *Orlando furioso* and Avellaneda's continuation. The "Criticism" section includes Riquer's "Cervantes and the Romances of Chivalry," E. C. Riley's "Novel and Romance in *Don Quixote*," Allen's "Levels of Fiction in *Don Quixote*," Herman Meyer's "[The Poetics of Quotation in *Don Quixote*]," Harry Levin's "The Quixotic Principle: Cervantes and Other Novelists," René Girard's "['Triangular' Desire in *Don Quixote*]," Robert Alter's "The Mirror of Knighthood and the World of Mirrors," Unamuno's "On the Reading and Interpretation of *Don Quixote*," Helena Percas de Ponseti's "The Cave of Montesinos: Cervantes' Art of Fiction," and Stephen Gilman's "The Apocryphal *Quixote*." It is still too early to tell whether the Douglas-Jones edition will gain widespread acceptance in American colleges and universities, but it has generated considerable interest among teachers, many of whom express an intention to use it when they next teach *Don Quixote* in English translation.

Anthologies

There is enormous resistance to the use of anthologies in teaching *Don Quixote*. "I find anthologies so poor in conveying the feeling of *Don Quixote*," declares one respondent to the survey, "that I avoid them at all costs." Others claim that students need access to the whole book even if only part of it is taught in class, for as one instructor explains, an anthology creates "a mistaken notion regarding the unity and complexity of a work; it obscures relationships of one part to another and can only give isolated impressions." Another respondent, himself a writer of fiction, states categorically that "you can not read and comment on novels...by sampling them." Many object to using selections made by other people, whose judgments about the relative importance of various episodes may not coincide with their own. One instructor overcame this problem by typing eighty pages from the novel and distributing them to all the students in a large survey class. Most teachers see only disadvantages in the use of anthologies, often adding that they never use them or do not "believe in" them.

Nevertheless, anthologies can sometimes serve a useful purpose. "Reading the complete text is always preferable but not always feasible in courses which try to cover a lot of material" writes one user of anthologies. Another admits to being "stymied" by the selections in the anthology she is using, but she feels that the nature of the course and the level of the students made it the only reasonable alternative. Others point out that anthologies allow students access to many different works at a relatively modest price, that even selected passages permit discussion of major problems and themes, and that anthologies enable students to compare different works and to place writers in their literary, cultural, and historical contexts.

For those who teach Cervantes in Spanish, two of the most commonly used anthologies are Ángel and Amelia Del Río's *Antología general de la literatura española* (1960) and Diego Marín's *Literatura española* (1968), both of which contain selections from *Don Quixote* in the first volume of a two-volume hardbound set. The Del Ríos reprint chapters 1, 2, 7, 8, 22, and 45 from part 1 and chapters 5, 7, 9, 17, 43, and 74 from part 2 of *Don Quixote* as well as excerpts from Cervantes' poetry, *La Galatea*, exemplary novels (none of which are given in their entirety), drama (including the complete *entremés* "La cueva de Salamanca"), and *Persiles y Sigismunda*. There are also a cursory introduction to Cervantes and footnotes on lexical matters. Proponents of this anthology claim that it provides ample selections and a useful if limited exposure to Cervantes' work.

Marín's selections from *Don Quixote* are much less extensive (pt. 1, chs. 1, 8; pt. 2, chs. 17, 18), but this anthology boasts a more substantial introduction and reprints one complete exemplary novel ("El licenciado Vidriera") and one *entremés* ("La cueva de Salamanca"). The notes relate to lexical problems and to the identification of characters, places, and literary allusions. A glossary of archaic usages at the end of the volume could be helpful to students. One person who uses this anthology believes that it offers students an enticing glimpse of the novel and allows the teacher to lecture on the overall structure of the book; however, another complains that it is frustrating because it contains too few passages from *Don Quixote*.

Other frequently used anthologies include Walter T. Pattison and Donald W. Bleznick's *Representative Spanish Authors* (3rd ed., 1971), Antonio Sánchez-Romeralo's *Antología de autores españoles* (1972), and Linton L. Barrett's *Five Centuries of Spanish Literature* (1962). The first volume of the Pattison-Bleznick contains chapters 1, 21, and 22 from part 1 and chapters 10, 41, and 74 from part 2. The notes and a brief introductory essay, "Cervantes and the Significance of the *Quijote*," are in English, and an extensive Spanish-English vocabulary appears at the end of the book. The first volume of Sánchez-Romeralo's anthology contains selections from chapters 1–3, 7–8, 16–17, 22, 25, and 30–31 from part 1 and 1, 10, 17,

22, 23, 48, and 74 from part 2. The notes are all written in English, but the introductory essay on Cervantes and *Don Quixote* is in Spanish. This anthology is attractively illustrated with paintings from the period, maps, and photographs of artifacts such as a knight's helmet; at the end of the volume there are a chronology of literary and historical events and an essential bibliography of secondary works. Barrett's compilation includes selections from chapters 1, 7, 8, 16, 19, and 21 in part 1 and chapter 74 from part 2 as well as reconstruction of the Dulcinea story with excerpts from part 1, chapters 13 and 25, and part 2, chapters 9–10, 25, and 32. The introductory material on "Don Quixote" and "Cervantes and the Modern Novel," the footnotes, and the intercalated summaries of the narrative are in English and addressed to students taking their first literature course in Spanish.

The only commonly used English-language anthology that includes *Don Quixote* is the two-volume *Norton Anthology of World Masterpieces*. Maynard Mack's note on the reading of literature in translation is reprinted at the end of each volume, and it is relevant to the teaching of Cervantes' novel in this context. P. M. Pasinetti edited the Renaissance section and wrote a general introduction in which he attempts to place Petrarch, Erasmus, Castiglione, Machiavelli, Rabelais, Montaigne, Cervantes, Marlowe, Shakespeare, Donne, Calderón, and Milton in a larger historical and literary context. This essay is followed by a separate biographical sketch for each author and a summary bibliography of works in English about him. The selections from *Don Quixote* include chapters 1–5, 7, 8, 18, 22, and 52 in part 1 and chapters 3, 12–17, 64, 65, 73, and 74 in part 2. These are divided into episodes like "I Know Who I Am, and Who I May Be, If I Choose," "Fighting the Windfalls," "Last Duel," and "Homecoming and Death." The notes and the text were adopted from the Putnam translation. Most teachers respect the scholarly seriousness of this anthology, although one person who teaches a "Literature since the Renaissance" course complains that *Don Quixote* appeared in the first volume, whereas most of the other assigned works were in the second volume. Norton, however, does publish a single-volume "Continental Edition" of this work; it is identical with the other except that it is slightly cheaper, because it does not contain any selections by English writers.

One other anthology is occasionally used in Spanish literature-in-translation courses: Seymour Resnick and Jeanne Pasmantier's *The Best of Spanish Literature in English Translation* (1976). The editors of this volume opted for the Cohen translation and included chapters 1, 2 and 8 from part 1 and chapters 42 and 45 from part 2 of *Don Quixote*, as well as the *entremés* "The Judge of the Divorce Court." They also provide a two-page introduction to the life and work of Cervantes but include neither footnotes nor summaries of omitted sections. At the end of the book, there is a useful bibliography of Spanish literary histories and anthologies of Spanish literature in English.

REQUIRED AND RECOMMENDED
FURTHER READING FOR STUDENTS

Some teachers of *Don Quixote* actively discourage students from consulting outside sources. They feel that the limited time available must be devoted to a reading of the text itself, that secondary materials detract from the experience of the text, or that students should be allowed to formulate their own critical judgments before sampling the vast and often contradictory array of interpretations in published scholarship on the novel. One respondent to the survey explains, "I teach literature as an aesthetic phenomenon and in human terms, hoping to make clear to students how this book might be relevant to their lives as a human document. . . . I avoid lengthy lectures on [scholarly topics], because I am much more preoccupied with showing students how to read, how to think, and how to write." Another says she prefers to send her students to music, art, and travel books to inspire them to read with enjoyment. Yet those who do not recommend further reading are in a definite minority, and teachers in more advanced courses often require considerable familiarity with the sources of *Don Quixote*, biographies, literary and cultural histories, critical commentaries, and subsequent literary works. The nature of these assignments varies according to the level of the students and the objectives of the particular course, but there is general agreement that such readings can broaden students' horizons, enhance their understanding and enjoyment of *Don Quixote*, and expose them to viewpoints that differ from those of the instructor.

To provide students with some guidance in this area, many teachers prepare annotated reading lists or set aside recommended books and articles on a reserve shelf in the library. Others refer students to a standard selective bibliography like those contained in the *Suma Cervantina* (1973) and the third volume of Murillo's edition.

Among the "sources" of *Don Quixote*, students are frequently required to read selections from the Bible, chivalric romances (*Amadís de Gaula, Tirante el blanco, Palmerín de Olivia, El caballero Cifar*), Ariosto's *Orlando furioso*, a pastoral novel (usually Jorge de Montemayor's *Diana*), a Moorish novel like *El Abencerraje*, and one of the picaresque novels (*Lazarillo de Tormes, Guzmán de Alfarache, El Buscón*). Most of these works are available in English translation, and several of the romances are conveniently collected in Roger and Laura Loomis' *Medieval Romances* (1956). *Amadis of Gaul* was translated and edited in 1974 by Edwin B. Place and Herbert C. Behm, and Avellaneda's *Don Quixote de la Mancha (Part II)* has been published in an English translation (1980) by Alberta Server and John Keller. Spanish versions of the romances are collected in Felicidad Buendía's *Libros de caballerías españolas* (1954). Teachers use these materials to illustrate the salient characteristics of different genres and to show how Cervantes drew upon, parodied, and transcended them.

Cervantes' other works are often studied in conjunction with *Don Quixote* to reveal the underlying unity of his writings, the range of his style, and the breadth of his originality. In particular, the exemplary novels and the *entreméses* help explain attitudes, ideas, themes, plot details, dialogue, and characterization. When teaching part 2 of the novel, some instructors like to have students read parts of Avellaneda's apocryphal continuation to show them why Cervantes responded to it as he did. Works by Góngora, Calderón, Quevedo, Lope de Vega, Shakespeare, Montaigne, Rabelais, Erasmus, and Grimmelshausen are sometimes used to illustrate dominant concerns of the period as well as differences in ideologies and world views. One teacher who assigns *Lazarillo, Don Quixote*, and *La vida es sueño* in a world literature course claims that "a 'comparative' study of these texts makes them richer in meaning for the students and also greatly contributes to a much better comprehension of the socio-historical and cultural context in which they were written."

Comparisons may also range across the boundaries of literary periodization, for, as one teacher remarks, it is often possible to provoke exciting new insights by comparing *Don Quixote* with "anything which is meaningful to members of the class." In fact, this practice seems to include everything from Plato's *Republic* (for the appearance-reality theme and the idealism-pragmatism conflict) and Homer's *Odyssey* (which exploits different levels of fictional reality and in which the hero, like Aeneas and Don Quixote, descends into the underworld) to Abbie Hoffman's *Revolution for the Hell of It* (for its rejection of accepted standards of behavior), William L. Shirer's *Rise and Fall of the Third Reich* (for Hitler's dementia), and Gerald Rosen's *The Carmen Miranda Memorial Flagpole* (for its ludic elements). In addition, there is the enormous list of works directly or indirectly influenced by *Don Quixote*: Fielding's *Joseph Andrews* and *Tom Jones*, Sterne's *Tristram Shandy*, Voltaire's *Candide*, Manzoni's *The Betrothed*, Dostoevsky's *The Idiot*, Flaubert's *Madame Bovary*, Twain's *Connecticut Yankee in King Arthur's Court* and *Tom Sawyer* as well as his *Adventures of Huckleberry Finn*, Melville's *Moby-Dick*, Goethe's *The Sufferings of Young Werther*, Jorge Amado's *Home Is the Sailor*, Pirandello's *The Late Mattia Pascal*, Dickens' *Pickwick Papers*, Stendhal's *The*

Red and the Black, Gogol's *Dead Souls*, Goncharov's *Oblomov*, many of Pérez Galdós' novels, Unamuno's *San Manuel Bueno Martyr* and *Mist*, Borges' "Pierre Menard, Author of *Don Quixote*," Joyce's *Ulysses*, García Márquez' *One Hundred Years of Solitude*, and Graham Greene's *Monsignor Quixote*. The list is endless, but teachers have reported success with students who have been encouraged to work out their own comparisons between these fictions and Cervantes' masterpiece, as well as between it and Lewis Carroll's *Alice in Wonderland*, Virginia Woolf's *Mrs. Dalloway*, Albert Camus's *The Stranger*, Kurt Vonnegut's *Slaughterhouse-Five*, F. Scott Fitzgerald's *Great Gatsby*, Zola's *Germinal*, Kafka's *The Trial*, Thurber's "Walter Mitty," Carlos Fuentes' *Terra nostra*, and Saul Bellow's *Henderson the Rain King*.

When teachers want students to read a standard biography or a "life and works" of Cervantes, they are most likely to assign William Byron's *Cervantes: A Biography*, Manuel Durán's *Cervantes*, Richard Predmore's luxuriously illustrated *Cervantes*, William Entwistle's *Cervantes*, or Aubrey Bell's *Cervantes*. Francisco Navarro y Ledesma's *Cervantes, the Man and the Genius*, Sebastián Juan Arbó's *Cervantes: The Man and His Time*, Fernando Diaz-Plaja's *Cervantes: The Life of a Genius*, and Malveena McKendrick's *Cervantes* have also been highly recommended. Bruno Frank's fictionalized biography *A Man Called Cervantes* is still readable and entertaining. Rodolfo Schevill's *Cervantes* has also been translated into English, and several teachers include it on their reading lists. Some students might enjoy the illustrations in *Cervantes: His Life, His Times, His Works*, ed. Mondadori, which includes sections on the author, his writings, his characters, and his critics as well as selections from *Don Quixote*.

For literary, cultural, and historical background material, teachers have recourse to a wide range of texts. Among those most frequently cited are J. H. Elliott's *Imperial Spain*, chapter 5 in John B. Trend's *The Civilization of Spain*, Otis Green's *Spain and the Western Tradition*, the chapters on Cervantes in Gerald Brenan's *Literature of the Spanish People*, Stanley Payne's *History of Spain and Portugal*, Américo Castro's *The Structure of Spanish History*, Salvador de Madariaga's *Spain*, Antonio Domínguez Ortiz' *The Golden Age of Spain*, Pierre Vilar's *Spain: A Brief History*, and R. O. Jones's *A Literary History of Spain*. Students who read Spanish are often referred to Ángel Del Río's two-volume *Historia de la literatura española*, Juan Alborg's *Historia de la literatura española*, Marín and Del Río's *Breve historia*, Juan Hurtado and Angel Palencia's somewhat outdated but still useful *Historia de la literatura española*, Ludwig Pfandl's *Cultura y costumbres*, and Antonia Ubieto Arteta's *Introducción a la historia de España*.

Because Cervantes' work bridges the Renaissance and the baroque eras, teachers sometimes advise students to read histories or studies of both periods: William Kennedy's *Rhetorical Norms in Renaissance Literature* or Wylie Sypher's *Four Stages of Renaissance Style* for the former and Frank Warnke's *Versions of the Baroque,* René Wellek's "The Concept of the Baroque in Literary Scholarship," or Morris Croll's "The Baroque Style in Prose" for the latter. Students who know Spanish are often sent to Aubrey Bell's *El renacimiento español,* Helmut Hatzfeld's *Estudios sobre el barroco,* and Emilio Orozco Diaz' *Manierismo y barroco.* A background in the history of ideas is provided by David Knowles's *The Evolution of Medieval Thought,* and several teachers have found Marcelin Defourneau's *Daily Life in Spain in the Golden Age* to be a useful compendium of information. A standard mythology like *Crowell's Handbook of Classical Mythology* by Edward Tripp, *Greek Myths* by Robert Graves, *Who's Who in Classical Mythology* by Michael Grant and J. Hazel, or Edith Hamilton's popular *Mythology* can help students understand some of the allusions in the book. One teacher assigns Montaigne's "Of Cannibals" to illustrate one Renaissance writer's critique of narrow-minded, superstitious thinking; Pico della Mirandola's "On the Dignity of Man" to provide a "characteristic Renaissance view of man" and a contrast with *Don Quixote;* and Bertrand Russell's essay on Descartes to promote discussion about the "relativity of truth and the breakdown of the Thomist world view."

The most popular and readily available collection of commentaries on *Don Quixote* is Lowry Nelson's *Cervantes: A Collection of Critical Essays,* which several teachers require their students to use as a textbook. It includes pieces by Brenan, Entwistle, Harry Levin, Thomas Mann, W. H. Auden, Leo Spitzer, Erich Auerbach, E. C. Riley, Carlos Blanco Aguinaga, and Edwin Honig as well as a chronology of important dates and a selected bibliography. A more ambitious collection—one that makes the work of foreign scholars available to American students—is *Cervantes across the Centuries,* edited by Ángel Flores and M. J. Benardete. In addition to essays by Jean Cassou, Ramón Menéndez Pidal, Joaquín Casalduero, Helmut Hatzfeld, Albert Morel-Fatio, Unamuno, Américo Castro, Benedetto Croce, and Waldo Frank, it contains interesting sections on the impact of *Don Quixote* in other countries and a list of musical adaptations of Cervantes' works. Flores and Benardete's earlier collection, *The Anatomy of* Don Quixote, is also sometimes recommended to students for its essays on the genesis of the work by Menéndez Pidal, the social and historical background by Morel-Fatio, the style by Hatzfeld, and "Hamlet and Don Quixote" by Turgenev. A somewhat less readily available collection, *Cervantes: A Critical Trajectory* edited by Raymond Barbera, is also occasionally recommended; it reprints essays by Auerbach, Turgenev, Coleridge, Heine, Unamuno, Ortega y Gasset, Pirandello, Madariaga, W. P. Ker, Mario Casella, Américo Castro, Pedro Salinas, and Wyndham Lewis. Important papers in both Spanish and English by contemporary scholars and critics are contained in *Cervantes and the Renaissance*, edited by Michael D. McGaha.

Spanish students are generally referred to the *Suma Cervantina*, edited by Avalle-Arce and Riley. The essays in this volume were written by leading scholars to provide an overview of Cervantes scholarship at that time; individual chapters deal with biography, each of the major works, general themes, and problems encountered in the study of Cervantes. An excellent bibliography, organized according to these chapter divisions, appears at the end of the book.

For beginning students, teachers have found that the most appropriate books and articles are Madariaga's *Don Quixote: An Introductory Essay in Psychology*, Durán's *Cervantes*, Margaret Church's Don Quixote: *Knight of La Mancha*, Richard Predmore's *The World of Don Quixote*, Mark Van Doren's *Don Quixote's Profession*, and frequently anthologized essays like Auden's "The Ironic Hero," Levin's "The Quixotic Principle," Auerbach's "The Enchanted Dulcinea," Turgenev's "Hamlet and Don Quixote," and Dorothy Van Ghent's "On *Don Quixote*" from her *The English Novel*. Lionel Trilling's "Manners, Morals, and the Novel," Alfred Schutz's "*Don Quixote* and the Problem of Reality," Oscar Mandel's "The Function of the Norm in *Don Quixote*," David Thorburn's "Fiction and Imagination in *Don Quixote*," William P. Ker's "Don Quixote," and Joseph Wood Krutch's "Miguel de Cervantes" are also sometimes made available to beginning students. Some teachers assign less well-known but important essays: Raymond Willis' "Sancho Panza: Prototype for the Modern Novel," George Haley's "The Narrator in *Don Quixote*: Maese Pedro's Puppet Show," E. C. Riley's "Three Versions of *Don Quixote*" and "Who's Who in *Don Quixote*? or, An Approach to the Problem of Identity," P. E. Russell's "*Don Quixote* as a Funny Book," J. M. Sobré's "Don Quixote, the Hero Upside-Down," Anthony Close's "Don Quixote's Love for Dulcinea," and "Sancho Panza: Wise Fool," Mary Mackey's "Rhetoric and Characterization in *Don Quixote*," Colbert Nepaulsingh's "Cervantes, *Don Quijote*: The Unity of Action," Victor Oelschläger's "Sancho's Zest for Quest," Lester Crocker's "*Don Quijote*: Epic of Frustration," and Geoffrey Stagg's "El sabio Cide Hamete Benengeli."

For more advanced students, the most frequently recommended titles include Ortega y Gasset's *Meditations on* Quixote, Unamuno's *Our Lord Don Quixote*, Ruth El Saffar's *Distance and Control in* Don Quixote,

E. C. Riley's *Cervantes's Theory of the Novel*, both parts of Allen's *Don Quixote: Hero or Fool?*, Alban Forcione's *Cervantes, Aristotle, and the Persiles*, and Leo Spitzer's "Linguistic Perspectivism in the *Don Quijote*" from his book *Linguistics and Literary History*. Howard Mancing's excellent study *The Chivalric World of* Don Quixote: *Style, Structure and Narrative Technique* should also be consulted by upper-level students, along with Leland Chambers' "Irony in the Final Chapter of the *Quijote*," Harold G. Jones's "Grisóstomo and Don Quixote: Death and Imitation," E. C. Riley's "Symbolism in *Don Quixote*, Part II, Chapter 73," Michael Bell's "The Structure of *Don Quixote*," Emilio Goggio's "The Dual Role of Dulcinea," Edward Dudley's "Don Quijote as Magus: The Rhetoric of Interpolation," Mancing's "The Comic Function of Chivalric Names in *Don Quijote*," Elias Rivers' "Talking and Writing in *Don Quixote*," Cesáreo Bandera's "Cervantes' *Quixote* and the Critical Illusion," Raymond Immerwahr on structural symmetry, C. A. Soons on Cide Hamete Benengeli, Elias Rivers on the prefatory material, Karl-Ludwig Selig on the battle of the sheep, Herman Iventosch on the Grisóstomo episode, Henry Mendelhoff on Maritornes, James Browne on the galley slaves, Gethin Hughes, Gloria Fry, Peter Dunn, E. C. Riley, and Robert Hollander on the Cave of Montesinos, Sidney Monas on the adventure of the lions, John Sinnigen on Camacho's wedding, and Bruce Wardropper, Harry Sieber, and Jürgen Hahn on the "Curioso impertinente."

Several important studies are only available in Spanish and are frequently assigned to students familiar with the language: Américo Castro's *El pensamiento de Cervantes* and *Hacia Cervantes*, Joaquín Casalduero's chapter-by-chapter commentary in his *Sentido y forma del* Quijote, Avalle-Arce's *Nuevos deslindes cervantinos* and *Don Quijote como forma de vida*, Ramiro de Maeztu's "Don Quijote o el amor," Durán's *La ambigüedad en el* Quijote, Félix Martínez Bonati's essays in *Dispositio*, and Maravall's *Utopía y contrautopía en el* Quijote. Castro's work on Cervantes has been especially influential; unfortunately, it has not yet been entirely translated into English, although two of his most important essays on *Don Quixote* do appear in his *An Idea of History*.

Finally, outside readings are sometimes assigned in order to place Cervantes' novel into a particular conceptual framework. For example, teachers who stress the techniques of narrative fiction and the role played by *Don Quixote* in the history of the novel often ask students to read Robert Scholes and Robert Kellogg's *Nature of Narrative*, Wayne Booth's *Rhetoric of Fiction*, Philip Stevick's *Theory of the Novel*, or Gyorgy Lukács' *Theory of the Novel*. One instructor discovered an original way of tracing stylistic threads in *Don Quixote* by relating them to similar concerns in the exemplary novels, which were read in conjunction with El Saffar's *Novel to Romance*. Another instructor taught *Don Quixote* as an example of the "myth of the hero." He asked students to read selections from Joseph Campbell's *The Hero with a Thousand Faces* and Carl Jung's *Man and His Symbols*; several others assigned parts of Michel Foucault's *The Order of Things*, in particular those that deal with *Don Quixote* and with perspectivism in Velázquez' *Las meninas*.

At a more elementary level, teachers are often confounded by the proliferation and availability of poorly prepared, inaccurate "study guides." If students feel a need for guidance in their first encounter with the novel, an instructor can profitably refer them to works like Margaret Church's *Don Quixote: Knight of La Mancha* or John Jay Allen's *Cervantes' Don Quixote*. The latter is an accurate, balanced, and useful brief introduction by a major Cervantine scholar. Although it was published by Monarch Notes, it should not be confused with Gregor Roy and Ralph Ronald's *Monarch Notes on Cervantes' Don Quixote*, which, like Marianne Sturman's *Cliffs Notes on Cervantes' Don Quixote*, contains pedestrian and misleading plot summaries, short biographical sketches, review questions, cursory bibliographies, and unimaginative discussions of style, characterization, and major themes. Daniel M. Crabb's *Pennant Key-Indexed Study Guide to Cervantes' Don Quixote* and Linton L. Barrett's *Barron's Simplified Approach to Cervantes' Don Quixote* are somewhat more reliable and reflect a basic critical understanding of the text, but they are not often displayed in bookstores. Teachers should be familiar with the contents of these pamphlets because students have an unfortunate tendency to read them in lieu of reading the book itself, a habit that obviously should be discouraged.

For lower-level Spanish students, Amelia Agostini de Del Río has prepared a *Compañero del estudiante del* Quijote which includes a table of dates, a short biography, an account of the relationship between Cervantes and Lope de Vega, the prologues to Cervantes' other published works, brief discussions of authors and texts that influenced Cervantes (Erasmus, León Hebreo, Raimundo Lulio, chivalric novels, *La Celestina*, *Orlando furioso*, *Lazarillo*, *El Abencerraje*, *Diana*, the popular ballads, Avellaneda's continuation), and a section on style and technique. For each chapter of the text, she provides a close textual reading, an explanation of literary and historical allusions, a list of themes for discussion, and a sampling of critical commentaries on the episode. At the end of the volume, she reprints extensive selections from the criticism and scholarship on the novel. Riquer's short, concise *Aproximación al* Quijote and Luis Morales Oliver's *Sinopsis de* Don Quijote have also proved useful to undergraduate students who are reading the novel for the first time.

THE INSTRUCTOR'S LIBRARY

Any essential bibliography for teachers of *Don Quixote* will be idiosyncratic and arbitrary to some degree, because each instructor gradually develops a sense for the works that are most important in shaping his or her approach to the novel. When people with no background in Hispanic studies are asked to teach *Don Quixote* in a Great Books or Masterpieces of World Literature course, they would do well to begin their preparation by consulting some of the works mentioned in the section on required and recommended further reading for students. As they become familiar with the field, they soon discover that an extraordinary amount of fine scholarship and criticism is available to them in both English and Spanish. One respondent to the survey insists that the best preparation for teaching *Don Quixote* is simply "the original text read and reread by the instructor," but others argue that instructors should do as much background reading as possible, and there is a general consensus that all teachers of the novel should know certain particularly valuable secondary works.

Because the following list is necessarily incomplete, instructors are encouraged to consult the standard bibliographies and the *Anales Cervantinos* (1951–62, 1971–   ). The *Anales* is an annual publication of the Instituto Miguel de Cervantes of the Consejo Superior de Investigaciones Científicas in Madrid; in addition to reviews of current scholarship, it publishes essays and notes (largely in Spanish, but also in English and French), texts relevant to the study of Cervantes, and a calendar of events. The Cervantes Society of America publishes a twice-yearly bulletin, *Cervantes*, which contains essays, reviews, and notes in Spanish and English. The society, which meets annually at the Modern Language Association convention, also publishes a newsletter and an annual volume. Anyone interested in the organization should write to John Jay Allen (Dept. of Spanish and Italian, Univ. of Kentucky, Lexington 40506).

Reference Works

Jeremiah Ford and Ruth Lansing's *Cervantes: A Tentative Bibliography* (1931) is seriously outdated, but it was a pioneering effort, and subsequent scholars remain indebted to it. Updated through 1962 by Raymond Grismer's *Cervantes: A Bibliography*, it was in turn superseded by José Simón Díaz' section on Cervantes in volume 8 of his monumental *Bibliografía de la literatura hispánica*. Several years later Dana B. Drake began publishing his Don Quixote *(1894–1970): A Selective, Annotated Bibliography* (1974, 1978, 1980). He chose 1894 as his starting point because Leopoldo Rius' three-volume *Bibliografía crítica* includes copious excerpts from critical commentaries before that date. The first two volumes of Drake's bibliography contain narrative summaries of 660 books and articles about Cervantes' novel. The subject index at the end of the second volume is helpful in locating items on particular topics, but the somewhat arbitrary selections and the alphabetical ordering (by authors' last names) render this work less useful than it might otherwise have been. Drake's third volume boasts a more rational plan of organization and contains summaries of books and articles on the reception of *Don Quixote* in Spain, France, Italy, England, Germany, Russia, Latin America, the United States, and elsewhere. For more recent scholarly work on Cervantes, teachers should consult bibliographies in the Murillo and Allen editions, the *Suma Cervantina,* the *Anales Cervantinos,* and the *MLA International Bibliography.*

In addition to the text editions of *Don Quixote,* teachers should be aware of a relatively recent facsimile of the first edition (1968) and several critical editions with significant annotations—in particular, those by Diego Clemencín (1833–39) and Rodríguez Marín (1947–49), the latter not to be confused with his earlier Clásicos Castellanos edition. Clemencín's notes are probably the finest ever compiled for the novel, and they still offer one of the best explications of the relation between *Don Quixote* and the romances of chivalry. These notes have been conveniently indexed by Charles F. Bradford in his *Índice de las notas de D. Diego Clemencín.* The four-volume *Don Quijote* in the *Obras completas* (1914–41), edited by Rodolfo Schevill and Adolfo Bonilla, has also been used as a definitive text for many years.

A fundamental source for the biographical study of Cervantes is Luis Astrana Marín's seven-volume *Vida ejemplar y heroica de Miguel de Cervantes Saavedra.* Although seldom read as a biography, it does reproduce a number of important documents. Those who know French might like to look at Jean Babelon's narrative biography, *Cervantes,* and those who know German could find it useful to read Werner Krauss's *Miguel de Cervantes: Leben und Werk.*

Teachers who encounter lexical difficulties with the original text may want to consult Covarrubias' *Tesoro de la lengua castellana o española* (1611). An encyclopedic dictionary compiled by a contemporary of Cervantes, it has been reprinted in a facsimile edition by Riquer. Although published more than a hundred years after Cervantes' death, the *Diccionario de autoridades* (1726) can also be useful in this regard, and it too is available in a modern edition. The second volume of Julio Cejador y Frauca's *La lengua de Cervantes* contains a dictionary and a concordance of principal words in *Don Quixote*; this enterprise was extended to the entire work of Cervantes and brought up-to-date in Carlos Fernández

Gómez' *Vocabulario de Cervantes*, which is particularly useful for comparing Cervantes' various usages of a particular word. Justo Caballero's *Guía-Diccionario del* Quijote can also help resolve textual questions.

Because Cervantes borrowed numerous phrases from proverbs and ballads, teachers often find it helpful to consult Gonzalo Correas' *Vocabulario de refranes y frases proverbiales* (1627), which Louis Combet has edited and annotated, or one of the more modern *refraneros* by José M. Sbarbi, Francisco Rodríguez Marín, Luis Martínez Kleiser, or Juana Campos and Ana Barella. Compilations of phrases and proverbs used in *Don Quixote* include those by Enrique de Cárcer, Juan Suñé Benages, and José Gella Iturriaga. Organized according to the chapters in the novel, Cárcer's book cites the passage in which a given proverb is found and then gives French, Portuguese, Italian, Catalan, English, and German translations of it. Suné Benages arranges his material alphabetically in various categories (idiomatic expressions, proverbs, adverbial phrases, etc.), defining the locutions and quoting the passages in which they appear. A list of expressions (organized alphabetically according to key words), proper names, and Latin locutions in *Don Quixote* can be found in Damián Estades Rodríquez' *El tesoro mágico*. General reference works that deal with the language of the period include Hayward Kenniston's *Syntax of Castilian Prose: The Sixteenth Century* and Martín Alonso Pedraz' *Enciclopedia del idioma*.

Richard Predmore's *Index* lists all references to proper names in the novel. *Cervantes' Place-Names*, by Eugene Torbert, provides a list of occurrences, etymologies, and geographical locations of all place names that appear in the works of Cervantes; it also discusses the particular significance these places had for the author. Enrique Ruiz-Fornells has undertaken the enormous task of compiling and publishing a complete concordance for *Don Quixote* and the apocryphal continuation; as of this date, the first two volumes (A–C) have appeared.

Background Studies

One of the best ways to obtain an overall view of sixteenth- and seventeenth-century Europe is to read pertinent sections in the third and fourth volumes of *The New Cambridge Modern History*—R. B. Wernham's *The Counter-Reformation and Price Revolution, 1559–1610* and J. P. Cooper's *The Decline of Spain and the Thirty Years War*. Fernand Braudel's classic *The Mediterranean and the Mediterranean World in the Age of Philip II* also provides a readable, authoritative account of the larger sociohistorical context in which Golden Age Spain played such an important role. Other valuable studies of this period include J. H. Elliot's

Europe Divided, Helmut G. Koenigsberger and George L. Mosse's *Europe in the Sixteenth Century*, and Henry Kamen's *The Iron Century: Social Change in Europe 1550–1660*.

There are also a number of histories that focus more specifically on Spain. R. Trevor Davies' *The Golden Century of Spain* and his *Spain in Decline* have served for many years as standard texts, but they have been to some extent superseded by more recent works like John Lynch's *Spain under the Hapsburgs*. Topics that were of particular interest to Cervantes have been treated in Kamen's *The Spanish Inquisition*, R. L. Kagan's *Students and Society in Early Modern Spain*, Irving A. Leonard's *Books of the Brave*, and I. A. Thompson's *War and Government in Habsburg Spain*. Although Stephen Gilman's *The Spain of Fernando de Rojas* deals primarily with the previous century, it clearly presents the *converso* problem in Spain, offering an extension and application of Américo Castro's cultural-historical theses. Economic conditions and their impact on Spanish society during this period are brilliantly discussed by E. J. Hamilton in his *American Treasure and the Price Revolution in Spain 1501–1650*; Ruth Pike's *Aristocrats and Traders* is also valuable in this context. Alfred Morel-Fatio presents a readable general account of the social and historical background in his contribution to *Cervantes across the Centuries*.

Unfortunately, many important works on this period are not available in English translation. For example, the third volume of Valentín Vásquez de Prada's *Historia económica y social de España* draws on materials that were not available to Hamilton, and Américo Castro's *La realidad histórica de España* and his *De la edad conflictiva* elaborate and sometimes modify the ideas he formulated earlier in translated works like his *Structure of Spanish History*. The fourth volume of Diaz Plaja's *La Historia de España en sus documentos* is not particularly readable as a history, but it does reprint many letters and documents from the age of Cervantes. Maravall's *Estado moderno y mentalidad social*, Riquer's *Caballeros andantes españoles*, Julio Caro Baroja's *Razas, pueblos y linajes*, Domínguez Ortíz' *El antiguo régimen*, Manuel Fernández Álvarez' *La sociedad española en la época del renacimiento*, Pinta Llorente's two-volume study of the Inquisition, and Antonio Rumeau de Armas' work on censorship also contain useful background materials.

For the intellectual history of Golden Age Spain, relatively little is available in English. Volume 3 of Marcial Solana's *Historia de la filosofía española* deals with Renaissance philosophy in Spain, and reliable accounts of Renaissance and Baroque thought are contained in the second and third volumes of José Luis Abellán's *Historia crítica del pensamiento español*. Maravall's two-volume *Estudios de historia del pensamiento español* and his *Factores de la idea del progreso en el renacimiento* are also valuable scholarly contributions in this area. The second volume of François Chatelet and G. Marret's *Histoire des idéologies*, entitled *De l' élise à l' etat*, contains background information on ideological developments in Spain, and Ludovik Osterc's *El pensamiento social y político del* Quijote offers a Marxist perspective on this aspect of Cervantes' thought. The *Historia de la espiritualidad* provides an overview of the major religious concerns of the period, but it should be supplemented by Marcel Bataillon's excellent *Erasmo y España*, particularly section 4 of chapter 14, and Antonio Vilanova's more specifically focused *Erasmo y Cervantes*. Paul M. Descouzis' two-volume *Cervantes a nueva luz* also discusses *Don Quixote* in the context of religious issues.

For teachers interested in the fine arts of the period, there are a number of reliable studies. James Lees-Milne's *Baroque in Spain and Portugal, and Its Antecedents* is a well-written introductory summary with an emphasis on architecture. George Kubler and Martin Soria's *Art and Architecture in Spain and Portugal* is a condensed but clear general discussion. Oskar Hagan's *Patterns and Principles of Spanish Art* contains a chapter on the age of Cervantes, and Bradley Smith's *Spain: A History in Art* presents a pictoral survey. The older *Spanish Art*, by Robert Tatlock and others, remains interesting for its chapters on the skilled crafts. The authoritative Spanish books on the subject are the twenty-two-volume *Ars hispaniae: Historia universal del arte hispánico* and Juan de Contreras' five-volume *Historia del arte hispánico*. Both treat Renaissance and Baroque art at length.

The themes of madness, play, and artistic representation are often discussed in classes where *Don Quixote* is taught, and some teachers find it useful to introduce materials on these topics. Michel Foucault's *Madness and Civilization* and Martine Bigeard's *La Folie et les fous littéraires en Espagne, 1500–1650* provide convenient points of departure for a consideration of madness, whereas Johan Huizinga's *Homo Ludens* and Roger Caillois's *Man, Play and Games* are relevant to the idea of play in Cervantes' novel. Two provocative studies of artistic representation are E. H. Gombrich's *Art and Illusion* and Rudolf Arnheim's *Art and Visual Perception.*

There is a considerable body of scholarship on the literary antecedents of *Don Quixote*, and Avalle-Arce cites several works on this topic in his chapter "Background Material on *Don Quixote*." In addition to the fundamental studies he mentions, teachers should know about Daniel Eisenberg's *Romances of Chivalry in the Spanish Golden Age* and Henry Thomas' older but still useful *Spanish and Portuguese Romances of Chivalry*. Most of the remaining literature on relevant chivalric, pastoral, and sentimental fiction is in Spanish: Francisco Márquez Villanueva's *Fuentes literarias cervantinas*, José Amezcua Gómez' *Libros de caballerías*

hispánicos, Armando Durán's *Estructura y técnicas de la novela sentimental y caballeresca,* and José Siles Artés' *El arte de la novela pastoril.* In
addition to the notes by Clemencín, those by Daniel Eisenberg in his
edition of *Espejo de príncipes y caballeros* provide insight into the relation
between *Don Quixote* and the romances of chivalry; furthermore, the
Espejo itself is an excellent example of the books with which Cervantes
was familiar. Marcelino Menéndez y Pelayo's three-volume *Orígenes de la
novela* was a groundbreaking effort in this area and the product of a
remarkably fertile mind; despite the proliferation of subsequent studies, it
deserves to be better known in the English-speaking world. The ballads on
which Cervantes drew so frequently are discussed in Diego Catalán's *Siete
siglos de romancero* and Menéndez Pidal's two-volume *Romancero
hispánico.* Sources for Cervantes' novel are also discussed in Maurice
Molho's *Cervantes: Raíces folklóricas,* Mac Barrick's "The Form and
Function of Folktales in *Don Quijote,*" and John Gilbeau's "Some Folk-
Motifs in *Don Quixote.*"

For Cervantes' relations with other authors—his predecessors as well as
his successors—instructors might want to consult the bibliographical
section on diffusion and literary relationships in the third volume of
Murillo's edition of *Don Quijote,* as well as the third volume of Dana
Drake's annotated bibliography. There is no single comprehensive work
on Cervantes' influence on subsequent writers; there is not even a
composite study of his impact on the English-American novel, although
there are many shorter pieces about his influence on individual writers.
Maurice Bardon's Don Quichotte *en France* and Ludmilla Turkevich's
Cervantes in Russia trace Cervantes' influence in France from 1605 to 1815
and in Russia from 1763 to 1940, and part 4 of Flores' *Cervantes across the
Centuries* is devoted to *Don Quixote*'s influence in England, France,
Germany, and Russia, but there is still much to be done in this domain.

· Several relatively recent books have explored particular aspects of *Don
Quixote*'s numerous literary successors. For example, Arturo Serrano
Plaja's "*Magic*" *Realism in Cervantes:* Don Quixote *as Seen through* Tom
Sawyer *and* The Idiot compares Cervantes' impact on Twain and
Dostoevsky, whereas Marthe Robert's *The Old and the New: From
Quixote to Kafka* analyzes the doublings of two quite different authors in
their protagonists to illustrate the novel's persistent concern with the
authority of literature and the undermining of that authority by the
movement of history. In *The Gates of Horn,* Harry Levin investigates
Cervantes' representation of disillusionment and traces elements of his
antiromanticism in Balzac, Stendhal, Flaubert, and Proust. René Girard's
Desire, Deceit, and the Novel employs *Don Quixote* as a paradigmatic
example of "triangular desire," which he sees as an underlying motif in

major novels by Stendhal, Proust, and Dostoevsky. In *Partial Magic*, Robert Alter discusses Cervantes' achievement as the exploitation of a dominant cultural crisis—the erosion of belief in the written word—and treats subsequent works by Sterne, Diderot, Faulkner, Woolf, Nabokov, Barth, Beckett, and Borges as confrontations with the same fundamental problem. Walter Reed's *An Exemplary History of the Novel: The Quixotic versus the Picaresque* appropriates *Don Quixote* as the primary exemplar of one narrative possibility in the history of the novel, and Alexander Welsh, in his *Reflections on the Hero as Quixote*, argues that Quixote represents a recurring attitude toward justice and individual identity in an arbitrary, ultimately incomprehensible universe.

Critical and Scholarly Approaches

One of the respondents to the preliminary survey remarks that "it is crucial for [the teacher] to understand the richness and the range of the critical tradition of the *Quixote*; it is clearly a case of poetic justice that an ambiguous work has provoked critical polemics and multiple possibilities for interpretation." Beginning teachers of the *Quixote* might well initiate themselves into this critical tradition by consulting works mentioned in the section "Required and Recommended Further Reading for Students." The demarcation line between advanced students and beginning instructors is a tenuous one, and their reading needs often overlap.

In recent years, proponents of a "hard" approach to the novel have contended that much of the "richness" and "range" of critical commentaries on *Don Quixote* can be traced to a misguided romanticization of the work. P. E. Russell adumbrates this line of argument in his *"Don Quixote* as a Funny Book,"* and Daniel Eisenberg defends it in his *"Don Quijote* and the Romances of Chivalry: The Need for a Reexamination,"* but the most fully developed version of the attack on "soft" interpretations is Anthony Close's *The Romantic Approach to* Don Quixote. Close argues that when Cervantes' novel became dissociated from the background of the chivalric literature it burlesqued, it became possible for the German Romantics, Casalduero, Unamuno, Ortega y Gasset, "Azorín," Américo Castro, and their followers to project national ideals, romantic symbolism, or allegorical intentions into the novel. Whether or not one agrees with Close's conclusions, his book should be read by all teachers of the novel: it provides a clear but skeptical overview of several major streams of Cervantine criticism during the past two hundred years. Mandel's "Function of the Norm in *Don Quixote"* and Allen's *Don Quixote: Hero or Fool?* should, however, be read in conjunction with Close to gain a balanced perspective on this critical controversy.

One recent study that Close would undoubtedly classify as "soft" is John Weiger's *The Individuated Self: Cervantes and the Emergence of the Individual*. It deals with the growing awareness of selfhood, and because this process is an immediate personal concern to many college students, one instructor in a world literature class found it to be a valuable source of ideas for teaching *Don Quixote*. In contrast, Arthur Efron's *Don Quixote and the Dulcineated World* is a "hard" approach insofar as it rejects the romanticizing trends of Cervantes scholarship, but it is highly idiosyncratic in arguing that *Don Quixote* is a farcical attack on the "Dulcinean" or conformist values that most people are conditioned to accept unquestioningly. Efron regards these values as products of repressed sexuality, and he views the novel itself as a repudiation of marriage, chastity, and other cultural ideals of its age. Obviously such interpretations can evoke a sympathetic response from students.

Two less controversial analyses often prove useful to teachers: Murillo's *The Golden Dial*, which deals with various modes of time in *Don Quixote*, and Raymond Willis' *The Phantom Chapters of the* Quijote, which investigates the apparently arbitrary chapter divisions in the novel to illustrate Cervantes' belief that life flows in an uninterrupted stream and cannot legitimately be truncated into discrete segments. Leonard Mades' *The Armor and the Brocade* and Harriet Frazier's *A Babble of Ancestral Voices* are also recommended for their chapters on Cervantes.

In Spanish, two of the most important linguistic studies of the novel are Helmut Hatzfeld's *El* Quijote *como obra de arte del lenguaje* and Ángel Rosenblat's *La lengua del* Quijote. The most frequently cited treatments of specific aspects in the novel include Márquez Villaneuva's *Personajes y temas del* Quijote, Helena Percas de Ponseti's two-volume *Cervantes y su concepto del arte*, Knud Togeby's *La estructura del* Quijote, Luis Rosales' *Cervantes y la libertad*, Gonzalo Torrente Ballester's *El* Quijote *como juego*, Guillermo Diaz-Plaja's *En torno a Cervantes*, Avalle-Arce's *Don Quijote como forma de vida*, Cesáreo Bandera's *Mimesis conflictiva*, Carlos Fuentes' *Cervantes o la crítica de la lectura*, Ciriaco Morón Arroyo's *Nuevas meditaciones del* Quijote, Carlos Varo's *Génesis y evolución del* Quijote, and the highly personal and digressive but often insightful *Ruta de Don Quijote* by José Martínez Ruiz ("Azorín"). Individual essays like Menéndez Pidal's "Un aspecto en la elaboración del *Quijote*" and those in Amado Alonso's *Materia y forma en poesía* and Francisco Ayala's *Experiencia e invención* and *Cervantes y Quevedo* are also useful.

In French, Paul Hazard's Don Quichotte: *Étude et analyse* was praised by one respondent as the best overall treatment of the novel, and the psychostructural approach in Louis Combet's *Cervantes; ou, Les Incertitudes du désir* was successfully employed in the classroom by another instructor, Viktor Schklovsky's provocative essay "Comment est fait Don Quichotte" is also available in French in his *Sur la théorie de la prose*. Cesare de Lollis' *Cervantes reazionario* has been recommended by instructors who read Italian.

AIDS TO TEACHING

There is considerable disagreement among teachers of *Don Quixote* about the use of slides, tapes, recordings, and films. Many simply do not use them, and some condemn them for detracting from the intellectual content of a course. "So far, I have seen no need to resort to audio-visual aids," remarks one respondent; another declares emphatically that he is not "an enthusiast of audio-visual aids"; yet another asserts that "a well-taught literature course for college or university students hardly needs Bandaid relief." Most teachers, however, recognize that such materials can help students appreciate the work, conceptualize the fictional world of Don Quixote, and relate it to their own concerns. "I don't presently use [audiovisual aids]," writes one teacher, "but I would be interested in learning more about them." Even those who are skeptical about the educational value of such devices often see some advantage to adopting them. "I do not think that these materials make an essential contribution to the students' understanding of the work," says one instructor, "but they provide a change of pace and a different angle for discussion."

One of the most common adjuncts to the teaching of *Don Quixote* is a personal slide collection consisting of illustrations to the various editions of the novel, scenes from the Spanish countryside, and paintings by Cervantes' contemporaries. Many teachers have used Joan Givanel y Mas's *Historia gráfica de Cervantes y del* Quijote as a source from which to make slides for classroom presentation; others have done the same with Claude Roger-Marx's boxed collection *Don Quichotte de Cervantes par cinquante artistes du XVIIe siècle à nos jours*. Two earlier volumes are also interesting in this respect: Manuel Heinrich's *Iconografía de las ediciones del* Quijote, which reproduces facsimile frontispieces from 611 editions printed in Spain and nineteen other countries, and H. S. Ashbee's *An Iconography of* Don Quixote, which lists illustrations and illustrated editions of the novel. Twenty-three prints are included at the end of Ashbee's book. Gustave Doré's illustrations are among the most popular, and they are all reprinted in a relatively recent Castilla edition (1947). One teacher describes them as inspiring, and another argues that "Doré's interpretations of some of the episodes are close to what the student should see in them." Individual works by Goya, Daumier, Picasso, and Dalí are also frequently used. Slides can be shown at the beginning of the course to demonstrate various artists' interpretations of Cervantes' characters, or they can be introduced during the discussion of corresponding episodes from the book. One teacher encourages students to choose from over two hundred illustrations in his private collection and organize a slide presentation with musical accompaniment at the end of the course. Another first discusses the visual appeal of a particular episode and then projects slides of illustrations from that episode as various artists have envisioned it.

A surprisingly large number of teachers have traveled to La Mancha and taken their own slides of sites mentioned in the novel. As one instructor observes, "these slides help students see the land, its people, and their artifacts as Don Quixote and his companion are said to have seen them." Even if one cannot travel to Spain, one can obtain slides and photographs for classroom use. The Spanish National Tourist Office publishes an illustrated pamphlet on La Mancha, and the Ministry of Culture distributes a free set of slides on Cervantes' life. The Ancora publishing firm sells a set of five slides, *La Mancha, tierras de Don Quijote*, and Eusebio Goicoechea Arrondo has put together a collection *La Mancha, tierra de Don Quijote*, which one instructor describes as a "very good and illuminating presentation [but] a bit romantic." There are also relevant pictures among the sixty slides in Alberto Sánchez' *Literatura española en imágenes*. Sites of Don Quixote's adventures, paintings, buildings Cervantes might have known, city panoramas, sixteenth-century sailing ships, and inns are reproduced in Astrana Marín's *Vida ejemplar*, and books like Mondadori's *Cervantes: His Life, His Times, His Works* or Predmore's *Cervantes* are good sources of illustrations. Students also seem to appreciate maps of Don Quixote's journey, which can be found in Riquer's Juventud edition or in José Terrero's "Las rutas de las tres salidas de Don Quijote de la Mancha."

The works of Velázquez, particularly *Las meninas*, are frequently shown during the teaching of *Don Quixote* to aid in explaining baroque art or to provide background on the appearance-reality theme and the technical use of chiaroscuro. One instructor uses *Las meninas* "to illustrate the way a work might capture the author/artist within it, and other paintings by Velázquez to show an interest in the period for the everyday and unglamorized aspects of existence that Cervantes was so concerned to capture." Another used *Los borrachos* in conjunction with Cervantes' treatment of the pastoral to illustrate the concept of demythologizing, and still another employed four Velázquez paintings to demonstrate what Ortega y Gasset called the prosification of myth. El Greco's work is introduced by some instructors "to help students understand the spiritual aspects of [*Don Quixote*]," whereas others situate the novel in a cultural context by showing slides that distinguish Renaissance, mannerist, and baroque tendencies in art. One instructor successfully showed Renaissance and baroque facades and altars to teach students the principles of symmetry and organization that are also incorporated in Cervantes' narrative.

Several film versions of *Don Quixote* are available for classroom showing. The two most popular are Grigori Kozintsev's 1957 Russian adaptation and Rafael Gil's 1948 Spanish movie with English subtitles. One instructor preferred the Kozintsev film as "the best I've seen to carry over to the students the feeling of the *Quixote*; it doesn't romanticize as Western films tend to do"; however, another favored Gil's version as a valuable contrast to the way in which students generally visualize the novel. G. W. Pabst's 1932 *Don Quixote* is also available in English, and there is a 1973 Australian filming of the ballet *Don Quixote* with Rudolf Nureyev. Several teachers have also obtained videotapes of the 1972 BBC production, *The Adventures of Don Quixote*.

Among the numerous recordings of *Don Quixote*, the most commonly used is a 1958 Folkways release in which Jorge Juan Rodríguez reads fifteen selected episodes (including the adventure of the windmills and Don Quixote's death) in Spanish; Folkways also distributes an English version of these selections read by Lester G. Crocker. A number of dialogues between Don Quixote and Sancho are dramatized on a 1966 Aguilar recording by Fernando Fernán Gómez and Agustín González, and Amado Alonso's readings of selected passages are available on an older Vocarium recording, *Don Quijote* (1956). The Spanish Music Center (New York) distributes an undated SMC Pro Arte record, *Lectura de Don Quixote*, that contains four episodes read by Eugenio Florit. A far more ambitious *Don Quijote de la Mancha* has been produced by the Juventud company on five cassettes with nearly thirty hours of playing time. Read by Juan Canas, these recordings are distributed primarily to the blind in the United States by the National Library Service in Washington, D.C. Audiotapes can be played in class to highlight particular episodes; they can also be deposited in a language laboratory or audiovisual center and made available to students. Some colleges and universities even have facilities that allow students to hear prepared tapes on a special telephone access line. One instructor copied selections from the available materials on cassettes, which students took home with them and studied at their own pace.

In addition to readings from the novel, lectures or discussions are also available in cassette form. A. Bartlett Giamatti's lecture *Don Quixote* deals with the influence of earlier literature (particularly *Orlando furioso*) on *Don Quixote*, and the Canadian Broadcasting Corporation's *Don Quixote as a Funny Book* reproduces a round-table discussion by three Cervantes scholars and a musicologist. A cassette specifically designed for instructional purposes is *Don Quixote of La Mancha*, produced by DAK Industries in North Hollywood, California. It includes excerpts from the novel in English and discussions of such themes as Cervantes' blend of pathos and slapstick, Sancho's function as a foil and philosophical counterpoint to Don Quixote, and the meaning of the book in the modern world. Several Spanish teachers have found the Cervantes tape in the Grandes Figuras de la Historia series to be "helpful as background," although at least one respondent thinks it is "of little use in communicating a sense of Cervantes' life." Entitled *Miguel de Cervantes y su tiempo*, it is distributed free by the Spanish Ministry of Culture.

A Nonesuch record, *The Pleasures of Cervantes (Vocal and Instrumental Music of Spain of the 15th, 16th, and 17th Centuries)*, provides good examples of the music of the period, and the Discos CBS cassette *Varios, Don Quijote de la Mancha* contains many lively songs on various episodes and characters from the novel. Among the musical adaptations of the Don Quixote theme, the two most popular versions for classroom use are Richard Strauss's tone poem *Don Quixote* and Dale Wasserman's *Man of La Mancha*, with lyrics by Joe Darion and music by Mitch Leigh. Several instructors employ excerpts from Jules Massenet's opera or Manuel de Falla's charming puppet opera, *El retablo de Maese Pedro*, and at least one teacher played Georg Philipp Telemann's *Don Quixote Suite* in class. The Strauss and Massenet compositions have been introduced to provoke discussions on "how a musical artist may be inspired by and try to render the spirit of the original," and at least one teacher played Falla's piece to demonstrate how well the composer had captured the spirit of that episode. In the area of popular music, Gordon Lightfoot has written and performed a song on Cervantes' theme in his 1972 album *Don Quixote*.

The most controversial adaptation is certainly *Man of La Mancha*, which is available in a film version with Peter O'Toole and Sophia Loren. The recordings from the original musical seem to provoke widely divergent responses from teachers. Those who identify it with their own romantic interpretations of *Don Quixote* regard it as a "modern adaptation of universal ideals" that inevitably conflict with reality. One proponent of this approach argues that the play's theme song, "The Impossible Dream," helps "students understand the essence of Don Quixote's character—the ability to dream the world as it is not." Several teachers in survey or world literature courses have students watch the film or read Wasserman's text and listen to the recording in order to "appreciate the totality and cohesiveness of the story, when they read only excerpts." Other Cervantes scholars consider *Man of La Mancha* a trivialization of *Don Quixote*, although even some of them have used it to show how the spirit of the original text can be misinterpreted in the modern age. One instructor in an advanced Spanish class discovered a particularly ingenious way of using *Man of La Mancha* to bring about a better understanding of Cervantes' novel. After the students had read part 1 of *Don Quixote*, he showed them a film version of the musical. After allowing them ample opportunity to express their admiration for it, he asked them to read Avellaneda's continuation. During subsequent discussions, the students began to perceive similarities between Wasserman's and Avellaneda's understanding of the Don Quixote figure, and this insight enabled them to comprehend Cervantes' reaction to the apocryphal continuation.

Commercially produced slides and filmstrips are not generally used in the teaching of *Don Quixote*, but they are frequently available in university and college libraries or learning centers; some of the sound recordings and visual images in these collections can be adapted for classroom use. The most ambitious of these projects is *Don Quijote de la Mancha* (1962), distributed by Educational Audio-Visual in Pleasantville, New York. This programmed approach to the novel consists of thirty-two filmstrips, sixteen half-hour audiotapes, and student manuals for independent listening. The 1,600 filmstrip frames have been chosen from numerous sources, and the actors (Fernando Ray and Francisco Rabal) read integrally from Cervantes' text. Other filmstrip and audiotape programs are available in Ancora's shorter Obras Maestras de la Literatura series (1956), in the *Encyclopedia Britannica* Great Classics of Literature series (1959), and in a Spanish National Radio production of *Don Quijote de la Mancha*. Audifilm has also brought out *Don Quijote de la Mancha*, consisting of 370 cartoonlike slides with ten dramatized half-hour audiotapes.

Part Two

APPROACHES

INTRODUCTION

There are as many different approaches to teaching *Don Quixote* as there are teachers of the novel, and each teacher generally modifies his or her approach according to the size, nature, and composition of a particular class. Yet all approaches are posited on some prior interpretation of the novel. Cervantes himself is a sort of teacher, and his work reflects a world view on which an effective teaching method can be based, but all instructors bring their own priorities, preoccupations, and viewpoints to the teaching of literature. What is actually presented in the classroom is a synthesis of the text, the available secondary resources, and one's own conception of the true, the significant, the beautiful, and the relevant.

The essays brought together in this volume reflect the wide range of possible approaches to *Don Quixote*. They are grouped into four sections. In the first, John J. Allen, Ruth El Saffar, and Howard Mancing reflect on the general questions that all teachers of the novel must consider in order to make it "come alive" for others. In the second section, six scholar-teachers explain the interpretive rationales behind their classroom treatments of *Don Quixote*. Daniel Eisenberg demonstrates the need to perceive the novel within the context of the chivalric romances and defends the "hard" approach, according to which *Don Quixote* is regarded primarily as a humorous creation. Ulrich Wicks tells how he presents the metafictional aspects of *Don Quixote* and encourages students to recognize the modern qualities produced by Cervantes' awareness of the medium in which he was writing. Peter Dunn's teaching is characterized by his careful attention to readers' responses to various aspects of the text, whereas Donald Bleznick's approach reflects the influence of Jungian psychology or myth criticism, and that of Carroll Johnson is based on a knowledge of Freudian psychoanalysis. The third section is devoted to three essays on the use of background information: Elias Rivers discusses the oral and written language traditions on which Cervantes drew, Norma Hutman explains her treatment of Don Quixote as a characteristic baroque man, and Avalle-Arce deals with the general problem of introducing background materials. In the final section, James Dayananda, Lewis Hutton, and Morgan Desmond describe innovative and successful ways of presenting *Don Quixote* to nonmajors. Each of these essays contains insights capable of generating new ideas for courses ranging from broad surveys of Western literature to specialized seminars on *Don Quixote*.

Our survey of Cervantes instructors reveals that many instructors have given serious thought to the articulation of their own goals and principles, although their reasons for teaching the book in a particular way differ enormously. Some use it to acquaint students with Golden Age Spain, employing slides and background lectures to depict the world in which *Don Quixote* was written. Others pursue a more philosophical approach: one respondent uses the novel to teach students that what we know and how we know it cannot be taken for granted. In terms of literary history, teachers also try to show students why and how *Don Quixote* is a modern novel. One instructor justifies this approach by arguing that *Don Quixote* "is seminal to the study of the novel..., because in one way or another it treats all the themes that are central to the novelistic tradition." Another acknowledges several of these objectives: "I expect students to come out with a better understanding of what is meant by a *novel*, of the interrelationships between art and life, and some glimpse of the Spanish character." Others believe that *Don Quixote* can help teach students how to read, how to enjoy and appreciate literature, how to write an intelligent paper, or how to develop the skills of critical interpretation.

In general, teachers want students to understand the text, to know the *Quixote* in depth, and to be exposed to a great masterpiece. They regard Cervantes' novel as a unique and special work that provides intense enjoyment if properly understood—an enjoyment that can lead to wisdom and understanding. "My first aim... is to enable the student to leave class saying 'What a great book!'" asserts one respondent to the survey. "Enjoyment opens the door to more profound learning, and so first I must facilitate the reading of a difficult, lengthy text." Another instructor comments that this enjoyment helps students to "learn something about the historic, cultural, and spiritual forces that shaped [the novel]." Still another sees it as a means of encouraging students to "get involved in the complexity and unity of the work" and to "appreciate the deep humanity of mind that informs it and the irony of such words as truth and reality," for he feels that a genuine appreciation of the work can stimulate personal growth. "A text as unique and rich as *Don Quixote* awakens intellectual and spiritual curiosity in the student, and since I believe that this is necessary to live," writes an instructor at a large state university, "this is what I pursue when I give the course." Many teachers are convinced that the novel should be related to their students' most deeply felt concerns. As one respondent explains, "the material in the *Quixote* must be related to contemporary attitudes and experiences, if it is to be vital....Cervantes continues to be important and universal because his problems are still with us, and his responses are attractive, even when they are not acceptable."

The manner in which these various objectives are realized in the classroom varies considerably. One highly respected Cervantes scholar lectures, pacing up and down the room and periodically glancing at his notes or entertaining a student's question; others engage almost entirely in free-wheeling discussions during which "the path twists and meanders." For many teachers, the most congenial format seems to involve some combination of lecture and discussion, although the degree of authority exercised by the instructor is not always the same. "I always press my own reading of the text," admits one respondent, whereas another encourages an atmosphere in which any categorical statement by the teacher or by a student can be countered immediately by an opposing statement. One instructor even refuses to lecture because he feels that his superior knowledge should never be the dominant factor in a classroom discussion. "Professors have been trained to lecture and students to listen," he writes, and that approach "effectively smothers any thinking on the part of the students."

Most teachers, however, readily accept responsibility for structuring the classroom experience. The usual approach to *Don Quixote* is chronological and includes the close textual analysis of selected episodes, although some instructors prefer to disregard the normal chapter sequence to highlight particular themes and motifs like role playing, illusion and reality, humor, realism, and the Dulcinea myth. Often, these two approaches are combined, and a specific topic is assigned for each day's discussion. Several teachers distribute outlines of the entire novel before discussing it to give students some idea of the overall structure while the class is discussing individual passages; others hand out summaries of chapters not treated in class.

Student participation in the interpretive process is fostered in several ways. One instructor insists that students first tell him what struck them as interesting or significant in the assigned readings; he then responds to or expands on what they have said. A similar method involves passing out a list of broad-based, thought-provoking questions the day before they are to be discussed; students are encouraged to prepare responses to these questions, and as their answers are discussed in class, the teacher guides them toward a mutually satisfying interpretation. Several instructors have students prepare questions for each class; in one case, these questions are rigorously graded at first, but the evaluative process fades into the background as the questions gradually become the focus for lively classroom discussions. Oral reports on specific themes, episodes, or critical commentaries are also frequently required as a way of ensuring student participation.

Some teachers engage their students by creating a particular atmosphere in the classroom. One instructor from a small liberal arts college has "dressed as a shepherdess for the pastoral lecture, as Dulcinea, [and] as the Duchess." Another explains her approach as

> laughter and shared recollections: the stuff that *Don Quixote* and classes about *Don Quixote* are made of....We begin the novel very slowly; I act parts out; the members of the class contribute to an oral résumé of the previous night's reading; we go over the passages from the text out loud....After the first three weeks of class, I begin to bear down on the students. I challenge them to read outside sources; we talk less about plot and more about significance and interpretation.

One teacher effectively establishes a dialectic between the picaresque (which he characterizes as a "chaotic view") and the Cervantine (which he defines as a "cosmic view"). He explains that this approach facilitates reference to subsequent authors and enables students to gain a better understanding of the complexity of Cervantes' mind. Another teacher adopts different critical approaches (historical, philosophical, theological, psychological, sociological, etc.) for analyzing successive episodes in the narrative. According to him, the advantage of this method is that students acquire an intimate familiarity with the text while simultaneously learning the principles of literary criticism. Others orient their teaching to cover specific topics like (1) the relation of the author to the book, the reader, and the fictional hero; (2) the psychological plausibility of Don Quixote's enterprise; (3) polarity and progress in the relation between Don Quixote and Sancho; and (4) Don Quixote's turning away from an obsession with personal glory and toward a concern for larger issues. One respondent to the survey refers to his method as "texts and contexts," because he emphasizes a close reading of the text while seeking to place it in five different contexts: (1) the cultural, literary, and ideological background;

(2) the complete works of Cervantes; (3) the generic traditions on which it drew; (4) the range of subsequent criticism; and (5) the possible responses of modern readers.

Courses or sections of courses on *Don Quixote* end in various ways. One teacher always devotes the final class session to a discussion of the human values in the work and the reasons why it is a classic. Another offers a lecture that synthesizes all preceding discussions about the novel. The lasting impact of *Don Quixote* on college and university students is hard to gauge, but one instructor testifies that students "can usually tell [him] at least one thing that is different about their own lives after having read and studied the *Quixote*." Another declares that "I would like *Don Quixote* to be as significant to my students as it is to me....There never has been a student who remained indifferent to the book."

Just as objectives differ from course to course and from instructor to instructor, assignments and standards of evaluation vary. Some teachers give frequent quizzes on factual matters. (Who is Grisóstomo? Why is Quixote called "The Knight of the Mournful Countenance"? Why does the canon stop writing his prose epic? What events does the Moorish translator omit and why?) Others encourage the memorization of passages (particularly proverbs) and ask students to identify them on examinations. Still others ask short-answer questions about the inns in the story, chivalric novels, religious ideas, the importance of bloodlines, demythification, the injection of everyday life into morally serious literature, the principle of "variety in unity," the opposition between narrative progression and aesthetic reiteration, differences between part 1 and part 2, madness, heroism, idealism versus realism, art and nature, the relation between Don Quixote and Sancho, enchantment, the role of women in the novel, Dulcinea, love, the pursuit of perfection, perspectivism, the interpenetration of literature and life, and the social implications of the work.

A representative sample of questions from examinations on *Don Quixote* include:

1. Why does Cervantes place the wineskin episode in the middle of the intercalated tale about the "Curioso impertinente"?
2. What elements of Cervantes' life are embodied in *Don Quixote*?
3. Does Cervantes sacrifice character to develop humor in the novel?
4. What is the role of women (or magic or religion) in *Don Quixote*?
5. Don Quixote is often mistaken for a picaresque hero; what might lead people into making this error?
6. Does Cervantes seek form and unity differently in part 1 and part 2?
7. What can be learned about Cervantes' attitude toward chivalric romances from a scrutiny of Don Quixote's library?

8. What is Cervantes' norm in *Don Quixote*, and is it embodied in any single character?
9. Was Sancho successful as a governor?
10. What is the relation between Don Quixote's meditations on the Golden Age and his knight-errantry?
11. Is Don Quixote out of touch with his times?
12. What is pastoral, picaresque, chivalric, sentimental, Moorish, and mirror-of-princes literature? How does Cervantes use these various modes of writing in *Don Quixote*?
13. Could Don Quixote ever become a pastoral hero?
14. In what ways is the Maese Padro episode (or the adventure of the lions, or the descent into the Cave of Montesinos, or the flight on Clavileño) an analogue to the text as a whole, and in what ways does it differ?
15. What are the romantic (or realistic) aspects of the Cardenio episode (or the adventure of the windmills)?
16. What is Sansón Carrasco's motivation?
17. What is the role of will in relation to the main character?
18. Why does Sancho beg his master not to die?
19. Was Don Quixote really quite lucid in areas that did not touch on knight-errantry, as the narrator claimed?
20. Why did Dickens, Flaubert, and Tolstoy call Cervantes the "father of the modern novel"?
21. What are the principal critical biases toward *Don Quixote*?
22. What evidence is there in today's world of a conflict between "the world of Don Quixote" and "the world of Sancho Panza"?
23. What school of interpretation of *Don Quixote* does Dale Wasserman's *Man of La Mancha* represent?
24. Edmund Wilson once wrote that he had been bored by everything he had ever known about Spain, that he had made a point of learning no Spanish, and that he had never "got through" *Don Quixote*. Write a letter to Wilson and comment on his statement.
25. Lionel Trilling stated that "all prose fiction is a variation on the theme of *Don Quixote*." Choose any novel with which you are familiar and comment on this contention.

Some teachers require oral reports on individual episodes from the novel, major themes, and critical or biographical studies of Cervantes. Paper topics range from the moral or stylistic appraisal of a single character, the interpretation of a short passage, the analysis of an episode within the thematic structure of the larger narrative, a consideration of the "Quixotification of Sancho and the Sanchification of Quixote," a discussion about the various narrators' roles or the nature of the "self-created hero," studies of differences between part 1 and part 2, or extended comparisons between *Don Quixote* and other literary works (e.g., *Don Juan, Franken-stein,* the *Odyssey,* and Jorge Amado's *Home Is the Sailor*). Somewhat less frequently, students are asked to review a Cervantes biography, compile a bibliography, prepare a research paper on background materials (e.g., the Moriscos in Spain or literary movements of the Golden Age), or present an abstract of their outside reading. In contrast, some professors refuse to give examinations in literature classes, and others discourage the use of secondary materials. There are even classes in which students' grades are almost entirely determined by their participation in class discussions.

A more traditional approach to the novel tends to preclude unorthodox attempts to provoke students into creative efforts. "Most [students] are not capable of any creative act," avers one instructor. Although his opinion definitely reflects a minority view, many teachers remain convinced that students can adequately express their creative impulses in traditional assignments. "The critical act is a creative act," writes one teacher, and another contends that "reading *Don Quixote* is about the most creative assignment I can imagine. Writing about it comes second. I try to encourage my students to see themselves in what Wolfgang Iser has called 'the role of the implied reader.'" Nevertheless, there are a substantial number of teachers who invite students to post unusual and provocative quotations on bulletin boards, collect proverbs from the book, or collate English versions of *Don Quixote* as a means of exploring problems of translation. For example, students have been asked to seek out Cervantes' own comments on translation and to evaluate the translation currently being used at their own university; on occasion, they have also been encouraged to interview people on the street about their images of Don Quixote and to collect newspaper items that allude to Quixote or "quixotism."

Several teachers require students to maintain a journal in which they "carry on a running dialogue with the reading matter, bringing up questions they want answered in class and relating what they read to materials studied in other courses, or, sometimes, to their own lives and interests." A few instructors allow students to compose poems or short stories in which a quixotic character confronts the contemporary world. One teacher specifically exhorted a class to "reproduce the theme, issues, and 'tone' of the original text." Sometimes students are given the opportunity to draw scenes from *Don Quixote* or to make posters for a departmental bulletin board. "Students have done paintings, sculptures, creative maps, and collages with Quixote themes" in one class, where they must submit a written explanation of their objectives with each creative project. In another, they can draw or use their photographic skills: "I have some fine original drawings students have done over the years," the teacher reports, "including a slide show of professional quality made by a student who was led into his career by this assignment." Students have performed dramatic readings of various episodes, staged the "Wedding of Camacho," produced *Man of La Mancha*, and videotaped original scenarios of "Don Quixote in the Modern World."

Whether instructors rely on traditional or less orthodox methods, however, they are unanimous in their attachment to Cervantes' great novel and in their conviction that it can be made accessible to students at all levels—a conviction tempered by the realization that appreciation of *Don Quixote* is enhanced by a familiarity with Cervantes' language, his culture, and his world. The following essays reflect this conviction, and I hope they will help others develop their own approaches to *Don Quixote*.

GENERAL CONSIDERATIONS

COPING WITH *DON QUIXOTE*

John J. Allen

"All prose fiction is a variation on the theme of *Don Quixote*," according to Lionel Trilling, for whom Cervantes posed "the problem of appearance and reality" (*Liberal Imagination* 203). In Harry Levin's opinion, *Don Quixote* is "the prototype of all realistic novels," exemplifying "the literary technique of systematic disillusionment" (*Gates of Horn* 47–48). René Girard begins his sweeping study of the modern novel with *Don Quixote*, specifically with "The Tale of Foolish Curiosity" from part 1. Both Wayne Booth and Marthe Robert consider Cervantes' use of the self-conscious narrator as central to the development of modern fiction, and Robert Alter's "partial magic" is, as it is for Borges, the magic of Cervantes.

Don Quixote has inspired painters from Goya to Picasso, playwrights from Beaumont and Fletcher to Dale Wasserman, and composers and songwriters from Strauss and Massenet to Joe Darion, Mitch Leigh, and Gordon Lightfoot. In recent years, virtually every figure of political significance in America, from Ralph Nader to Jimmy Carter to Ronald Reagan, has tilted at windmills in the cartoons of our newspapers and magazines.

Novelists have been the most enthusiastic admirers of this "paradigmatic novel of novels," as Alter calls it in his foreword to Marthe Robert's *The Old and the New* (ix). Levin reminds us that

> Defoe was proud to acknowledge "the Quixotism of R. Crusoe."
> Marivaux's first novel, *Pharsamon*, was subtitled *Le Don Quichotte*

français. Fielding brought out a comedy, *Don Quixote in England*, before announcing—on the title page of *Joseph Andrews*—that his first novel had been "written in [imitation of] the manner of Cervantes." Faulkner read *Don Quixote* every year, "as some do the Bible."   (44–48)

Stendhal and Flaubert both acknowledged it as a primary influence on them, Kazantzakis dedicated *Alexis Sorbas* to Sancho Panza, and Turgenev wrote a classic essay on the book. Many have shared Tristram Shandy's sentiments about "the peerless knight of *La Mancha*, whom, by the bye, with all his follies, I love more, and would actually have gone further to have paid a visit to, than the greatest hero of antiquity." After World War II, André Malraux remarked that only three books, *Robinson Crusoe*, *Don Quixote*, and *The Idiot* (the first and last both profoundly influenced by the second) were truly meaningful to the survivors of prisons and concentration camps (119–20). Finally, we have the words of a contemporary novelist, Robert Coover, who acknowledges the debt of the modern novel to Cervantes:

> Your stories...exemplified the dual nature of all good narrative art: they struggled against the unconscious mythic residue in human life and sought to synthesize the unsynthesizable, sallied forth against adolescent thought-modes and exhausted art forms, and returned home with new complexities. In fact your creation of a synthesis between poetic analogy and literal history...gave birth to the Novel—perhaps above all else your works were exemplars of a revolution in narrative fiction, a revolution which governs us—not unlike the way you found yourself abused by the conventions of the Romance—to this very day.   (77)

The range of the novel's appeal astonishes quite as much as the extent of it. Catholic thinkers find their Catholicism vindicated by it, reformers find their criticism of the status quo supported, and Marxists discover that it prefigured their analysis of capitalist society. Throughout modern history, *Don Quixote* has inspired everything from ballads to ballet. How are we, as teachers, to cope with such a prodigious book?

There are so many innovations in Cervantes' novel—so many elements of previous works are refined and brought to perfection in it—that even a partial list is staggering: the creation of a self-conscious narrator, the illusion of the autonomous character as achieved by the subversion of narrative reliability, the integration of a multiplicity of styles, the assimilation of many different narrative genres, the profusion of various levels of fictionality, the transformation of events into experience through the manipulation of point of view, the elaboration of a subtle and pervasive irony, the masterful use of dialogue in the creation and development of character. The fundamental problem of the relation between art and life is developed in *Don Quixote* with respect to every conceivable set of paired opposites: illusion-reality, lies-truth, fiction-fact, poetry-history, mystery-revelation. Moreover, Cervantes' shift from action and passion per se to the development of character involved impressive perceptions of the way people change, dream, and fantasize.

Anyone who has taught *Don Quixote* has become involved in the complications of Cervantes' narrative, but it is always useful to remind students that the book entails the story of readers reading, or misreading, and of writers writing, or failing to write. Don Quixote's reading drives him mad, and his final regret is that he has no time left to read a different kind of book. The author's reading is said to have provoked him to write the novel. All the important characters of part 2 are readers of part 1, and most of the principals in both parts are readers of chivalric romances and other kinds of fiction. Both Don Quixote and the canon are would-be writers, and Ginés de Pasamonte is glimpsed at a moment when he is between two parts of the book he is writing. The "humanist" guide to the Cave of Montesinos is a professional author. As a writer, Cide Hamete is potentially so prolific that he asks to be praised for his restraint in limiting himself, as he has, in part 2. In the text, there is explicit discussion and criticism not only of narrative fiction but of drama and lyric as well. Books and manuscripts are bought and sold, handled, read aloud, acted out, annotated, translated, criticized, printed, plagiarized, burned, buried, and even kicked around by the devils of hell. Because the production and consumption of fiction are primary activities in *Don Quixote*, it is an ideal text for the teacher of literature.

The responsibility of introducing students to a work that has had such a profound impact on the most serious and discriminating minds of the past three hundred years is an awesome one, and the incredibly diverse array of interpretations can only dismay us further. Northrop Frye's injunction that we bring to literature "an understanding as little inadequate as possible" has never seemed more appropriate. Fortunately, *Don Quixote* resists emasculation and destruction in the classroom more tenaciously than any other work I know. It gets through to students despite the teacher's biases and obfuscations and pedantry, partly because such shortcomings are satirized in Cervantes' characters and narrators and thus easily discounted. Don Quixote's declaration that "there are some who wear themselves out in learning and proving things that once known and proved are not worth a penny to the understanding or memory" has always struck me as an apt inscription for the portico of a university library. When I teach *Don*

Quixote, I try to acknowledge my consciousness of inadequacy and partiality at the outset, as much to protect myself from exposure by Cervantes as for the benefit of my students. If I seem at times (in class or in print) to be more presumptuous, it is because so much is at stake in the interpretation of this book. Cervantes' novel fairly begs to be argued over, as a look at the history of *Quixote* criticism reveals. But there is a good explanation for this phenomenon. When the imagined world in a work of fiction approaches the scope and complexity of the world we live in, we perceive the interpretation of the one as a test of our adequacy to comprehend the other, however different they may be from one another in actuality.

As I see it, the study of literature is essentially a response to the question "Whence comes this power?" We study literature not primarily in order to appreciate it but in response to an intuitive appreciation. When students are told that the study of *Don Quixote* will lead to an appreciation of its power, we should not be surprised if their response to our analysis is "So what?" The effect is similar to that of needing to explain a joke to someone who hasn't found it funny. Unamuno suggests this perspective when he turns a classical aphorism on its head. "To be able to love something, one must first know it" is a characteristic instance of Roman banality, but it acquires a new sense when Unamuno transforms it into the maxim: "to be able to know something, one must first love it" (92).

My ideal student is one who comes to me with a copy of *Don Quixote* and says, "I love this book; help me find out why." A professor of comparative literature with whom I took a great books course many years ago asked us the following question on the final examination: "Which of the books we have read this term did you like least, and to what defect in yourself do you attribute your lack of appreciation?" An intuitive response to literature is a prerequisite for study, not a result of it. What a teacher can do is to explore with students how and why Cervantes affects us as he does.

Epictetus observed that "men are disturbed not by things, but by the views that they take of them." The humanities in colleges and universities study the views people take of things. Certainly this approach is fundamental to the study of literature, where relations between a fictional world and readers' perceptions of their own world provide keys to an understanding of the author's attitude toward life. Lionel Trilling has said that "a primary function of art and thought is to liberate the individual from the tyranny of his culture in the environmental sense and to permit him to stand beyond it in an autonomy of perception and judgment" (*Beyond Culture* xiii). The narrowing of this statement to the liberating function of art allows us to think about the unique value of literature, and therefore of *Don Quixote*, but still from the focus of "an autonomy of perception and judgment."

Do we get beyond ourselves or our culture by amassing facts about other times and other cultures? Not necessarily. Although *Don Quixote* abounds with information about sixteenth-century Spanish customs and institutions, there is far more about such matters in the history books. Wayne Booth says that "our stories criticize each other as expressions of how life is (*Rhetoric* 69). The reaction to *Don Quixote* is never "That's interesting. I didn't know that." It is: "That's right. That *is* the way things are, the way people are, the way I am." Of course Don Quixote is not you or I, but he is not as distant as the subjects of biography or clinical case histories. He is halfway between these two levels of reality, and that is precisely the value of Don Quixote and his world. As an individual, I can't judge myself properly, because I am too involved with myself; I will rationalize my failures and shortcomings. In contrast, I can't judge you, because I don't know enough about you and my ignorance will cause me to oversimplify and distort. By eliciting the reader's imaginative participation, fiction mediates between these overly subjective and overly objective positions. My relation with Don Quixote is a seamless fabric of empathy, omniscient understanding, and judgment that is impossible to achieve in "real life" either with others or with myself. As Benjamin DeMott declares, "fiction alone draws us out from the cage of self into caring, knowledgeable concern for the life that is not our own....Reading and writing fiction equals judging yourself from outside, judging another from within" (25, 81). This conviction is related to an idea expressed more abstractly by David Couzens Hoy in *The Critical Circle:* "Essential to the understanding of the art work is a movement toward self-understanding in the interpreter" (136–37). It is a movement, in Trilling's words, toward "an autonomy of perception and judgment," beyond the tyranny of our twentieth-century American culture.

All great fiction works in this way, and *Don Quixote* is no exception. But *Don Quixote* is also the story of a reader whose imaginative participation in literature distorts his perception and overcomes his judgment, so that it constitutes a lesson in how to read as part of its "expression of how life is." *Don Quixote* will continue to be read, and it will continue to move its readers powerfully. We will continue to teach it, thereby ensuring a larger readership than the book would otherwise command, and, insofar as we are able, we will help our students to reach "an understanding as little inadequate as possible" of how Cervantes has involved them and so many before them in such a profoundly affecting experience. It is difficult to imagine a text—even a hypothetical one—more relevant to a student's education in the humanities, and it is our responsibility as teachers to encourage students to grasp this relevance.

COUGHING IN INK AND LITERARY COFFINS

Ruth El Saffar

Throw away the lights, the definitions,
And say of what you see in the dark

That it is this or that it is that,
But do not use the rotted names.

Wallace Stevens

Robert Bly, in one of his wide-ranging, free-wheeling poetry readings, proclaimed literature professors the murderers of Shakespeare, Blake, Hardy, Yeats, and their kind. His indictment was redolent of hyperbole, but it was warmly received by an audience primed to swallow every morsel of wisdom that fell from his lips. Bly may have had the Pied Piper's hypnotic power, but that alone does not explain the enthusiasm generated by this particular observation. In the years since I myself joined in applauding his denunciation of those who teach the world's great writers in packaged, predigested units, I have returned again and again to his statement.

As professors of literature, we cannot fail to note that *something* seems to be expiring in the humanities departments of our colleges and universities. Interest in the masterpieces of Western culture is eroding before our eyes, and enrollments in humanities classes are declining. Although we tend to regard ourselves as helpless observers rather than active participants in this process, I would like to suggest that we momentarily lay aside our visions of a Great Conspiracy (devised by the malign forces of Business, Technology, and the Economy) and consider how we might recapture our own original excitement of reading our favorite writers and how we can transmit that excitement to our students.

We might well begin with Cervantes. Let us think back to that (perhaps mythical) time when we read *Don Quixote* for the fun of it. Was there laughter then at Sancho's outrageous failures to render chivalric prose by memory to the priest and the barber? Did we do mental flip-flops, like Don Diego de Miranda and his son, in our attempts to decide whether or not the Knight of La Mancha was really mad? Did we hope that Dulcinea might somehow appear, and did we suffer with Don Quixote as he stumbled ever more painfully toward his end? Did we feel betrayed when the hero renounced all that went before as pure folly?

These are embarrassing questions. They invite us to reexperience a naive reading of a great masterpiece—to reactivate some of the emotive responses that years of academic training have taught us to ignore or explain away. We respond to this demand much as Roger Ebert might respond if, after delivering a sophisticated movie review, he were asked, "Yes, but did you cry when you saw it?" As professional scholars and teachers of literature, we are more comfortable talking about technique, irony, authorial distance, narrators, and narratees—in short, about anything other than the visceral feelings awakened by the reading of a text.

I am not suggesting here that we transform literature classes into feel-ins or that we renounce all critical terminologies. I am simply urging a reassessment of our role as undergraduate teachers and an acknowledgment of the primary, unsophisticated joys of reading and other forms of make-believe.

Before proceeding with this exercise, we need to consider whether we can still read *Don Quixote* naively. The text comes to us heavily burdened with erudite commentary, the work of centuries of scholarship. Anthony Close, in his *The Romantic Approach to* Don Quixote, has persuasively argued that we cannot possibly free our readings of *Don Quixote* from two hundred years of Romantic and post-Romantic interpretations. Yet the basic problem is even more serious than Close's argument suggests. The text may be laden with critical garments that obscure its original form, but it is also enshrouded with an aura of sacredness that prevents present-day readers from approaching it in a spirit of playfulness. In its hallowed presence, students and teachers alike may feel that outbursts of laughter are signs of disrespect that must be suppressed. Canonized and dogmatized, the text becomes its own antithesis, subject to the very erosion about which we have just been complaining.

In this way, critics and teachers with the best of intentions have often made *Don Quixote* virtually unapproachable. To rescue it, we must seek to recall our own naive reading of the book, but if we cannot do that, we must at least begin to look at it for signs of its own iconoclasm. *Don Quixote* is above all a book about breaking down conventions and well-tried literary forms. It was written by an author who, poorly trained in scholarship, said of secondary sources: "I am too spiritless and lazy by nature to go about looking for authors to say for me what I can say myself without them" (pt. 1, prologue; p. 27).[1] *Don Quixote* is also a book about the joys—and dangers—of reading. If we are to recover it, we must stop "coughing in ink" and get down to the business of pleasure.

It might help to remember that Cervantes—or at least his surrogate, the Second Author in part 1, chapters 8–9—was addicted to reading. He read any bit of paper that floated past, and much of what he read was trash. Like popular romances today, chivalric and pastoral novels had "hooked" a good many people in sixteenth- and seventeenth-century Spain. Cervantes knew that writers had to tell a good tale if they expected to attract readers, and although he protested vehemently against the tastes of a reading public overfed on pulp romances, he aimed for that very market, and *Don Quixote* succeeded in capturing it.

Undergraduate students may read romances, but many, perhaps most, do not have a reading habit. We may therefore have to appeal to them through their collective experiences with the likes of *Fantasy Island*, *Quincy*, and *M°A°S°H*. We must seek to reach our students where they are; we must come to understand what it is in cheap, sentimental, violent, and abusively exploitative mass entertainment that holds an audience. I believe that the drawing power of popular literature lies in a taste for imaginative participation in the lives, experiences, feelings, fears, and aspirations of others, and I am convinced that this taste can be shaped into an appreciation of finer works of art.

The hunger for fantasy and the desire for relief from the oppression of day-to-day life are the seeds from which all loftier appreciations of literature and life will grow. The seed, of course, is neither the flower nor the fruit. It needs cultivating. It would be foolish indeed to begin our garden by throwing out the seeds because they are small, dull-looking, and enclosed in shells. All too often we have evaded the mud and muck of cultivation by shaming those students who read *Don Quixote* and thought they were supposed to laugh, or those who became excited over William Blake. If we take away the expectation that students will find interesting, hilarious, absurd, and tragic figures in *Don Quixote*, we may have lost them at the beginning. They may plow through the text with us, but they won't tell their friends to sign up for the course the next time it is offered.

For our own sake and for the sake of our students, we need to treat *Don Quixote* first and foremost as a wonderful, delightful reading experience. Students might be requested to note down and read in class the sections they especially like. They might be encouraged to ask and answer the numerous questions that naturally arise: Why does Sancho stay with Don Quixote? Is Don Quixote really mad? Why did Cervantes have his hero recant? Debates about such questions might be staged, or the students might be challenged to discover modern equivalents for characters and situations in the novel. The issues that literary scholars have been trained to focus on follow with surprising predictability after such "naive" opening questions have been posed, because the very practice of literary criticism developed in response to questions which needed answers.

If we take *Don Quixote* out of its temple and carry it off to a local bar, a Fourth of July parade, an aerobics class, or the university coffee shop, we suddenly discover how much it has to say to us and about us. It celebrates the life of an early seventeenth-century reader who, like today's aficionados of soap operas and cheap fiction, needed stiff draughts of fantasy in order to endure an otherwise humdrum existence. It was written by an author who realized that, if his book were to have any touch of erudition, it would have to come from faked footnotes, ready-made quotations, and stock mythological characters (pt. 1, prologue; pp. 27–30).

When we begin to relax with *Don Quixote* and to feel free walking in and out of its many doors, we see that life inside the text is not really so different from life outside it. This marvelous looking-glass effect enables us to listen with Juan Palomeque, his family, Cardenio, Dorotea, and the barber as the priest reads us a story (pt. 1, ch. 33). In part 2, we discover that we have been hoodwinked as often by the narrator as Don Quixote has been by those who set out to fool him. This trick is revealed in the episode of the Knight of the Mirrors (pt. 2, ch. 14), Camacho's wedding (pt. 2, ch. 21), Master Peter (pt. 2, ch. 25), the pinching of Don Quixote and Doña Rodríguez (pt. 2, chs. 48, 50), the talking head (pt. 2, ch. 62), and the Knight of the White Moon (pt. 2, ch. 65). In each case, Cervantes waits until we have participated with Don Quixote in his confusion before telling us how that confusion was engineered. As readers and as characters we are frequently doubled within the work, becoming both participants in and observers of a story that moves across the screen of our imagination.

Once we allow ourselves and our classes to enjoy the text, we can begin to show our students how the doors to *Don Quixote* swing both ways. We can point out that, even as Cervantes urges us into his house of fiction through the humor and pathos of his main characters, he warns us to keep our distance. The jolt that most first readers of the novel experience when they come to Don Quixote's recantation and death is really only a delayed reaction to a long chain of less obvious hints that literature, however fascinating, can also destroy. Throughout the novel, Cervantes strives to hold readers out of his fictional world while beckoning them to enter. He portrays his fantasy-drunk hero as seriously deranged and even dangerous, as Andrés (pt. 1, ch. 4), the Basque gentleman (pt. 1, ch. 8), Juan Palomeque (pt. 1, chs. 16–17), the *encamisado* Alonso López (pt. 1, ch. 19), and the goatherd Eugenio (pt. 1, ch. 52) would all testify. If Don Quixote manages to frighten and sometimes injure people during his journey, he is an even greater menace to himself, for he suffers a badly torn ear, the loss of several molars, and innumerable beatings, tramplings, clawings, and humiliations. Readers are implicitly warned that they identify with Don Quixote's blind passion for literary "reality" only at their own risk.

Furthermore, Cervantes stops the novel in the middle of an episode to declare that the author has run out of material; he breaks the work into chapters and parts in unlikely places, and he deliberately withholds information. These literary devices remind readers that the work is a fabrication, not to be confused with their own lives. The play with levels of literary style, the multiplication of possible names for the same object, the different perceptions of the same reality from different vantage points all subvert our tendency to confuse words and things and to think that one view of the world contains all truth.[2]

In this regard, Cervantes is his own best teacher. Like Plato's famed *pharmakon*, *Don Quixote* is both the poison and the cure: Cervantes lures us into his book and shows us its charms, but he also warns us against its dangers.[3] He would have us accompany Don Quixote and Sancho and he wants us to enjoy the journey, but he also teaches us to let go of the fiction and to see the book for what it is. In short, he would have us learn, through his work, to be in the world but not of it.

Don Quixote contains within it the birth, flowering, and death of the novel it is reputed to have introduced into Western letters. It writes us into the text by mirroring our fantasy-hungry selves, but it also writes us back out by constantly exposing its own literary techniques. Authors like Fielding, Galdós, Balzac, and Dickens have elaborated the fantasy element of Cervantes' masterpiece, entangling their readers deeply in the lives of everyday characters like themselves. Others, like Sterne, Unamuno, and Proust, have emulated the self-consciousness of Cervantes' artistry, drawing from *Don Quixote* a model for representing the dilemma of an author who, trying through words to capture experience, makes this dilemma the subject matter of his novel. Yet Cervantes' ability to fix the reader at a magical spot midway between identification and detachment has rarely, if ever, been duplicated.

As teachers we should follow Cervantes' lead into and out of *Don Quixote*. He is our best guide. Let us find our students' equivalents of Don Quixote's romances of chivalry. They do exist, even if we don't approve. Cervantes did not approve of Don Quixote's reading tastes either, but he obviously indulged in them himself, just as we surreptitiously indulge in second-rate television programs. We can then show students how their passion for fantasy is mirrored in *Don Quixote*. When some level of identification has been established, students should be encouraged to react naturally to what they are reading. Their own questions should eventually guide them to secondary sources. One should take time with the first twenty chapters, indulge in the pleasures of the text, and disregard fears of oversimplification. In my experience, *Don Quixote* has the capacity to satisfy all readers from Sancho Panza to deconstructionists. The more students know, the more it has to tell them. But the doors must be left open so that the text will continue to be a discovery for each student according to his or her own lights.

If, at the end of the course, students have become a little less frightened of literary icons and a little more enthusiastic about the possibilities of a story from another age and another culture, perhaps we can keep the lid off our coffin and the ink out of our lungs and belie Yeats's vision of scholars, a vision not so very different from that of Bly, or Cervantes:

> All shuffle then; all cough in ink
> All wear the carpet with their shoes
> All think what other people think;
> All know the man their neighbour knows.
> Lord, what would they say
> Did their Catullus walk that way?

NOTES

[1]*The Adventures of Don Quixote*, trans. J. M. Cohen.

[2]The break at the end of chapter 8 is discussed in George Haley and in F. W. Locke. The disconformity between the narrative flow and the formal subdivisions of the work has been treated by Raymond Willis in *The Phantom Chapters of the Quijote*, and a general discussion of the author's sleight of hand is contained in my *Distance and Control in* Don Quixote (esp. ch. 4). Levels of literary style are described in Angel Rosenblat, and the use of names to describe things is insightfully discussed in Leo Spitzer, Michel Foucault's *The Order of Things*, and Manuel Durán's *La ambigüedad en el* Quijote.

[3]The *pharmakon* is a metaphor for beguiling rhetoric that leads one, just as *eros* does, away from the center. It appears in Plato's *Phaedrus* and is used extensively by Cesáreo Bandera in his introduction to *Mimesis Conflictiva* and by René Girard in *Violence and the Sacred*.

THREE APPROACHES TO *DON QUIXOTE*

Howard Mancing

It always saddens me when I hear of a college or university where the course on *Don Quixote* is unpopular or has the reputation of being taught badly. What can such a course be like, I wonder; how can a teacher have contrived to make the book uninteresting? On the other hand, it is always gratifying to know of a *Quixote* course that is brilliantly taught (as was the one I took as a graduate student) or to hear about an inspirational professor who wins outstanding teaching awards for a course on the novel. I have often felt that my colleagues might legitimately feel a certain envy when they contemplate my job: reading and discussing with good students that greatest of all novels, *Don Quixote*. For me, it is more a privilege than a chore to teach works by authors whose genius and originality is unquestioned—Homer Dante, Shakespeare, Goethe, Baudelaire, Joyce, Proust, and, of course, Cervantes.

In this brief essay, I would like to offer some observations on three approaches to *Don Quixote*. The first approach is formal, a flexible model for dealing with the work according to the interests and capabilities of the students in a particular course. The second is thematic, a consideration of how a single question can provide a unified way of reading and discussing various elements in the book. The third is comparative, an attempt to present and assess the intertextuality of the Quixotic tradition in literature.

I

"My history...will require a commentary to make it intelligible" (pt. 2, ch. 3; p. 441).[1] *Don Quixote* is a long and formidable book to read for the first time. Like many "classics," it is more often begun than finished. Perhaps the ideal way to encounter it for the first time is to read it slowly, a few chapters at a time, with others who can discuss what has just been read and reevaluate previous impressions in the light of the new material. In other words, *Don Quixote* is an excellent text for the traditional classroom situation.

The role of a teacher in this situation might well be what Salvador de Madariaga would call a "reader's guide to *Don Quixote*." A comparison can be made with Vergil, who guides Dante through the Inferno and answers the right questions at the right time. The mix of lecture and discussion in any given class period should vary according to the material read for that day and the responses and reactions of the students. On those days when the students are expansive, insightful, original, or excited, the dominant mode is usually discussion—which may stray far from the assigned chapters but never from the novel itself. On other days, the instructor might lecture on the material and expect relatively few contributions from the students. Some classes are devoted to detailed examinations of brief textual passages, others to broader thematic concerns. The key is flexibility: if a student comment leads to a consideration of a reader's ethical reaction to a specific character or to an examination of the social realities of Moriscos and *conversos* in Renaissance Spain, these matters should be discussed. If they have not already been considered, they can easily be raised when reading about Don Diego de Miranda (pt. 2, ch. 16) or Roque Guinart (pt. 2, ch. 54), respectively. There are many critical problems to be discussed: the reader's ethical reaction to the protagonist (i.e., does the reader laugh at or sympathize with Don Quixote?), Cervantes' stance vis-à-vis Renaissance literary theories, the psychological evolution of Don Quixote and Sancho, the pervasive influence of the romances of chivalry, levels of fiction and the metafictional problems of the text, varieties of style, word play and onomastic humor, intricacies of structure and plot, the use of Cervantes' text by novelists from Avellaneda to Saul Bellow. These matters can be discussed repeatedly throughout the course, and attitudes toward them can be revised whenever new textual material necessitates a change. Each class period and each course can be unique, shaped by circumstance and modulated by student interest and response. All the basics should have been covered by the end of the semester, but the order and the emphasis always seem to vary.

The theme of reality versus appearance provides a good example of how this flexible approach can operate. The problem is basic to *Don Quixote,* and I assume that no class on the novel can avoid a consideration of it. We might lecture to the students or have them participate in a discussion on this subject as it arises in connection with Don Quixote's arrival at the first inn/castle (pt. 1, ch. 2), his encounter with the windmills/giants (pt. 1, ch.

8), or his appropriation of the barber's basin/Mambrino's helmet (pt. 1, ch. 21). The problem is also adumbrated in Don Quixote's explicit comment, "what seems to you a barber's basin seems to me Mambrino's helmet, and to another it will seem something else" (pt. 1, ch. 25; p. 180), and in the dispute that culminates in a vote at Juan Palomeque's inn (pt. 1, chs. 44–45). Instead of following a more formal, planned structure, we might simply raise the appearance-reality issue at any or all of these points and discuss it as thoroughly as a particular class requires.

In my most recent Don Quixote class, the students repeatedly returned to questions about the nature of reality. Lines were drawn between two camps: those who adhered to a subjective (Quixotic) interpretation of reality and those who defended a more empirical (Panzaic) view. Finally, when Sancho presented his "basin/helmet" compromise (pt. 1, ch. 44; p. 355), two extraordinary students entered into a spontaneous debate. Both had extensive philosophical and theological training and had studied the Bible at length: one was a devotee of Oriental and subjectivistic philosophies, the other a traditional Roman Catholic with seminary experience. As they began to argue, I simply sat down and listened with the other students for the remainder of the period. Paradoxically, it was one of the most exciting classes I ever "taught."

By the end of a semester devoted to Don Quixote, students should be familiar with the text. They should know the characters and scenes of the novel, and they should be able to recognize major aspects of style, structure, narrative technique, and theme. They ought as well to have considered the cultural and social context in which the book was written. But above all, they should have enjoyed themselves and achieved personal growth as a result of the intellectual and aesthetic experience of reading and discussing of the book.

II

"He hit upon the strangest notion that ever madman in this world hit upon, ... that he should make a knight-errant of himself" (pt. 1, ch. 1; p. 27). What does it mean that Don Quixote chooses to become a knight-errant in imitation of his literary models? A thorough consideration of the implications of this question can lend a logical thematic unity to any teaching of Cervantes' masterpiece. The novel's point of departure is Alonso Quixano's existential need to justify his life by choosing to lead a new one that has been inspired by books. To be an authentic knight-errant, Don Quixote employs archaic and formulaic speech; in fact, everything he says and does is based on a conscious imitation of what he has read. As the novel progresses, he sometimes betrays his own standards of chivalry and makes concessions to reality. When other characters enter the novel, they either conform to his imagined world of chivalry or they undermine it. In a few instances, they both conform to it and undermine it, but the crucial point is that style, theme, characterization, and structure in *Don Quixote* all depend on a choice made by the protagonist in the first chapter.

For this reason, the intertextual premise of *Don Quixote* cannot be ignored. To read and understand Cervantes' novel on more than a superficial level, one should have read (or have become familiar with) *Amadís de Gaula* and other sixteenth-century Spanish romances of chivalry. The presence of these books in *Don Quixote* cannot be overestimated. References and allusions to them abound; they are parodied, paraphrased, and satirized by virtually every narrator and character in the book, from the mad ravings of Alonso Quixano in part 1, chapter 1 to his definitive recantation in part 2, chapter 74. The intertextuality that begins with the romances of chivalry is soon extended to pastoral and picaresque fiction, varieties of theater, and popular and erudite poetry. *Don Quixote* is, as much as anything else, a book about books: the art of writing and narrating books, the effects of reading books, and the consequences of attempting to live one's life according to the norms of a literary text.

A number of themes and issues that might seem unrelated can nevertheless be subsumed under the general rubric of chivalry. Although the theme of imitation reappears throughout the novel, it is most directly explored in part 1, chapter 25, when Don Quixote gratuitously emulates Amadís de Gaula's self-imposed penance for love. The issue of the book's narrator is raised during Don Quixote's first sally, when the knight imagines the "sage magician" who will write the chronicle of his chivalrous deeds, and it becomes increasingly complicated as the fictional historian Cide Hamete Benengeli assumes ever greater importance. Furthermore, the problem of reality versus appearances is repeatedly raised in terms of chivalric legend: inn versus castle, windmills versus giants, barber's basin versus enchanted helmet.

III

"For me alone was Don Quixote born, and I for him; it was his to act and mine to write; we two together make but one" (pt. 2, ch. 74; p. 830). Like most of those who have taught *Don Quixote*, I have made some attempt to illustrate the universality of the work and its enduring inspirational quality. I have had students read the text and listen to the music of *Man of La Mancha* in order to compare the characters and themes with those of Cervantes' novel. I have devoted classes to playing Richard Strauss's lovely tone poem *Don Quixote*. I have amassed a collection of slides by artists like

Goya, Doré, Daumier, Dalí, Picasso, Herreros, and others who have illustrated Cervantes' story and interpreted his characters in a visual medium. I have required students to write papers comparing *Don Quixote* with other novels. But I have never systematically attempted to incorporate the hundreds of literary works inspired directly or indirectly by *Don Quixote* into my classes. Indeed, it would be a quixotic endeavor to structure an entire class around the intertextual relations involving *Don Quixote* and all subsequent literature.

In *Meditations on* Quixote, José Ortega y Gasset has written that "every novel bears *Quixote* within it like an inner filigree" (162). This presence is most obvious in the many novels that are self-proclaimed sequels to *Don Quixote*—works from Avellaneda's apocryphal continuation in 1614 to Torcuato Miguel's *La vuelta de Don Quijote* in 1979. It is also reflected in novels where the protagonists are namesakes of Cervantes' knight-errant: Charlotte Lennox' *The Female Quixote*, G. K. Chesterton's *The Return of Don Quixote*, José Larraz' *¡Don Quijancho, maestro!* and Richard Powell's *Don Quixote, U.S.A.* There are also stories in which secondary characters from the novel are featured—Diego San José's *Ginés de Pasamonte* or Robin Chapman's excellent *The Duchess's Diary*. But the case need not always be so obvious. Parson Adams, Mr. Pickwick, Emma Bovary, Prince Myshkin, Isidora Rufete, George F. Babbitt, Eugene Henderson, Alonso Cordero (in Herbert Lobsenz' *Vangel Griffin*), Celestino Marcilla (in Henry de Montherlant's *Chaos and Night*), and Colonel Vorotyntsev (in Alexander Solzhenitsyn's *August 1914*) range from the ridiculous to the sublime, from the obvious to the enigmatic; they are as different from each other as are their authors. Yet they have one basic trait in common: they are all consciously modeled on Don Quixote. What are the protean qualities that inspire such radically different progeny? To what extent does an awareness or ignorance of quixotic elements affect our readings of these books? Can one fully appreciate them without knowing *Don Quixote*? How does one react to literature that seeks its inspiration in previous literary texts? How does one evaluate it?

Even protagonists that are not based directly and consciously on Don Quixote may exhibit quixotic features. All characters who read books or watch television or movies and dream of alternative realities experience the same dilemma that made Alonso Quixano choose to become Don Quixote: Catherine Morland in *Northanger Abbey*, Maggie Tulliver in *The Mill on the Floss*, Isabel Archer in *The Portrait of a Lady*, Etienne Lantier in *Germinal*, Loretta Wendall in Joyce Carol Oates's *Them*, Chance in Jerzy Kosinski's *Being There*, Isadora Wing in Erica Jong's *Fear of Flying*, and Jack Twiller in William Kotzwinkle's *Jack in the Box*. It is an intriguing challenge for students to read some of these books and to contemplate the power of Don Quixote's timeless story as told and retold in infinite variety.

The conscious Cervantine presence in various modes of literature is not limited to the endless parade of Quixotic characters. The metafictional tradition of the novel that discusses itself as it is being written/read clearly begins with Cervantes and includes great practitioners from Laurence Sterne to Michel Butor and John Barth. Some of the greatest Spanish and Spanish-American writers—Galdós, Unamuno, Azorín, Borges—have been virtually obsessed with *Don Quixote*, returning to it repeatedly and incorporating it with great originality into their own works. Many of the best modern Hispanic poets—Rubén Darío, Manuel Machado, Antonio Machado, Enrique de Mesa, León Felipe, Jorge Guillén, Gerardo Diego, Borges, Gabriel Celaya, and Blas de Otero—have written major poems inspired by *Don Quixote*. Is there a more seminal work of literature than Cervantes' novel?

"All prose fiction is a variation on the theme of *Don Quixote*," according to Lionel Trilling in his essay "Manners, Morals, and the Novel" (203). "That's the struggle of humanity, to recruit others to your version of what's real," theorizes the protagonist of Saul Bellow's *Adventures of Augie March* (402). "We are all in flight from the real reality. That is the basic definition of *Homo sapiens*," observes John Fowles as he interrupts *The French Lieutenant's Woman* to comment on the characters and the work (82). These writers have all felt the impact of Cervantes, but none of them has ever made a more profound statement on what it means to be human than Cervantes did in *Don Quixote*. More than any literary figure I have ever encountered, Don Quixote symbolizes existence in the modern world.

Cervantes' novel is perhaps best read for the first time in the traditional classroom setting. But if a work of art is to maintain its immediacy and relevance, it must improve with repeated readings, which must be undertaken by the student alone. We who teach *Don Quixote* can introduce the novel to new readers and guide them through their first encounter with the text, but, like Vergil, we can only go so far. If our students rarely encounter a Beatrice or a Dulcinea to take them further, they must nevertheless realize that the paradise of literary appreciation can only be reached in a solitary dialogue between themselves and the text.

NOTE

[1]Here and throughout, I quote *Don Quixote: The Ormsby Translation, Revised*, ed. Joseph R. Jones and Kenneth Douglas.

CRITICAL APPROACHES AND THE TEACHING OF *DON QUIXOTE*

TEACHING *DON QUIXOTE* AS A FUNNY BOOK

Daniel Eisenberg

> If I understand it correctly, this
> book of yours...is an attack on the
> romances of chivalry,...despised
> by many, yet praised by many more.
>
> *Don Quixote*, pt. 1, prologue

Cervantes wrote *Don Quixote* to make us laugh at the amusing mis-
adventures of a burlesque knight-errant. By so doing, he hoped to end the
great popularity of romances of chivalry, in which the deeds of knights-
errant are portrayed; he saw these works as deficient, incapable of
properly entertaining their readers. At the same time, he wished to supply
what the romances could not offer: entertainment that was not only
harmless but beneficial.

Many modern critics are reluctant to see *Don Quixote* this way, which is
the way Cervantes' contemporaries saw it. Even Philip III testified to this
fact; on hearing a student laugh uproariously, he concluded that the
"student is either beside himself, or reading *Don Quixote*" (Russell 318).
The modern resistance to this interpretation may arise from nationalism
("*Don Quixote* portrays the spirit of Spain, so it cannot be comic"), the low

prestige of humorous writing ("Since *Don Quixote* is a classic, it cannot be a funny book"), the belief that we should not laugh at a fictional character's misfortunes, or a simple lack of familiarity with Cervantes' literary and cultural milieu. Some ignore the humor altogether: Luis Murillo's recent bibliography does not even include "humor in *Don Quixote*" as a category, and it misplaces Peter Russell's fundamental article "*Don Quixote* as a Funny Book" under the heading "*Don Quixote* in England."

Cervantes certainly had secondary purposes, as well as secondary sources, and I do not mean to imply that the study of sources or of humor is anything like a comprehensive approach to *Don Quixote*. Yet to claim that *Don Quixote* is not primarily a work of humor is to claim that it is a failure. As Russell has shown, Spanish as well as foreign readers of the time unanimously considered *Don Quixote* a funny book.

If Cervantes had a "true" purpose, it eludes even modern critics, who cannot agree on any alternative interpretation. What Oscar Mandel (in "The Function of the Norm in *Don Quixote*") has called the "soft" approach—one that sees Quixote as admirable rather than ridiculous—is a product of the Romantic movement's exaltation of suffering. The influence of that movement on contemporary interpretations of *Don Quixote* remains strong (see Anthony Close, *The Romantic Approach to* Don Quixote).

To a degree, the Romantic misinterpretation of *Don Quixote* is a result of the book's success: the romances of chivalry that Cervantes attacked are, in fact, no longer read. Yet the teacher or scholar who wishes to understand the work must begin with an examination of its stated topic and with some knowledge of its protagonist's preferred reading. The failure to begin at the beginning accounts for much of the current confusion in *Quixote* criticism.

The favorite pleasure and escape reading of the Spanish Renaissance, the romances of chivalry (which I treat extensively in *Romances of Chivalry in the Spanish Golden Age*) exercised considerable influence on both culture and literature, an influence that has still not been adequately explored. The chivalric romances both reflected values and helped to shape them. They reminded soldiers that Christianity should be promoted as well as defended and that infidels should be vanquished and converted or killed; the Spaniards acted on this belief in the New World as well as in Europe. The chivalric novels stressed the pleasant (and minimized the unpleasant) aspects of traveling to little-known parts of the world; chivalric names like "California" and "Patagonia" were applied to strange lands. The Emperor Charles V, the most powerful and expansionist ruler Spain ever had, was a great fan of such works. They even had an influence on the church; the soldier Loyola, for example, was to some degree inspired by them to found that quasi-military, mobile, practical order of "soldiers of Christ," the

Jesuits. The romances were far too expensive for the poor, but illiterate people who heard them read were enchanted. In short, the books were addicting.

This addiction was all the more serious because the books were not only bad literature; they were also pernicious, at least according to many thoughtful writers of the period. The chivalric romances distracted readers from the essential task of saving their souls. They taught young men how to win, not only the heart, but also the body of a young woman. They undermined the institution of marriage and the authority of parents, and they encouraged youths to leave home on foolish endeavors. Cervantes was hardly the first to feel that the chivalric romances should be suppressed. He chose burlesque, and a fictional demonstration of the books' negative effects, as his means of attack.

To one who has read romances of chivalry, *Don Quixote* is a hilarious book. The protagonist of a romance was always young, handsome, and strong. Don Quixote is old, rides a broken-down horse, wears armor patched with cardboard, and claims a special competence in making birdcages and toothpicks (pt. 2, ch. 6). The knights of the romances traveled through colorful parts of the world, such as China, North Africa, and Asia Minor. Often they went to countries like England and Greece, noted for their "chivalric" history; they never visited Spain. Don Quixote tries to be a knight in Spain, and in one of its least attractive regions: the treeless, desertlike, underpopulated plain of La Mancha. References to this region constitute a pervasive jest: Don Quixote is famous "not only in Spain, but throughout La Mancha," and Dulcinea is not only "the most beautiful creature in the world, but even the most beautiful of La Mancha." The very name Don Quixote *de la Mancha* is one of the most prominent jokes in the book. A *mancha* 'stain' is exactly what a knight should avoid.

Whereas the knights-errant were accompanied by respectful admirers of chivalry, Don Quixote chooses a fat, garrulous, ignorant, greedy, unhappily married peasant as his squire. Knights performed useful deeds—restoring queens to their thrones, helping kings repel invaders, and eliminating menaces to the public order. Don Quixote sets prisoners free, attacks armies of sheep, and bothers merchants peacefully going about their own business. In his mad lust for glory, he also attacks windmills, wineskins, and puppets. Pigs run over him, and the narrator pronounces it "an adventure." Whereas people in distress asked knights to come to their rescue, Andrés specifically requests Don Quixote not to complicate his life with any more help (pt. 1, ch. 31). On the one occasion when Don Quixote's help is urgently and sincerely sought—when someone really needs assistance—he does nothing (pt. 1, ch. 44).

As Don Quixote, expert on chivalric culture, tells us, knights were usually in love. But those knights were of royal blood, and they fell in love with women of similar rank. Don Quixote, an impoverished lesser noble, chooses to love a peasant girl who has a loud voice and smells like a man (pt. 1, chs. 25, 32). Her virtue is repeatedly questioned in the novel; in the introductory sonnet of the Caballero del Febo, for example, we discover that only because of Don Quixote could one pretend that Dulcinea was chaste. Sancho is surprisingly enthusiastic about Aldonza Lorenzo (pt. 1, ch. 25), and this enthusiasm may have something to do with his wife's jealousy, of which he complains in part 2, chapters 22 and 25.

Don Quixote's other contacts with women are no more successful, and they are equally funny. If beautiful women and princesses fall in love with the attractive, competent young knights of the romances, Don Quixote has to seize, and hold on to, a prostitute so repulsive that she would make anyone but a mule driver vomit (pt. 1, ch. 16). Women leave him dangling by the wrist (pt. 1, ch. 43), throw cats in his room while he sleeps (pt. 2, ch. 46), and discuss his *caspa* (a dandrufflike disease of the scalp) in verse (pt. 2, ch. 44).

These, of course, are not the only unchaste women in the book. The point needs to be made that one of the book's humorous elements involves its many sexual and excretory allusions, a fact of considerable interest to contemporary American students. Such material was, of course, never found in the romances of chivalry, but it did have a long tradition in humorous writing. In *Don Quixote*, people smell (pt. 1, chs. 16, 20, 31; pt. 2, ch. 10). They have bugs (pt. 2, ch. 29). They urinate (pt. 2, ch. 52). Women menstruate, or rather, enchanted women fail to do so (pt. 2, ch. 23). Unmarried women get pregnant (pt. 2, ch. 52). Sancho's donkey farts, and this event is declared by its owner to be a good omen, as Donald McGrady has pointed out in "The *Sospiros* of Sancho's Donkey." Obscene words are used and disussed (pt. 1, ch. 25; pt. 2, chs. 12, 29). On occasion, the hero himself appears quite indecently dressed (pt. 1, chs. 25, 35).

If I have elaborated on the comic side of Don Quixote, ignoring his altruistic goals and wise and eloquent words, as well as his companion, the wise fool Sancho, it is because this crucial element is the one most often missed by modern readers. I offer a more comprehensive view in my forthcoming book *A Study of* Don Quixote.

Teaching *Don Quixote* as a funny book can improve student motivation, for students, like most people, are more interested in entertainment than in philosophy. In many ways, however, this approach is devilishly difficult. I have never had a student who has read a single romance of chivalry or one who has seen the Cantinflas movie *Don Quijote cabalga de nuevo* (also released as *Un Quijote sin mancha*), the adaption that is most faithful, humoristically and geographically, to the novel.

Many have seen *Man of La Mancha*, and one of my first tasks is to undo the damage caused by that adaptation and by the misleading statements found in literature textbooks: to convince students that it is permissible to laugh. With some I never succeed. Most, however, cannot help but laugh, following the example I set for them when I explain the book from the perspective of the chivalric romances.

To help students appreciate the humor, I often translate it into contemporary terms. "Don Quixote de la Mancha" is like saying "Don Quixote of Taylor County," a similarly remote and relatively uncultured place. Many popular comedians use misfortune or impotence to elicit laughter: Woody Allen, for example, who dresses inappropriately, misunderstands what is said to him, is incompetent with machinery, doesn't know how to get the girl, yet wins our heart all the same. The inns, filled with colorful characters, I compare to truck stops, and the mule driver, satisfied with Maritornes, to a truck driver.

Approaching *Don Quixote* from a "hard" perspective means paying close attention to Cervantes' language. His subtle, precise, and colorful use of words, still inadequately studied, accounts for much of the book's charm and status as a classic but also makes it difficult for students to understand and appreciate. No existing edition is properly annotated for students with immature skills in Spanish. "Read it slowly; he wrote it slowly," I optimistically advise them. I also recommend reading aloud.

This problem is compounded when dealing with *Don Quixote* in translation, and I recommend that no one teach or even read *Don Quixote* in English without first reading the comments on existing translations by Russell ("*Don Quixote* as a Funny Book") and John Jay Allen ("*Traduttori Traditori: Don Quixote* in English"). Russell unequivocally states that no translation since the eighteenth century is faithful to the spirit of the work, and Allen shows that all versions are marred by serious inaccuracies. Allen's call for a new translation has been answered by Jones' and Douglas' revision of Ormsby's translation; however, Shelton's version (London, 1612–20) is the most faithful to the spirit of the original, though inaccurate in many details and not available in a form suitable for classroom use. I believe, though, that the Spaniards are correct when they claim that *Don Quixote*, like much verbal humor, is to some extent untranslatable. Some levels of style and some chivalric archaisms and proverbs can be reproduced in English, but the vivid dialogue, with lines like "allá van reyes do quieren leyes" (pt. 2, ch. 5), "¿Católicas? ¡Mi padre!" (pt. 1, ch. 47), "Muéreme yo luego" (pt. 1, ch. 10), "señor mío de mi alma" (pt. 1, ch. 12), and "paciencia y barajar" (pt. 2, ch. 23), can only be explained, never translated.

Teaching *Don Quixote* as a funny book means teaching Golden Age Spanish, for which a survey course—often the students' only previous preparation—is inadequate. I endlessly explain linguistic features: the use of the second-person plural, metathesis ("*dalde*" for "dadle"), the future subjunctive, the different use of object pronouns, the unfamiliar or archaic words and constructions ("un su marido"), the proverbs and their implications ("a buen callar llaman Sancho"), and the changing levels of style. In addition, some of the action, and the implications of what characters or narrators say, must be explicated. As Riquer has pointed out (in his essay "Cervantes y la caballeresca" in the *Suma Cervantina*), even Spanish students may not know what a barber's basin is, and without such knowledge some of the humor is obviously lost.

There is, unfortunately, never enough time to discuss all this in depth. It would take about two years, and that type of study is impossible in an American university, if it is still possible anywhere. I have often had to teach not merely *Don Quixote* but all of Cervantes in a ten-week quarter. Although a course on Cervantes provides a good context in which to teach *Don Quixote*—most of the students will never study the complete opus of any other Spanish author—the undergraduate students I teach at Florida State cannot read the entire *Quixote*, much less the other works of Cervantes, in such a short period of time. Because I would rather have them read a lesser assignment well than a longer one superficially, I feel obliged to delete portions of the novel in preparing my syllabus. I usually choose for deletion—how I hate to write this!—such sections as the intercalated tales of part 1 and most of part 2 after the departure from the Duke's castle.

The length of *Don Quixote* and the difficulty my students experience in reading it impose three restrictions on my teaching of the novel. Since reading the text is the first priority, and there is not enough time even for that, I do not ask students to write papers. Moreover, I do not expect them to read anything other than the text itself. I specifically ask undergraduates not to seek out books on *Don Quixote* or on Cervantes. At best they are likely to find a Romantic interpretation; at worst, they will consult books like Dominique Aubier's highly misleading *Don Quichotte, prophète d'Israël*. I do give graduate students a summary history of *Quixote* criticism and a bibliography of suggested readings; this list includes, among others, Riley, Forcione, Allen, El Saffar, and Riquer. I discuss the differing views of these critics, and I teach students how to use bibliographical tools (like the listings and commentaries in *Anales Cervantinos*) to orient themselves in the huge Cervantine bibliography. I describe the life and personality of Cervantes and discuss how they are reflected in his work. I lecture on the romances of chivalry and the parody of chivalric customs, style, and adventures; on the author's Horatian intent to give us lessons for living along with the humor; on Don Quixote's madness and Golden Age attitudes toward it; on the differences between the two parts; on the levels of reality and fiction found in the work; and on the continuation of Avellaneda, his interpretation of part 1, and its influence on the authentic part 2.

If all of this is done "simply, with meaningful, pure, and well-placed words" (pt. 1, prologue), the students—most of them—will come to the conclusion that I have reached, that *Don Quixote* is a brilliantly successful funny book. It is no chore to teach *Don Quixote* from this perspective. It's a different experience for me every time. Every time I go through the book, I find something new and funny in it. Every time I am amused, and pleased, and I wish it were possible to bring Cervantes back to life for one of those leisurely conversations at which he was so adept. "Quien a buen árbol se arrima, buena sombra le cobija" 'He who stays near a good tree, is covered by good shadow' (pt. 2, ch. 32). *Vale.*

METAFICTION IN *DON QUIXOTE*: WHAT IS THE AUTHOR UP TO?

Ulrich Wicks

Embedding is an articulation of the most essential property of all narrative. For the embedding narrative is the *narrative of a narrative*. By telling the story of another narrative, the first narrative achieves its fundamental theme and at the same time is reflected in this image of itself. The embedded narrative is the image of that great abstract narrative of which all the others are merely infinitesimal parts as well as the image of the embedding narrative which directly precedes it.

Tzvetan Todorov, "Narrative-Men"

"Y ¿a qué se atiene el autor?" When Don Quixote poses this question, he is repeating what all students indirectly and directly ask in their every encounter with a literary work: "What is the author up to?" (pt. 2, ch. 4; p. 494).[1] For Don Quixote, this is a naive question; for *Don Quixote*, it is a very problematic one: we shift uneasily in our relation to the book and wonder about the fictions of Don Quixote himself in relation to *Don Quixote* itself. By focusing on this passage, we can guide students to a fuller understanding of the complex narrativity Cervantes created.

Earlier in this scene, Quixote learns from Sansón Carrasco that the story of his knight-errantry is in print all over Spain. "Does the author by any chance promise a second part?" Don Quixote asks, to which Sansón replies: "Yes, he does... but he says he has not found it, and does not know who has it. And so we are in doubt whether it will come out or not. Indeed, some say that second parts are never any good, and others say that enough has been written about Don Quixote. So it is doubtful whether there will be a second part." Yet we *are* reading the second part, even as we hear it being speculated on. At this point Sancho adds, "we should be in the field by now, undoing injuries and setting right wrongs, as is the use and custom of good knights errant" (pt. 2, ch. 4; p. 494). This conversation is perhaps the most extraordinary in world literature: two characters are talking about the book that created them and is now a best-seller in the world they "live" in. When Quixote first set out, he imagined the future history of his life: "Who can doubt that in ages to come, when the authentic story of my famous deeds comes to light, the sage who writes of them will say, when he comes to tell of my first expedition so early in the morning..." (pt. 1, ch. 2; p. 36). Now that the story is in print, he calls Cide Hamete Benengeli "an ignorant chatterer [who]...set himself to write it down blindly and without any method, and let it turn out anyhow" (pt. 2, ch. 3; pp. 489–90). Quixote, as we know from the beginning, has been the kind of reader who blindly refuses to distinguish between actuality and fiction, reality and illusion; in fact, he is such a bad reader that he never tries to separate fiction making from experiential reality. Now that there is a chronicle circulating about his adventures, he is quick to point out every discrepancy between what he thinks has happened and what other readers tell him the author "reported." This is a distinction he never made in his mad reading of chivalric novels. Ironically, he hasn't read this book about himself; we are now reading the sequel, which in turn is about Quixote *not* reading. Part 2 of *Don Quixote* is thus a book about a fiction-crazed man who doesn't bother to read a book about his own life. He believed everything in the books of chivalry, but he now believes—on the basis of hearsay—that everything in his own life story is false. Echoing Quixote's question about Cide Hamete, students and teachers of the book are obliged to ask, "What is Cervantes up to?"

Reading *Don Quixote* is an unsettling experience. Like Mann's *Death in Venice*, which is about a writer writing (and a writer writing about that writer writing), like Beckett's *Waiting for Godot*, which is about actors acting (and a playwright who doesn't give them a play in which to act), and like Flaubert's *Madame Bovary*, which is also about a reader reading badly (and a writer writing about reading), *Don Quixote* is a self-reflexive work: the acts of reading, the responses of readers, and the implications of reading—both within the narrative and outside it—are the real substance of the book. The character of Don Quixote is created from books and recreated in books. Cervantes himself is both author and reader. As Quixote changes the world around him, so Cervantes makes us alter our perspectives on fiction and on the differences between what we conventionally and simplistically call "imaginary" and "real." After the adventure of the fullers, Don Quixote tells Sancho that "not everyone is sufficiently intelligent to be able to see things from the right point of view" (pt. 1, ch. 20; p. 159). Shortly afterward, having won the barber's basin he calls Mambrino's helmet, he says that "its metamorphosis is of no consequence to me, who knows what it really is" (pt. 1, ch. 21; p. 163). He later adds that "what seems to you to be a barber's basin appears to me to be Mambrino's helmet, and to another as something else" (pt. 1, ch. 25; p. 204). The multiple points of view Don Quixote himself uses to explain or justify his relations to perceived and conceived reality are the same strategies that students must develop in their relation to the book. The act of reading is a sallying forth that—like Quixote's adventures *in* the fiction—makes readers constantly aware *of* the fiction. What, indeed, is the author up to?

If reading *Don Quixote* upsets conventional received ideas about reality and illusion, then teaching it is an even more unsettling experience. But it is also maddening fun. In some ways, the use of the book in a course is analogous to Cervantes' use of Quixote's sallies; students discover that reading *Don Quixote* is an adventure that alters their approach to other books in the course, and the instructor finds that the novel is seminal to all innovative fiction written over the past four hundred years. Students and teachers soon realize that they have much to learn—about themselves, about the nature of reality, about the nature of fiction. *Don Quixote* is about all of these, but it is above all about fiction making itself—why it does what it does and how it does it. No writer since Cervantes has written a more provocative fiction about fiction.

Don Quixote, often called (in Trilling's phrase) "the great forefather of the novel," is also the prototypical metafiction. The term "metafiction" was apparently coined by William Gass in his *Fiction and the Figures of Life*. He claims that it applies to those works in which "the forms of fiction serve as the material upon which further forms can be imposed" (24–25) and adds that it "is characteristic of this kind of writing to give overt expression to its nature, provide its own evaluation…" (109). In *Partial Magic: The Novel as a Self-Conscious Genre*, Robert Alter describes this same self-reflexiveness:

> Knowing that a fiction is, after all, only a fiction, is potentially subversive of any meaningful reality that might be attributed to the fiction, while assenting imaginatively to the reality of a represented action is a step in a process that could undermine or bewilder what one ordinarily thinks of as his sense of reality.… The imagination, then, is alternately, or even simultaneously, the supreme instrument of human realization and the eternal snare of delusion of a creature doomed to futility. (15, 18)

The nature of self-reflexiveness can easily be illustrated for students by referring to examples from the visual arts. In Velázquez' *Las meninas* (1656), for example, we see the artist himself, looking at his canvas, the back of which is facing us in the left side of the picture; the king and queen are situated behind us, outside the picture, but reflected in a small mirror that faces us. Velázquez is simultaneously inside and outside his own frame, painting it and painting himself painting. "The entire picture," Michel Foucault observes in *The Order of Things*, "is looking out at a scene for which it is itself a scene"; "representation undertakes to represent itself" and offers itself "as representation in its pure form" (14, 16). In Magritte's *The Human Condition I* (1933), a canvas inside the canvas coincides almost completely with the "real" scene behind it as seen through a window; in fact, the canvas inside the canvas is a recurrent theme throughout Magritte's work. His *In Praise of Dialectic* (1937) shows an exterior view of a window opening into a building to reveal an exterior view. Escher, too, provides many examples, like his *Print Gallery* (1956), in which a painting inside a gallery extends outside it to become the town in which the gallery is located. In *Gödel, Escher, Bach*, Douglas R. Hofstadter examines the nature of this self-reference by wrestling with such paradoxes as "The following sentence is false. The preceding sentence is true." This set of self-contradictory propositions has a visual analogue in Escher's *Drawing Hands* (1948), in which a hand draws the hand that draws it; the viewer is unable to tell which hand is "real" and which is the representation.

Hofstadter calls such infinite self-reference "strange loopiness," and he defines it as a phenomenon that "occurs whenever, by moving upwards (or downwards) through the levels of some hierarchical system, we unexpectedly find ourselves right back where we started" (10). In meta-art, we cannot contemplate, or immerse ourselves in, the representation without simultaneously contemplating the elusiveness of the frame itself. Ultimately, the phenomenon of metafictionality forces us to think about the nature of the medium in which the work presents itself. Referring specifically to Saul Steinberg's version of Escher's drawing hands, E. H. Gombrich writes:

> We have no clue as to which is meant to be the real and which the image; each interpretation is equally probable, but neither, as such, is consistent. If proof were needed of the kinship between the language of art and the language of words, it could be found in this drawing. For the perplexing effect of this self-reference is very similar to the paradoxes beloved of philosophers: the Cretan who says all Cretans lie, or the simple blackboard with only one statement on it which runs, "The only statement on this blackboard is untrue." If it is true it is untrue and if untrue true. There is a limit to the information language can convey without introducing such devices as quotation marks that differentiate between what logicians call "language" and "metalanguage." There is a limit to what

pictures can represent without differentiating between what belongs to the picture and what belongs to the intended reality.

(238–39)

It is precisely this blurring of the intended reality that characterizes
metafictionality in a specific work. To make the signifier opaque rather
than transparent is a sign of metafictionality, which, when we detect it,
makes us orient ourselves differently in relation to the signified. We are no
longer absorbed into the illusion; rather, we are made aware of the power
of the signifying work to absorb us. Don Quixote's many adventures are
lessons on how *not* to read or view or listen. Students can learn from them
that distance—aesthetic, emotional, and rhetorical—is vital in the act of
reading.

Cervantes puts his readers on guard from the moment he writes a
prologue about not writing a prologue; a self-reference to his own *Galatea*
(pt. 1, ch. 6) is another signal that this narrative is going to call attention to
itself *as* narrative. When students reach chapters 8 and 9 of part 1, where
Cide Hamete and the Moorish translator are introduced, they are in a
position to recognize that Cervantes is playing with his narrative just as Don
Quixote is playing with, and being played with by, the world around him.
The great game of illusion, allusion, and elusion—all of which trace their
roots to the Latin *ludere* 'to play'—has begun in earnest. From this point on,
the narrative itself creates and destroys illusions in the same way that Don
Quixote's narrative-nourished imagination does. The translator often
doubts the reliability of Cide Hamete, and Cide Hamete doubts himself.
The narrator, who calls himself the "second author," praises both Cide
Hamete and the translator, but he also occasionally questions the accuracy
of their accounts. Throughout, the narrator comments, the translator
comments, and Cide Hamete comments. In part 2 Don Quixote himself has
the opportunity to comment on a narrative that has already been presented
to us in its multilayered form. What *is* the author up to?

After considering the traditional approaches to *Don Quixote*, students
are likely to be thrown for a "strange loop" when they are asked to consider
it as a metafiction. They have been exposed to self-reflexiveness in movies,
cartoon strips, and television shows (especially in commercials), but
they've never really examined the phenomenon as *Don Quixote* asks them
to examine it, and as Don Quixote himself never really does. They do
become aware of what Jean Cassou, comparing the book with Brueghel's
The Land of Cockaigne (1567), calls "infinitely varied perspectives.…
Reality changes with the eye of the beholder," and "thus is reality shattered
into manifold illusion" (Flores and Benardete, *Cervantes across the*

Centuries 7–8). But in general students want to struggle with the diegesis (the created illusion of Don Quixote and his world) and to ignore the extradiegetic (the creating illusion of the narrative process itself). It's disturbing enough for them to deal with Don Quixote confronting a hostile world that nevertheless nourishes his illusions; the elaborate machinations by the Duke and Duchess far exceed anything Don Quixote ever imagined, and Sansón Carrasco's schemes to get him home require more radical alterations of "reality" than any Quixote ever contrived. But it is even more disturbing for students to face Cervantes' metafictional game, because it implicates each of them in Don Quixote's dilemma. It makes them suspect that people may be the prisoners of their own illusions, not of the real world in which actual demands are made. This realization produces a simultaneous pleasure and uneasiness in our students; it enchants and disenchants at the same time. As Gérard Genette explains in his *Narrative Discourse*, "The most troubling thing about metalepsis indeed lies in this unacceptable and insistent hypothesis, that the extradiegetic is perhaps always diegetic, and that the narrator and his narratees—you and I—perhaps belong to some narrative" (236). Cervantes recognized this relation, and he wove it into *Don Quixote*, which itself projected the problem into the very fabric of subsequent fiction making. Sterne's *Tristram Shandy*, Gide's *The Counterfeiters*, Borges' *Labyrinths*, and Barth's *Lost in the Funhouse* all play with the metafictional dimension of narrative that Cervantes first probed so thoroughly in *Don Quixote*.

To show students the magic of *Don Quixote*, I use several key episodes in addition to the one in which the protagonist asks what the author is up to. One is the long episode involving Cardenio, who says of Don Quixote: "It is so strange and rare that I do not know whether anyone trying to invent such a character in fiction would have the genius to succeed" (pt. 1, ch. 30; p. 267). Yet we are reading about such a character, and, as his adventures unfold, reality seems much stranger and rarer than that which Don Quixote's fiction-fed mind has conceived. The Spanish countryside is full of romances and pastorals that rival the improbabilities in the books of chivalry. An inn becomes a place of "enchantment" (pt. 1, ch. 45), and it is certainly a place of coincidence: Lucinda and Ferdinand meet Cardenio and Dorothea there (pt. 1, ch. 36), the captive meets his brother (pt. 1, ch. 42), and the barber appears (pt. 1, ch. 44). The diegetic world Cervantes creates is in fact more magical than that evoked in the chivalric novels, which everyone regards as improbable.

Another key episode is the puppet show, during which Don Quixote fails to maintain an appropriate distance between himself as viewer and the presentation of a fiction. Because the performance does not conform to his book-bred notions, Quixote slashes the puppets to bits and finally justifies his action by blaming it on enchanters who "persecute me [and] are always placing before my eyes shapes like these, and then changing and transforming them to look like whatever they please" (pt. 2, ch. 26; p. 643). This episode is a paradigm of the reader's relation to *Don Quixote* or to any work of fiction. Just as Pasamonte (himself a character imitating literature) can spellbind Quixote into believing the puppets real, so Cervantes, who creates this illusion of an illusion, has been spellbinding us. The puppet show is like *Don Quixote*, drawing in the viewer and then exposing the illusion.

A third key episode in my approach to the novel is the dialogue between Quixote and Don Álvaro Tarfe, a character in Avellaneda's false continuation. In this episode, Cervantes simultaneously acknowledges and destroys the work of his rival by bringing a character from it into his own fictional world. "Let me affirm once more that I didn't see what I did see, and that what happened to me didn't happen," says Don Álvaro (pt. 2, ch. 72; p. 928). From the moment Don Quixote becomes aware of a book about his exploits, the narrative is filled with problematic illusions of this kind. Don Quixote and Sancho Panza are not aware of their existence in a book, but they are aware of the existence of a book about them. Quixote and Sancho have their "real" existence to contend with, a book existence that coincides with their "real" past, and another book existence that ostensibly grew out of their first book existence but not out of their "real" lives. Cervantes' fiction is thus like a Borgesian infinity of mirrors, mixing the apparent real with the presumed illusory in a created world where perceived events are more fabulous than those reported in books. In this world, Don Quixote is a perfect knight-errant; in fact, he is the *only* one. This is the great metafictional paradox of *Don Quixote*: because he is book-bred, he seems all the more real for being the protagonist in a book that seeks to debunk the works that bred him.

The narrative techniques Cervantes uses to achieve his metafictional effects have been thoroughly studied. Leo Spitzer's "Linguistic Perspectivism in *Don Quijote*," E. C. Riley's *Cervantes's Theory of the Novel*, George Haley's "The Narrator in *Don Quijote*: Maese Pedro's Puppet Show," Ruth El Saffar's *Distance and Control in* Don Quixote, and John J. Allen's *Don Quixote: Hero or Fool?* all provide excellent discussions of the problem. In addition, I would make available to students Hofstadter's *Gödel, Escher, Bach*, Patrick Hughes and George Brecht's *Vicious Circles and Infinity*, and Raymond Smullyan's *What Is the Name of This Book?*, all of which deal with paradoxes of the kind posed by *Don Quixote*. Finally, students are likely to be intrigued by Borges' "Pierre Menard, Author of the *Quixote*" and "Partial Magic in the *Quixote*," which can be found in his *Labyrinths*. Borges builds on the narrative games created by Cervantes. In "Partial

Magic" he asks, "Why does it disturb us that Don Quixote be a reader of the *Quixote* and Hamlet a spectator of *Hamlet?* I believe I have found the reason: these inversions suggest that if the characters of a fictional work can be readers or spectators, we, its readers or spectators, can be fictitious" (196). Perhaps we are all, as Borges has implied in some of his stories, characters in a vast cosmic fiction.

After discovering that ten years elapse between parts 1 and 2 of *Don Quixote* and that a month passes before Quixote learns of the existence of a book about him, a student once asked me, "What's Cervantes *doing?*" I first referred the student to Don Quixote's words, "But now I declare that appearances are not always to be trusted" (pt. 2, ch. 11; p. 535). I then flipped through the passages in which Quixote rationalizes what happens to him—and what happened to the book about him—as the work of an enchanter. I said that Cervantes was aiming for verbal enchantment and explained that *enchantment* comes from a Latin root meaning "incantation" and that *Don Quixote*, like Dante's *Divine Comedy*, is one of the truly enchanting—incantatory—books in world literature. It consumes itself in the act of telling; it is an illusive, allusive, and elusive work—a verbal "ouroboros," a vicious circle like a snake devouring its own tail. (And when the snake-circle is given a twist, it becomes a figure eight, the sign for infinity.)

With all its paradoxes and ironies, metafiction as exemplified in *Don Quixote* is both centrifugal and centripetal: it absorbs us into the story, but it also distances us so that we see fiction making as an infinite circle, like that metafictional moment created by Shakespeare in *Julius Caesar* when Cassius and Brutus, ostensibly living the "real" event, speculate on its future fictionalization (3.1. 111–14). Cervantes' narrative is full of moments like this, metafictional shocks of recognition that jolt us out of the story and into an awareness of story making, just as Don Quixote himself is drawn into and then literally thrown out of his adventures. Cervantes' great metafictional narrative restores to us the magic of reality, and it restories for us the reality of illusion. *Don Quixote* teaches students more about the workings of fiction making than any other book I know; exploring the metafiction of Cervantes' narrative helps them become flexible and sophisticated readers, aware of the intricacies of verbal enchantment.

NOTE

[1]All quotations are from J. M. Cohen's translation, *The Adventures of Don Quixote.*

GETTING STARTED: *DON QUIXOTE* AND THE READER'S RESPONSE

Peter Dunn

Students who come to a course on *Don Quixote* carry with them a weighty object that is assumed to be a long novel. The perception that it is long and the supposition that it is a novel will tend to form a response to it even before the opening lines have been read. What I have to say concerns the initial stages of this encounter with the text, and I propose to treat it under the aspects of extension and genre as well as beginnings.

I

What consequences does length have for author and reader? Students will of course ponder this question at intervals as they read, but they can also be asked to reflect on it at the outset and to recall their previous reading of novels, stories, and poems. Perhaps a student in the class will suggest that short poems and stories are like simple organisms insofar as they have but a single center or organizing principle, be it an anecdote, an insight, a flash of epigrammatic wit, or a sudden shift of awareness. Such works require us to encompass the beginning and the end in a single view. We might explain how this can be achieved by the transformation of a simple structural model like that of Tsvetan Todorov in his *Grammaire du* Décaméron. Is a long novel merely a succession of such moments, or does the largeness of scale entail different modes of organization? Like a short story, a novel must surprise us, but would we read on if we did not have some shadowy expectation of a particular kind of ending? Is the author one of those who plan it all ahead, like God about to create the world and all eternity, foreseeing it in all its wholeness and variety? Or does the story appear to be the work of artist Matisse seated before his unfinished canvas, speculating on what might happen to the lines of force and tensions of color if he were to put a smudge of red ochre just *there*—and so on, moment by moment, choice by choice?

Such preliminary discussion may lead to a working hypothesis (which we must be ready to refine, modify, or abandon). If we are lucky, this hypothesis will be both neat and capacious, like Albert Cook's suggestion, in *The Meaning of Fiction*, that there are plots of "design" and plots of "process," that "we can distinguish between plots whose causality seems contained in their beginning, and plots whose causality generates itself anew through the middle and end in such a way that by the end we are on totally unexpected ground" (16–17). Distinctions like this are never as sharp and categories are never as exclusive as they at first appear to be, but such a binary division of the field does serve to organize the perceptions of the reader. We can proceed from this distinction to suggest that plots of design demand to be seen as wholes, with the author removed from sight, just as an architect is absent from his building, whereas plots of process unfold in such a way that we are compelled to attend to the shifting tensions and the changing perspectives within the narrative. In this case, the author, or a surrogate narrator, is often present in the work as a mediator. Whereas the remote author of the plot of design may, like Homer, let the work stand forth in self-sufficiency, the narrator of the plot of process may intrude with expressions of surprise or puzzlement or offer some conjecture to explain strange events or conduct. Before students reach the end of *Don Quixote* part 1, they should be able to recognize that Cervantes uses both kinds of plot and that sometimes he places one next to, or inside, the other. They should then be asked to look closely at these relations and to examine the ways in which contiguous plots affect one another. Eventually the class will be able to move toward a generalization: for example, that Cervantes accepts formal distinctions in order to override them. Any such generalization must, of course, be supported by evidence taken from other levels of the text. Moving beyond this level of generality, the class can be shown how the mixing of plot types and social levels, modes (comic, tragic, romance, etc.), and levels of discourse (narrative, expository, authorial irony, etc.) produce the illusion of a complete, inclusive world.

By starting with what is familiar to all readers—the existence of stories with plots—we make other avenues of approach more accessible. For example, once the students have read far enough to perceive that *Don Quixote* is not a formally tight composition, it becomes easier to explain the parody of the romances of chivalry. These were loose and episodic but subject to broad generic rules, and Don Quixote's adventures also take on this rambling form. Students will come to appreciate how Cervantes made use of his readers' familiarity with the romances, adopting the chivalric genre but distancing himself from it ideologically. Each time that Rocinante is permitted to choose the road to follow, we are made aware of the presence of the chivalric romances in the world of the reader. The same is true of both the episodic plot that Cervantes pushes to absurdity and the ideological-structural cliché that identifies chance with divine providence in the life of the hero. The teacher can thus move from plot to genre and to the experience of generic expectation. This expectation operates in the act of approaching a text, in perceiving its structure, and in detecting and responding to the interpretive codes built into it.

Here, then, is a first glimpse of Cervantes as he plays the game of author in accord with certain preconceptions of his readers, satisfying their expectations on one level while defeating them on another. Further discussion can lead from reader expectations back to the concept of "plot," its difference from "action," and its essential *literariness*.

In short, the instructor can lead from discussion of plot into the narrative art of Cervantes or go beyond it into various topics in narrative theory. For example, the analysis of some incidents into their constituents of action and function could prepare the way for an introduction to the general theories of Propp, Brémond, or Greimas. Alternatively, patterns and continuities in the novel's structure may be carefully compared with patterns and continuities in cultures or in the life of an individual person. These broader topics could be developed in one or more lectures, but they could equally well become special projects for a student or for a group within the class.

II

Readers normally anticipate that a novel will establish a relation with their own empirical reality. They expect to find a certain density of description, a fictional world constituted by reference to familiar objects, usages, habits, conventions, and institutions and presented within a unified sequence of actions. This frame of temporal continuity has served traditionally as a metaphor for causality in the minds of readers and interpreters. The familiarity of this fictional world, which is not felt to need commentary, helps to elicit the reader's assent to what happens there. We take this so much for granted that exceptional worlds are assigned to special categories labeled "historical," "fantastic," "Gothic," "science fiction," and so on.

The world (that is to say, the empirical reality) presented in *Don Quixote* will not be familiar to our students. Would it have seemed accurate, realistic to Cervantes' readers? And does it matter to us, now, how Spanish readers read it then? The answers to these questions will not be apparent to students without assistance. It is, however, worth recalling what we noted a little while back concerning the formal resemblances between *Don Quixote* and the romances of chivalry. It is clearly important that Cervantes' readers had also read the kind of stories that the knight read. The literature that drove the poor gentleman insane was part of the empirical reality of the first readers; the novel would not work as parody if this were not so.

We can also help our students bridge the gap between our world and Cervantes' very different one by ensuring that they have appropriate historical and biographical information. Not all such information is appropriate, and we must take care to explain the relevance of whatever information we have judged to be necessary. Students are entitled to know why what is usually "background" is being placed in the foreground. At the same time, we must be sensitive to the risks of handling biographical material in such a way as to support current myths such as "Cervantes the idealist hero" or "Don Quixote the projection of Cervantes" or (Unamuno's inversion of the previous example) "Cervantes the shadow of Don Quixote."

We can go some way toward closing the gap by annotating the world as it appears in the book, even if we cannot reconstruct in ourselves the experience of a seventeenth-century Spanish reader situated in the contemporary social, political, and religious reality. We can produce maps, show the dusty roads of La Mancha, and explain that the "hero" set out in a region where the routes of travelers and herdsmen met and crossed. We can make that world credible: it is sparsely populated, but people continually come and go in it, and whenever the knight looks for a castle he finds an inn. A large part of the reality that continually thwarts Don Quixote is strongly encoded in the text, not because the author has "loaded the dice" against his creature, but because it is made up of elements already existing in the real world.

Students require some information about the romances of chivalry, those aristocratic fantasies in whose empty landscapes castles are like friendly or hostile space stations. On this basis we can establish some features of the structure of resemblance/difference that characterizes parody. The open expanse of La Mancha is the best approximation that Spain could offer to the landscape of the romances. It simply happens not to have castles and knights, just people going about some very familiar and typical activities, at least in the early chapters. The familiarity and the intense physicality of the world that Don Quixote encounters is meant to ring true, we may assume, because its immediate purpose is to make the romances ring false. In other words, we cannot experience directly the first Spanish readers' sense of the reality of the world evoked in the book, but we can indirectly affirm its authenticity. A sense of its authenticity is necessary if we are to recognize the incongruity between this reality and the expectations that Don Quixote repeatedly imposes on it. To a large extent the text specifies what we need to know about it. The knight shared with his early readers his familiarity with romantic fiction and also his everyday experiences in an empirical reality that invalidated that fiction for the readers (though not, obviously, for him). Like certain holy men, Don Quixote tries to be in the world but not of it.

If we examine a map of the villages and roads of La Mancha—Argamasilla, Quintanar de la Orden, El Toboso, Puerto Lápice—and set it against the larger map of Spain, another fact comes into view: the distance that separates that region from the centers of power, wealth, and influence. La Mancha is hardly the place to be if one wants to change the world, as Don Quixote does, nor is it that "wilderness" into which spiritual leaders typically withdraw to gain strength before going forth into the "world." Even pacific change through preaching requires that one address crowds. La Mancha is neither "wilderness" nor "world" in the sense of the familiar dichotomy. In part 2 Don Quixote does leave La Mancha and touch the sources of power—the Duke and Duchess, the city of Barcelona, the printing press, the Spanish navy—and their energy helps to destroy him. What this change means for the hero's mission can be discussed later, but students will be better prepared for it if they have acquired early in the reading sequence an ability to recognize the political and symbolic geography of Spain.

III

The endings of works of literature have probably been studied far more than beginnings have, but how the author breaks the primordial silence is of more than conventional significance. In a sense, beginnings are arbitrary: a realistic novel, for example, with its illusion of a before and an after could, by definition, have started at some other point than where it does. Jane Austen could have dispensed with the opening sentence of *Pride and Prejudice*—"It is a truth universally acknowledged, that a single man in possession of a good fortune must be in want of a wife"—and proceeded directly to the business of narrating. We recognize, though, that however arbitrary beginnings may be, there is a logic to the effective beginning. Jane Austen's universal "truth" descends bathetically to the prejudice of a particular class, time, and place, thereby setting the ironic tone that pervades the rest of the novel. In *Lazarillo de Tormes*, Lázaro's "Well, first of all Your Honor should know that I am called Lázaro de Tormes..." lets us see that we are eavesdropping (by design) on one side of a dialogue already in progress—or what is meant to look like a dialogue. The uncertainties of the beginning, and its obvious slant toward one party who commands all the words while the other remains silent, have already provided essential cues both as to what we are reading and as to how we are to interpret it. Similarly, *Don Quixote* needs to be read with particular attention paid to its beginning, because in the first two chapters the rules are established from which all the rest is generated.

"In a certain village in La Mancha...."[1] This phrase, taken by Cervantes from a narrative ballad, makes the novel begin with a quotation and thereby manifests immediately the novel's *literary* nature, counter to the narrator's repeated claims to be writing documented history. The following phrase, "which I do not wish to name," asserts the presence of an author. The uncertainty about Don Quixote's original surname (Quesada? Quixada? Quexana?) marks that author as fallible yet scrupulous. It is not difficult to discern the springs of the comedy in the incongruities between person and persona, between the protagonist's self and his assumed role. A middle-aged village nonentity poses as a glamorous romantic hero, his soaring ambition and lofty rhetoric backed by a rusty sword and a shaky nag. This double linguistic invention, in which Cervantes purportedly commences writing his "history" and the obscure hidalgo transforms himself into a hero by a willful act of language, traces its origin back to fictitious acts of *reading* by that hidalgo. Romantic fiction is read as fact and made to serve as the model for life; the protagonist is consumed by a passion to remake himself, to write himself into a history under the aegis of Amadís de Gaula, whose rhetoric he adopts in order to validate his own acts. Within the book, the figure of the author is less that of a writer than that of a reader who continually exclaims over what he has just read. Fact and fiction, art and life, reading and writing loop repeatedly back so that each one mirrors the other.

At the moment the knight assumes his new role, he buries his old self and recreates himself in and through language. The new role is reaffirmed by the act of renaming: himself, his horse, his lady. The act is repeated and extended at intervals as he incorporates others into his world. We may therefore regard his existence as Don Quixote as a ceaseless attempt to fix and retain this convergence of self and role, to sustain the new identity by asserting it in every new situation and eventuality. Of course, this linguistic willfulness and violence cannot prevent what is forcibly joined from pulling against the unnatural union. The more Don Quixote imposes sameness on the world, the more difference takes its revenge and the more precarious both he and the book of his life become. The discrepancy between the quest and its champion is made even more absurd by him and by his bravado. The epic seriousness of the narrator is called into question by the banality of his protagonist's acts and of the world in which he operates. The veracity of the author who identifies himself with his story and warrants the truth of this strange and unheard-of tale is in turn made suspect by it. Within Don Quixote himself the join is never sealed, the transformation never complete, so the contradictions multiply. He can adjust his words to the chivalric models, but his acts remain travesties. Unable to suppress the everyday world that is his field of operation, he declares that it is manipulated by jealous enchanters. For the Quixote who inhabits the fictional world of chivalric fantasy, the ordinary world has become strange, subject to laws that he cannot comprehend. It fails to fit the paradigms derived from his reading and must be explained as the irruptions of demonic forces. For him the world of chivalry is normal, whereas our prosaic world of gravitation, of the inertia of solid moving bodies, of empirical cause and effect is a ceaseless succession of marvels. Thanks to this peculiar dialectic, the enchanters enable Don Quixote to reenter a world from which he has alienated himself. By a curious reversal, therefore, he becomes capable of retrieving a reality that he has suppressed. Students will no doubt suggest some modern analogues of this phenomenon. Indeed, the entire subject of enchantment offers abundant topics for student papers and presentations.

The introduction of Sancho Panza into the story really marks a new beginning, although his presence may also be seen as enlarging the range of polarities and deepening the existential level of the text. The dialectical oppositions will be reflected in the relations between Don Quixote and Sancho. Each of them struggles to master a role, not only in relation to the world and in the eyes of others, but also in his own eyes and in those of his companion. These struggles have social dimensions and are expressed through the codes of master-servant relations and through the literary code of chivalry. Looking beyond the encounters with travelers and the other varied but passing events, students will find that the one constant feature of the narrative is the dialogue between these two men and the subtle play of power and dependence that unites them. For most students it is not difficult to look through the individual characters to the symbolic possibilities suggested by their relation: the ascetic versus the sensual, the self-sacrificing versus the self-gratifying, the altruistic versus the worldly, and so on. Don Quixote himself, not surprisingly, encourages this kind of reading. We must make sure, however, that the ironies are not overlooked. The knight, after all, finds gratification in his pursuit of fame, and his fury in wielding the sword may raise some questions concerning his asceticism.

Besides, other contrasts, on the social level, are less flattering to Don Quixote. One character is a rentier consuming his patrimony with books of fantasy; the other is a tiller of the soil, who made the earth produce until his master seduced him with promises of power and wealth. The master is barren, while the servant nourishes a family.

As they read further into the book, students must meet, and try to account for, the difficulty of passing a final judgment about either one of this famous pair or about the two of them together. The title of John Jay Allen's book, *Don Quixote: Hero or Fool?* reflects this difficulty. How is it that any judgment we make will have eventually to be reversed? Do the contraries cancel out, coexist in intolerable contradictions, or somehow fertilize each other? Are these equivocations characteristic of the entire book? Can we know, for example, what is folly and what is wisdom? Are we sure that what looks like wisdom at one moment will not appear as folly at another? We may seem to have strayed too far from the subject of the initial expectations of the readers in their encounter with the text, but we have really been showing that this process is a ceaseless one from the beginning to the end of our reading. As we read, each new act or event or decision or remark modifies the existing expectations partly by satisfying them and partly by delaying or diverting them. Before we have read very far, the range of conscious and unconscious expectations has become enormously complex. If we could stop and analyze them at any moment, we would find long-range expectations, immediate expectations, and others that fall somewhere between the two. We expect from the start that Don Quixote's mission will fail, but we do not know how or when, or how close to success he will come, or how conscious he will be of his failure. Then, when we see a pair of characters, one tall and skinny, the other short and fat, we sense an archetypal combination, the pairing of universal contraries that may well draw into its field of attraction all the inconsistencies— the love and the resentment, the sacrifices and the petty treacheries—of which human relations are capable. Taking the widest view, we expect the book to be the story of the knight's adventures and his inevitable defeat. We discover, perhaps on the tenth or twentieth reading, that it is the record of the conversations of Don Quixote and Sancho Panza, because those marvelous colloquies really represent the empirical reality of all readers in any time or place who yearn for companionship even as they crave freedom.

I conclude by briefly mentioning some of the implications that arise from this great novel. At the beginning of Don Quixote's career, the innkeeper who performs the mockery of knighting him tells, with heavy irony, of his "virtuous" career as an errant youth. When the knight stops people on the road, he makes them give an account of themselves. Before long, the book has become a densely woven tapestry of stories presented as the tellers' personal experiences. Within the world of the book, none of these stories is intended as pure entertainment. Rather, lives are transposed into words, and discourse becomes art through the skill of the speaker and the acclamation of the listeners. As the tellers reveal their compulsive fantasies and expose the threads of desire and deception, of chance and causality, the listeners are not passive; their curiosity has elicited the stories, and they respond with amazement, a whole range of emotions, and with judgment. Don Quixote is clearly not the only character who lives his life in response to stories and fictional models. This observation leads necessarily beyond literature. Do we ever escape from fictions in our lives and in the way we think? Can we separate beyond doubt entertaining fictions from normative ones? (*Amadís de Gaula* was normative for Don Quixote and partly exemplary for some readers, but it is not normative at all for us.) We approach new situations and people with a stock of fictions—stereotypes or expectations about "how things will go." Fantasies of desire or fear— fictions again—often distort our perceptions. Think of how often we encounter the words "image" or "scenario" in public statements. Such problems attest to the book's universality. Even so, the instructor cannot allow these topics to wholly divert the student's attention from the book. The real object of inquiry must be how they arise in Cervantes' novel and what function they perform there.

The three sections of this essay present three initial perceptions that can be explored, defined, and extended so as to lead inductively to (1) paradigmatic or extrinsic categories of genre and social reference, (2) the syntagmatic or intrinsic categories of plot and pattern, and (3) the parodic and comic modes. Rather than start with an exposition of critical theory, I prefer to move from a nontechnical reading toward the discovery of method, system, and technical vocabulary. What the class discovers about the different levels of the text can be synthesized several times in the semester. Denis Donoghue described the process informally when he wrote, "Perhaps the reader brings to the reading something like a hypothesis, an informal set of expectations based upon his sense of the kind of book in hand . . . and the drift of the first few pages. He then plays off his reading of the words and sentences against his general impression of the work. Pre-understanding involves something like intuition, guesswork, or a set of hunches" (*Ferocious Alphabets* 33). In this brief essay, I have suggested how teachers can approach Cervantes' text as an object that directs the reader to refine and revise these hunches, provoking a continuous current of interpretation in the classroom.[2]

NOTES

[1]*The Adventures of Don Quixote*, trans. J. M. Cohen.

[2]Those who would like to pursue some of the ideas suggested in this essay might begin by consulting Wayne Booth, *The Rhetoric of Fiction;* Norman Friedman; Wolfgang Iser; Frank Kermode; Robert Scholes and Robert Kellogg; and Alfred Schutz.

DON QUIXOTE AND THE ACT OF READING:
A MULTIPERSPECTIVIST APPROACH

Edward H. Friedman

It would be appropriate to speak of pedagogical effort as an example of rhetorical strategy, because one who teaches adds form to substance, structures the unstructured, and seeks to persuade artfully. *Don Quixote* is complex, consistently inconsistent, self-reflective, and entertaining, a text in which "telling" competes with "showing" to amplify and obscure messages. The purported intention—the destruction of the chivalric romances—may be verified or ignored, depending on the method employed to decode Cervantes' treatment of satire and whatever material extends beyond satire. A comprehensive analysis of the text should stress its diversity and the problematic nature of both its humor and its points of reference. My strategy for teaching *Don Quixote* relies on what I consider the motivating force behind Cervantes' creation: multiperspectivism. That is, I attempt to provide students with a multiperspectivist approach to the multiperspectivist object par excellence.

Don Quixote may be seen as a novel and as a theory of the novel or of writing in general. It is at once the story of Don Quixote and the story of the creation of the text, and this dichotomy continually builds upon itself. The literary representation of the birth and death of an anachronistic knight-errant (and voracious reader) heralds not only the birth of the modern novel but also the emergence of a new dichotomy, that of story versus history—or the writing of fiction versus the writing of history—and ultimately the dichotomy of the power or impotence of the word. In *Don Quixote*, Cervantes makes statements about art and about the world, and he integrates reaction to the creative process into the creative product. It is a novel that reads between its own lines, exalting in its literariness and making the storyteller a theorist, critic, and polemicist as well. A consideration of the *Quixote*, according to this view, must be as open as possible, both to analysis of the novel and to analysis of criticism. The text must be read critically, and commentary—in and of the text—must be read metacritically, to delineate the structures of the literary enterprise. Varying critical approaches represent not a choosing of sides but rather a compendium of potential insights into a text, a means toward a deeper appreciation of text, context, and criticism. In the *Quixote* and in light of Cervantes' preoccupation with the written word, the act of reading becomes an analogue of an analogue, the subject and object of experience.

In a one-semester course on *Don Quixote*, an instructor has the opportunity to explore the text from a number of focal points.[1] To allow the students to be critically informed yet relatively free of critical prejudices, I spend two or three weeks "preparing" them for a confrontation with the text. We discuss concepts that will form part of a reading of the *Quixote*, but with referents other than the novel itself. Offering a theoretical framework and an examination of selected literary conventions, the background material serves the text by fostering direct reader response. As an introduction to critical vocabulary, critical models, and critical thought, this stage setting is important for subsequent study of *Don Quixote*. Without prescribing or predetermining an interpretation, the introduction aims to identify major questions posed by the literary text. Guidance at this point may allow the students to "discover" the *Quixote* for themselves and to establish their own priorities regarding the mechanisms and meanings of the text. The relations between these topics and the *Quixote* may be discussed and reexamined throughout the semester. The readings include:

1. Michel Foucault's essay on Velázquez' *Las meninas* in *The Order of Things*.
2. Three poems: Lope de Vega's "Soneto de repente" ("Un soneto me manda hacer Violante"), Juan Ramón Jiménez' "Vino, primero, pura," and Vicente Huidobro's "Arte poética."
3. "*Hamlet* Q.E.D." and "Metatheatre: Shakespeare and Calderón" from Lionel Abel's *Metatheatre*.
4. "The Idealization of Reality: Garcilasso de la Vega" and "The Exaltation of Reality: Luis de Góngora" from Pedro Salinas' *Reality and the Poet in Spanish Poetry*.
5. Selections on narrative reliability from Wayne Booth's *The Rhetoric of Fiction* and selections on the author-narrator-reader relation from Seymour Chatman's *Story and Discourse*.

6. Edward H. Friedman's "Chaos Restored: Authorial Control and Ambiguity in *Lazarillo de Tormes*" and Edwin Williamson's "The Conflict between Author and Protagonist in Quevedo's *Buscón.*"
7. Brief selections from three self-conscious novels: Sterne's *Tristram Shandy*, Unamuno's *Niebla*, and Gerald Rosen's *The Carmen Miranda Memorial Flagpole.*
8. "The Historical Text as Literary Artifact" from Hayden White's *Tropics of Discourse.*
9. Julio Cortázar's short story "La noche boca arriba" ("The Night Face Up").
10. M. K. Read's article "Man against Language: A Linguistic Perspective on the Theme of Alienation in the *Libro de buen amor.*"

Foucault's essay treats the question of multiperspectivism in baroque art, a form that features art within art and stresses the presence of artists in their works. This painting about painting exemplifies, by analogy to another medium, the literary phenomenon of intertextuality and the metanovel, both of which deal with texts within texts. Foucault orients, reorients, and disorients the viewer of the painting to capture the multiple visual and conceptual possibilities evoked by the representational space. There is much for the eye to see and for the mind to perceive. Certain works, including *Las meninas* and *Don Quixote*, call attention to the complexities and the infinite beauty of visual and verbal images. The artist becomes an actor within the tableau to lend preeminence to the created object. By doing so, the artist inverts the traditional hierarchy of the real over the imaginary and challenges the concepts of absolute reality and uniformity of perception. The Velázquez on the canvas of *Las meninas* is a counterpart of the Cervantes in the prologues to *Don Quixote*, who is fictionalized to separate self from other and thus distinguishable from the Cervantes who is composing the text. The mental jolt produced by the unexpected presence demands a constant evaluation and reevaluation of the perceptual field, and this is a fundamental message in the art of Velázquez as well as in the art of Cervantes.

The selections by Lope, Jiménez, and Huidobro are metapoems, works in which form merges with meaning, an example of medium as message. Lope's humorous treatment of the composition of a sonnet makes the reader aware of the conventions that direct the poet's art. "Vino, primero, pura" outlines Jiménez' progression toward purity of poetic expression yet paradoxically makes use of the rhetorical structures the poet pretends to have rejected. Huidobro puts his creationist theory into practice in a poetic manifesto that seeks a new reality in the realm of literature, a reality ruled by a poet who functions as a "little God." The poems promote a view toward literary points of reference and toward a definable, accumulative movement in the text. The *Quixote* may be considered an extension of each of these self-referential planes, magnified and converted into narrative terms. The fusion of process and product, as seen in the poems, underscores the central dichotomies of Cervantes' novel and makes clear his juxtaposition of the creative act with the object of creation.

In *Metatheatre*, Abel draws on the force of the dramatic imagination as manifested by playwrights and by dramatis personae who are aware of their own theatricality and thereby serve to illustrate life-dream and world-stage metaphors. Abel regards *Hamlet* as a play that works against type (tragedy) to produce a new dramatic form (metatheater); the protagonist becomes a metaphorical dramatist who attempts to rewrite life's scenario. The literary character, in a manner of speaking, confronts and supersedes his creator by competing for the creator's role. Don Quixote is precisely this type of character, with the *Amadís de Gaula* as his pretext (pre-text) and those who surround him as his supporting cast. In rejecting present reality, Don Quixote invents a new order, which he invites and challenges others to accept. The common denominator of the metatheatrical variations is role playing as it relates to identity and authenticity, key factors in the tension between literary reality and "objective" reality.

Salinas' study of Garcilaso and Góngora is essentially a presentation of the transition from one literary classification to another, from Renaissance poetry to baroque poetry. Before discussing Salinas' thesis, students should read the well-known carpe diem sonnets "En tanto que de rosa y de azucena" (Garcilaso) and "Mientras por competir con tu cabello" (Góngora), poems that reflect what Salinas refers to as the "idealization" and "exaltation" of reality. Góngora's conversion of material reality into an aesthetic or poetic reality relates to the concept of the literary macrocosm, in which the written word contains and dominates objective phenomena. The literary macrocosm offers a reality dependent on its own system of conventions rather than on "objective" reality. Cervantes and the baroque poets glorify this difference by exploiting the linguistic and semantic powers of the word, those properties that have no analogue in the real world. As opposed to the aim of nineteenth-century realism, the goal is not to approximate objective reality but to surpass it by making the literary text a comprehensive and self-contained vehicle of expression.

Booth's *Rhetoric of Fiction* and Chatman's *Story and Discourse* focus on the act and art of narrative discourse. The dichotomy between what is communicated and the way in which it is communicated offers an approach to the structure of the *Quixote* and specifically to the interplay between novelistic theory and practice in Cervantes' fiction. The diverse narrators of the *Quixote* challenge narrative reliability and expand the role of the reader while providing formal analogues of conceptual issues raised in the text, issues such as truth and the power of the word. The articles on *Lazarillo de Tormes* and *El Buscón* center on the tension that exists at various levels of narration. The rhetorical strategies of a multifaceted narrator compete with those of an implied author. It is this ironic relation between the participants in narrative discourse that the picaresque mode incorporates into the text and that Cervantes intensifies in the *Quixote*. The structure and the substructure of these works are inseparable from the question of point of view; discourse becomes part of the story. The discussion of narrative perspective in the picaresque novel leads— historically and structurally—to Cervantes' discursive complications and variations.

The selections from *Tristram Shandy, Niebla,* and *The Carmen Miranda Memorial Flagpole* illustrate the presence and the continuity of self-consciousness in the novel. The broad humor of these works does not preclude an agonizingly serious search for authenticity. Sterne emphasizes the problems of compositional time and place, echoing Cervantes' precognitive rejection of novelistic realism. Unamuno presents the conflict between the literary and the nonliterary, a reciprocal struggle between two worlds that both counteract each other and depend on each other for existence. This struggle culminates in a debate between an author who fictionalizes himself and a character who wants to extend his identity beyond fiction. Augusto Pérez' authenticity lies in his deviation from human attributes, in the justification of his status as a fictional being. It is not his suffering but his literariness that makes him exist. Only when Augusto begins to emulate the extratextual author does he show signs of mortality; conversely, there can be little refutation of the immortality of the Unamuno who emerges in chapters 31–33 of *Niebla*. Within the confines of the text, Augusto Pérez and Don Miguel de Unamuno are immortal because they are not subject to human destruction. Beyond the text, Unamuno is less vulnerable to temporality because he exists in the text and because his literary analogue gives him faith in eternity. Like his predecessors, Rosen subordinates objective reality to literary reality in an ambiguous and self-contradictory text, supposedly written by the accountant twin brother of an absent novelist yet featuring a denial of the textual premises by a psychiatrist, Dr. S. Freudenberg, who intervenes in the prologue. The three works offer examples of the self-conscious, self-referential text and help students to comprehend Cervantes' preoccupation with the process of creation and with the meaningful flouting of narrative conventions.

White's essay is an effective companion piece to the *Quixote*, which might well be termed a literary text as historical artifact. For White, historical narratives are "verbal fictions, the content of which are as much *invented* as *found* and the forms of which have more in common with their counterparts in literature than they have with those in the sciences" (82). *Don Quixote* purports to be a true history, despite considerable evidence to the contrary. In this way it broaches issues of historical truth and questions the structures of historical consciousness. The shift from the unwritten to the written implies dependence on literary models, often without formal recognition of the problematic nature of this transition. The contradictory "true history" of Don Quixote is ironically faithful to the conventions of the preceding century's historical chronicles, and White's analysis foregrounds the historicist fallacies and fictionalized facts that Cervantes scrutinizes in the *Quixote*.

In "La noche boca arriba," Cortázar begins with a story that alternates "real" and "dream" visions as told by an apparently reliable narrator. Upon this structure he superimposes an apparent reversal of the two visions, transforming the dream into reality and reality into dream. But the reversal is only apparent. In fact, the change is rather from a reliable to an unreliable narrator, who calls both the real and the illusory into question by fusing and confusing them. The manipulative skills of the fictional narrator and the ambiguities of the text oblige the reader to contemplate a puzzle without a solution, a puzzle not unlike the *Quixote*. The short story and the novel lend themselves to an examination of the elements that produce meanings in narrative and of questions that make answers impossible or irrelevant.

Read's approach to the *Libro de buen amor* stresses the "deepening awareness in European culture of the problematic nature of language" (260). Relying on both classical and contemporary models, Read analyzes the linguistic bases that underlie Juan Ruiz' text. This type of criticism seeks to define a linguistic "deep structure" and to focus on language as the determining factor in the articulation of textual significance. The article addresses itself to the question of verbal potentiality and verbal indeterminacies: types and levels of language, linguistic reality, the individual in control of language, and language in control of the individual. In *Don Quixote*, Cervantes presents the powers and the limitations of the word: the text is a display of discursive possibilities, as well as a self-critical commentary on the distance between signifier and signified.

These readings are discussed by the class and supplemented with a brief overview of Spanish literature: the Golden Age as a literary and historical period; the emergence of the novel, with special attention to the influence of the Italian *novella;* idealistic trends; the picaresque mode; Cervantine fiction from the *Galatea* to the *Persiles;* and baroque style. The students are then ready to read the text of the *Quixote*, an experience that I hope they will approach with a heightened sense of critical perspective.

The prologue and the first chapter of *Don Quixote*, part 1, introduce the novelistic systems that provide a basis for Cervantes' dialectic. The fictional author grapples with literary conventions, Don Quixote wrestles with chivalric conventions, and they both anticipate moments of truth with a demanding reading public distanced from the practice of knight-errantry. The dialectic gains momentum with the appearance of Cide Hamete Benengeli's manuscript in chapter 9. From the beginning, the reader must learn to follow the linear plot (the adventures of Don Quixote), the metaplot (the writing of the text and intratextual commentary), the values expressed in the various episodes, the linguistic levels, and the ways in which meaning is produced in the text. In addition to these broader considerations, I ask each student to follow a particular topic as it appears throughout this section of the novel: metatheatrical elements, reality versus fantasy, satire of the chivalric romances, the temporal scope of the novel, Don Quixote's madness, the role of Sancho Panza, variations on the theme of love, the function of the intercalated stories, intertextuality. This exercise helps to ensure a close reading of the novel and to give each student an opportunity to participate in class discussions.

The class spends approximately eight weeks reading the *Quixote*. After completing part 1, students write brief essays on a specific facet of the text: literary self-consciousness in part 1; plots, subplots, and the organization of literary material; the creation of Don Quixote by the author, the narrator(s), and the character himself; the concept of reality in part 1. The essays require students to think comprehensively about the text and to synthesize critical principles while allowing the instructor to identify problems and to work toward resolving them in presenting part 2.

In part 2, the literary machinery of the first part continues, intensified by an acknowledgment of the 1605 text and Avellaneda's spurious sequel. Part 1 determines the direction of part 2, affecting story, tone, and theory within the text and guiding the textual composition. The second part creates a new dialectic, the elements of which form the basis for an analysis of the 1615 text. The individual episodes relate contextually to what has preceded them, calling for a continuous synthesis. For example, the Duke and Duchess are readers of the *Quixote* who, like Don Quixote himself, alter reality to conform to the demands of fiction. They ridicule the knight, but they also emulate him, compounding and confusing the literary worlds-within-worlds. As the narrative progresses, the points of reference become increasingly complex, and this complexity between internal and external markers defines the dialectic of part 2.

Having stressed the relation between the two parts, I ask students to write another brief essay on one of the following topics in order to find new sources of synthesis: the *Quixote* of 1605 in the *Quixote* of 1615, Dulcinea del Toboso versus Barataria Island, the significance of the Duke and Duchess in the structure of *Don Quixote*, the function of the intercalated stories in part 2 and their relation to those in part 1.

The remaining weeks are devoted to a survey of critical studies of the *Quixote*. The objective in this part of the course is twofold: to discover new ways of examining the text and to seek a broader understanding of critical models. I have used Miguel de Unamuno's *Our Lord Don Quixote*, E. C. Riley's *Cervantes's Theory of the Novel*, Gonzalo Torrente Ballester's *El Quijote como juego*, Carlos Fuentes' *Cervantes o la crítica de la lectura*, John J. Allen's *Don Quixote: Hero or Fool?*, parts 1 and 2, and Anthony Close's *The Romantic Approach to Don Quixote*, as well as works by Cesáreo Bandera, Arthur Efron, Ruth El Saffar, R. M. Flores, Félix Martínez-Bonati, Helena Percas de Ponseti, Elias Rivers, Cesare Segre, John G. Weiger, and others. In the bibliography, as in the *Quixote* itself, juxtaposition is crucial. Unamuno's commentary is a perfect example of what Close designates as the "Romantic approach," which he rejects as a viable reading of the text. For Torrente Ballester, Don Quixote is neither a hero nor a fool but an actor consciously practicing his craft; this distanced, metatheatrical view stands in sharp contrast with Allen's emphasis on reader response. To test their critical and metacritical skills, I ask students to write several one-page abstracts of selected studies. The term paper (approximately ten pages) is an analysis of one episode from the *Quixote*, including a commentary on three or four articles.[2]

Just as the *Quixote* complements and contradicts itself, so the critical tradition of the *Quixote* forms a complementary and contradictory "text," and the validity of each text rests on the creation of tension. In his metahistorical exploration of levels of consciousness, Hayden White would undoubtedly see here a movement through the major tropes (metaphor, metonymy, synecdoche) toward the dominant trope of irony. At every stage I would add an emphasis on oxymoron in this antinovelistic novel, this ahistorical history. The act of reading and the critical act call for a reconciliation of the irreconcilable, leading to the pleasure of Cervantes' text and its usefulness. Cervantes elevates the written word by investigating its multiple possibilities, by granting a privileged status to the peculiar reality of literature. The self-referentiality of *Don Quixote* is part of its story and part of its beauty. By viewing the problematic elements of the text as indispensable to the study of the text, the reader may in turn exalt the *Quixote* and texts in general. If all goes according to plan, the students and the instructor will be profoundly affected, as was Alonso Quijano, by their reading.[3]

NOTES

[1] The 400-level course described in this paper is taught in Spanish; however, the basic format may be modified for a graduate seminar on Golden Age prose fiction, a course on the Spanish novel in English translation, or a course on masterpieces of world literature.

[2] Undergraduate students have the option of a final examination. A two-hour exam might require them, for example, to discuss the structural and theoretical significance of ten of the following elements: *Amadís de Gaula*, the Cave of Montesinos, "El curioso impertinente," the Duke and Duchess, Dorotea, the canon of Toledo, Ginés de Pasamonte, Marcela and Grisóstomo, Camacho's wedding, Ricote, Cide Hamete Benengeli, Sansón Carrasco, Barataria Island, and Alonso Quijano. Another section could ask for a discussion of the text as it relates to the concepts of metatheater, the baroque, story/discourse, and intertextuality.

[3] I would like to express my gratitude to Elias Rivers and Harry Sieber, masterful guides to *Don Quixote*, and to my students at Arizona State University.

AN ARCHETYPAL APPROACH TO *DON QUIXOTE*

Donald W. Bleznick

An archetypal approach to literature helps us to understand why certain literary works have an enduring and universal appeal. Anthropology, psychology, and comparative religion all reveal recurrent patterns in the thought and behavior of human beings. These patterns emerge in widely separated points in space and time, and they support the idea that we share aspects of our psychic functioning with our ancestors and with people from different cultures throughout the world. This perspective was originally stated by the British anthropologist James G. Frazer (1854–1941), especially in his monumental *The Golden Bough* (1890–1915), where he demonstrated in great detail that there are essential similarities of belief among people everywhere and in all ages. The writings of Carl G. Jung (1875–1961) went beyond Frazer's examination of mythology. Jung popularized the term "archetype" (i.e., motif, image, or thematic pattern) and applied it to "primordial images" that predate the recorded history of mankind. For him, these recurrent archetypes were "inherited forms of psychic behavior" constituting the "collective unconscious" of the human race.

Jung studied recurring archetypes chiefly as they appeared in dreams. On the basis of his work in this area, he theorized that "the psyche contains all the images that have ever given rise to myths" (*Archetypes* 7)[1] For Jung and for many literary critics who have followed his lead, myths are not inventions but representations that reflect real, vital perceptions of the human psyche and express the manner in which people experience the world. Mircea Eliade (1907–   ) has carried this approach even further by demonstrating how myths articulate fundamental truths of human beings in the universe, how they link members of a tribe or nation together in a spiritual bond that transcends time, and how different mythologies have similar underlying themes and patterns.

Aware of how deeply myth affects the reader, writers in all epochs have consciously or unconsciously embedded archetypes in the structures, characters, and images of their narratives. When these archetypes are utilized appropriately, they evoke a responsive chord in the reader, because they are part of the "collective unconscious" that everyone shares with everyone else. In a sense, each reader's psyche has vicariously experienced the feelings, thoughts, and episodes that characters experience in a work of fiction. Archetypal criticism examines these archetypes as they appear in literary texts and thus helps us grasp fundamental truths about ourselves and our fellow human beings. This is why the archetypal approach can have such a profound impact on undergraduate students. In an early essay from *Our Lord Don Quixote*, Unamuno declared that the Spanish people created Don Quixote, that "Cervantes was merely the instrument by which sixteenth-century Spain gave birth to Don Quixote.... Cervantes is no more than the minister and representative of humanity; that is why his work was great" (456). This contention suggests that Cervantes was endowed with special powers that enabled him to express the genuine values, concerns, and yearnings of his compatriots—the psychic raw materials that readers unconsciously recognized and understood as parts of themselves.

For example, Cervantes clearly availed himself of the universal myth of the hero. Heroes generally emerge at critical junctures in a society's history, and they serve to reconfirm its basic values and hopes, which have somehow been placed in jeopardy. In Golden Age Spain, the people were undergoing a spiritual crisis, in part as a reaction to the Reformation but also as the result of deep social malaise. Despite the apparent greatness of the Hapsburg empire, the country was suffering from chronic economic weakness and a visible decline in political competence and power. Within this context, Don Quixote is a hero, although his unusual behavior and his failures in part 1 would seem to indicate otherwise. Like the traditional culture hero or savior, he undertakes a perilous journey to fulfill a mission. At the end of part 2, he may be compared to the hero who fades away or dies to atone for the sins of those for whom he has sacrificed himself. Psychologists view this journey as symbolic of the process by which the individual attains psychological maturity.

The analysis I use in the classroom takes this insight as its starting point and encompasses the totality of the life of Alonso Quixano, the real name of Cervantes' protagonist. Except for the beginning and ending of the novel, Quixano assumes the role of Don Quixote, the persona, or social mask, that he adopts in an attempt to realize his desire to right the ills of the world. His experiences as Don Quixote are essential to his "individuation" (Jung's term for psychic growth) and to his attainment of maturity, which occurs when he recognizes the folly of knight-errantry and accepts authentic Spanish religion. In presenting the adventures of Don Quixote, Cervantes depicts the psyche's journey from the primordial pool of the unconscious to a higher level of consciousness and knowledge. It is Cervantes' masterful rehearsal of this universal pattern—embodied in the hero archetype—that enables *Don Quixote* to retain its vitality and immediacy for millions of Spaniards and others who continue to read it, and it is on this basis that students can most readily respond to its greatness.

At the age of fifty, after having spent many years reading novels of chivalry, Quixano chooses to become a knight-errant, because these books and their anachronistic world offer him apparently suitable models of behavior for his quest. Students can easily see how he relies on chivalric models in subjecting himself to an initiatory rite of passage: he obeys the prescribed ritual for obtaining knightly arms, keeps the required vigil over them, obtains a horse, selects his lady, and has himself dubbed a knight by the innkeeper. Knowing that chivalric tales employ names that reveal the essence of one's persona, he invents a name that links his original one with a symbol of knighthood, for the word *quixote* comes from the Catalan *cuixot* 'thigh piece,' the armor that protects the thigh. Just as knights assume new names at different stages of their careers, Don Quixote becomes known successively as the Knight of the Sorrowful Countenance and the Knight of the Lions; he even contemplates adopting the name Quixotiz when he considers settling down to a pastoral life.

The Hero archetype is not the only one that students encounter as they read *Don Quixote*. Early in his career, Quixote declares that he intends to restore the Golden Age, an archetype common to all mythologies. Yet his efforts to revive an era of peace, harmony, truth, and justice are repeatedly thwarted. To explain his failures, he refers back to the chivalric novels and insists that jealous sorcerers are conspiring against him. Recent studies in mythology, psychology, and comparative religion reveal that enchanters, witches, demons, dragons, and monsters stand for the inexplicable forces that imperil an orderly balance in the lives of individuals and societies. In Jungian terms, the credence that people like Don Quixote lend to the power that invisible forces exert over them derives from the shadow, the weak side, the unconscious that can intrude into the conscious realm without warning. Jung has described how the shadow can be projected onto other people as a means of covering up one's own faults or weaknesses. Most of Don Quixote's behavior (especially in part 1) can be interpreted as a childlike, primitive phase of personality development during which he refuses to accept responsibility for his own failures. When *Don Quixote* is presented in this manner, students recognize that Cervantes' hero finally becomes an adult only after his defeat by the Knight of the White Moon (pt. 2, ch. 64), for at this point Quixote blames his incapacity to sustain his role as knight-errant on his own weakness and not on the machinations of enchanters.

Another dimension of the novel can also be convincingly explained to students in terms of Jungian archetypes. The chivalric code requires that Don Quixote have a lady inspire him in his exploits, and he chooses Dulcinea. In Jung's terminology, she symbolizes the "anima," the female element in a man's psyche, that which opposes the influence of the shadow (i.e., the enchanters). The anima is like the soul. As Jung writes in his *Archetypes and the Collective Unconscious*, "It is the living thing in man, that which lives of itself and causes life. . . . She makes us believe in credible things, that life may be lived . . ." (26–27). In his conversations with the Duchess, who claims that Dulcinea is a figment of his imagination, Don Quixote is unconcerned, because, from his point of view, Dulcinea is a real person who possesses all the noble characteristics associated with a lady fair (pt. 2, ch. 32). As the mediator between Don Quixote's conscious self and Quixano's inner world, she guides the protagonist to a higher, more spiritual quality of life.

When teaching *Don Quixote* according to the archetypal approach, it is crucial to discuss the Cave of Montesinos episode (pt. 2, chs. 22–23), for it reveals Don Quixote's progress toward a mature state of self-awareness. His descent into a subterranean cavern parallels the infernal journeys recorded in diverse mythologies throughout the world and in literary works like Vergil's *Aeneid* and Dante's *Divine Comedy*. These visits to hell constitute initiatory rites, during which the hero penetrates into the unconscious for the purpose of gaining new insight and knowledge. They may transform the hero's personality, as they do in *Don Quixote*. When Quixote enters the womb of the earth, he has his first opportunity to encounter genuine knights and to experience the reality of knight-errantry. During this intense contact with the roots of his own knighthood, he reaches the threshold of self-consciousness. For the first time, he has misgivings about the nobility and goodness of the chivalric life. His consciousness must assimilate the woeful plight of heroes and a mercenary Dulcinea who requests a loan of six *reales* to buy a new cotton shirt. He is later plagued with doubts about the validity of this flawed dream, but it has supplied him a more realistic understanding of life, even if he is not yet ready to accept it.

The disillusioning and maturing processes triggered by this psychic shock can be illustrated for students by discussing some of the subsequent episodes. Shortly after Quixote's dream, Sancho is delighted to discover that his master accepts an inn as a real inn and does not transform it into a castle. During Maese Pedro's puppet show (pt. 2, ch. 25), Don Quixote intrudes into the fictional world of the puppets and smashes them to pieces, but immediately after this incident his anger subsides, and he avers that enchanters had caused him to misinterpret reality. The humiliating and degenerate game of chivalry imposed upon him by the Duke and the Duchess (pt. 2, chs. 30–57) furthers Quixote's progressive disillusionment with his profession, and he decides to leave their castle when he realizes that he has done nothing there to accomplish his goals.

Don Quixote and Sancho's imaginary flight on Clavileño (pt. 2, ch. 41) also has archetypal significance, for it too promotes a greater degree of self-awareness in Cervantes' hero. Don Quixote has encountered the archetype of magic flight in his readings, and he accepts the idea that the wooden horse can transport him five thousand leagues to Candaya, where he will presumably defeat the wicked enchanter and giant Malambruno. This episode is the only one in which Don Quixote uses magic to accomplish a feat, and it demonstrates his desire to transcend his own human limitations. Sancho gives a detailed account of what he "saw" on that flight, but Quixote doubts the authenticity of the adventure and says that Sancho was either lying or dreaming. By the end of the chapter, Quixote understands that his perception of reality is not a uniquely and absolutely true version of life's events; he even offers to accept Sancho's account of their ride on Clavileño if Sancho will accept his story of what occurred in the Cave of Montesinos. It is not difficult for students to perceive that Quixote's spark and drive wane considerably after he leaves the ducal palace (pt. 2, ch. 58). When he and Sancho encounter a dozen men dressed as peasants and guarding four objects veiled with white sheets, Don Quixote does not spring spontaneously into action, as he might have done at an earlier time. On the contrary, he politely inquires about their mission and never doubts their explanation that they are bearing images of Saint George, Saint Martin, Saint James, and Saint Paul to be placed on a village altar. On examining the uncovered images, he contrasts the works of the saints with his own efforts, and he confesses that he does not know what he is accomplishing through his own labors. He even adds: "But should my Dulcinea del Toboso be released from the pains she suffers because of her enchantment, my fortune being improved and *my mind righted*, it may be I shall direct my steps along a better path than I am now following" (pt. 2, ch. 58; p. 839; italics mine).[2]

At this point Cervantes is obviously preparing his readers for the imminent demise of the Don Quixote persona, which occurs on the beach at Barcelona (pt. 2, ch. 64), where Sansón Carrasco, disguised as the Knight of the White Moon, succeeds in his second attempt to defeat Don Quixote in knightly combat and to send him back to the peaceful, "sane" life of Alonso Quixano. In his first attempt, Carrasco had disguised himself as the Knight of the Mirrors, but Don Quixote had refused to see his own reality "mirrored" in his antagonist's armor; in the second attempt, Cervantes' hero succumbs to the "moon," which suggests death in the mythic tradition. Banished from knight-errantry for at least a year, Don Quixote tries to find a new persona. He briefly toys with the idea of substituting one fictional existence for another—a pastoral illusion for a chivalric one. Thus desire reflects a universal longing for paradise and signifies a higher state of consciousness, even holding out the promise of immortality, a personal goal that Quixote acknowledges on numerous occasions. The pastoral dream is ephemeral, however, and Quixano is destined to cast aside fictional models for the spiritual certainty of Christianity. In terms that students can readily comprehend, he has attained a more mature and realistic view of the world. When he and Sancho are trampled by six hundred pigs, he stops Sancho from slaughtering several of them (pt. 2, ch. 68). These pigs are pigs and not warring armies, as the sheep had been in part 1. The affront to Quixote's dignity is ascribed, not to enchantment, but to divine will in retribution for his sins, and after scrutinizing every female countenance he passes on the road back to his village, he despairs of ever seeing Dulcinea again. At this point, the persona of Don Quixote is on the verge of vanishing.

When Quixote and Sancho are about to enter their village, Sancho kneels and shouts, "Open your eyes, my beloved country, and see your son Sancho Panza returning—if not rich yet well beaten. Open your arms and receive your son Don Quixote too, who, though conquered by another, *has conquered himself*—which, as I have heard him say, is the very best kind of victory" (pt. 2, ch. 72; p. 930; italics mine). Through Sancho, Cervantes is informing his readers that Alonso Quixano's experiences as a knight-errant have demonstrated the inadequacy of the chivalric life as a means of completing the process of individuation. Although the Don Quixote persona has failed, Quixano achieves a genuine victory in his realization that the ills of the world cannot be cured by extraordinary feats of knightly valor. Cervantes' central message thus reaffirms the Spaniards' obligation to renew their allegiance to Catholicism, the most vital constant of their culture and the only authentic expression of a true Spaniard's life.

This dimension of Cervantes' archetypal novel can be illustrated for students by comparing the childlike Don Quixote with Don Diego de Miranda, the Knight of the Green Coat—a well-adjusted, mature Spanish gentleman who radiates goodness, charity, and peace without cultivating ambitions of vainglory. Miranda is a good husband and father. He pursues the simple life. He is "devoted to Our Lady, and always trusts in the infinite mercy of our Lord God" (pt. 2, ch. 16; p. 567). How vastly different is this ideal Spaniard from the would-be knight-errant who is more concerned with the renown of his own exploits than with the primacy of God's will. Sancho had once affirmed that "it's better to be a humble little friar, of any order you like, than a valiant and errant knight. A couple of dozen lashings have more effect with God than a couple of thousand lance-thrusts, even against giants, or hobgoblins, or dragons." At that point Don Quixote replied, "*Chivalry is a religion*, and there are sainted knights in glory" (pt. 2, ch. 8; pp. 519–20; italics mine). This statement reveals his fanatical belief in chivalry, which contrasts with the balanced religious faith of a complete Spanish gentleman like Don Diego.

In *The Sacred and the Profane*, Eliade observes that it is rare to find "a drastically nonreligious experience of the whole life" and that "vague memories of abolished religious practices and even a nostalgia for them" remain in nonreligious views of life (181). This observation is certainly valid for the secular world of twentieth-century American students, and in Golden Age Spain, imbued with Christian zeal since the Middle Ages, the life of a culture hero quite naturally reinforced the religion practiced by the people from whom Quixote's own consciousness has sprung. Alonso Quixano is a good man who seeks his own redemption as well as that of his compatriots, and when he discovers his true identity, he simultaneously reaffirms the quintessence of Spanish existence—its religious faith. The fever from which he suffers on returning home is, in this context, a divinely ordained purge of the Don Quixote persona. Fever can be equated with fire, a symbol of transformation and regeneration, a purifier and a destroyer of evil forces. When Alonso Quixano awakens, his first words are: "Blessed be Almighty God, who has vouchsafed me this great blessing! Indeed his mercies are boundless, nor can the sins of men limit or hinder them" (pt. 2, ch. 74; p. 935). At this point, he has attained unity with the true Christian God, and he can safely renounce the pursuit of chivalry. He knows who he is and can resume his true identity as Alonso Quixano the Good. Having completed the process of individuation, he has no more worlds to conquer, no more stages through which he must ascend. He has successfully overcome the trials that a universal culture hero must encounter. During his journey, he has achieved self-understanding, and his fictional experiences illustrate for the benefit of his fellow Spaniards that the good life must be based on genuine Christian principles. The notary who records his last will and testament says that, by recanting his past life, Alonso Quixano can die more serenely and in a more Christian manner than any knight-errant in the books of chivalry (pt. 2, ch. 74). Cervantes purposely failed to identify his hero's birthplace so that Don Quixote could stand for all the inhabitants of La Mancha; in actuality, he stood for much more. The story of his adventures reveals a truth relevant not only to the people of La Mancha but to all Spaniards and to all human beings. Because the archetypal approach makes students aware of this universal dimension of Cervantes' masterpiece, it is particularly well suited for use in the classroom.

NOTES

[1]In the same text, Jung equates myths with psychic phenomena: "He [primitive man] simply didn't know that the psyche contains all the images that have ever given rise to myths, and that our unconscious is an acting and suffering subject with an inner drama which primitive man rediscovers, by means of analogy, in the processes of nature both great and small" (*Archetypes* 7). Jung later expands on this point: "The primitive mentality does not *invent* myths, it *experiences* them. Myths are original revelations of the preconscious psyche, involuntary statements about unconscious psychic happenings, and anything but allegories of physical processes. Myths, on the contrary, have a vital meaning. Not merely do they represent, they are the psychic life of the primitive tribe, which immediately falls to pieces when it loses its mythological heritage, like a man who has lost his soul" (154).

[2]*The Adventures of Don Quixote*, trans. J. M. Cohen. All subsequent quotations are from this edition.

PSYCHOANALYSIS AND *DON QUIXOTE*

Carroll B. Johnson

In the Department of Spanish and Portuguese at UCLA we offer two courses in *Don Quixote*, one at the undergraduate level for Spanish majors and others who can read Spanish and have some familiarity with Spanish literary history, the other a seminar for advanced graduate students who have just completed a graduate course in Cervantes' other works. Because these courses and their students differ, the application of psychoanalytic categories must also differ. This chapter deals mainly with the presence of Freudian psychology in an undergraduate course; it alludes only briefly to what might be termed a full-blown "psychoanalytical approach" to *Don Quixote* at the preprofessional level.

In a class on *Don Quixote* for undergraduates, the instructor must present a generalist's view of the work. I always begin by attempting to locate Cervantes' novel in literary history, by referring to earlier traditions and works that came before it and that it incorporates, for it is in relation to this context that *Don Quixote* takes on some of its own meanings. Even a cursory examination of these intertextual relations is time-consuming, especially with students who are generally unfamiliar with the chivalric tradition, the pastoral, the picaresque, and the Byzantine romance. For this reason, I devote several class periods to a discussion of these genres, emphasizing the prose romances of chivalry (especially *Amadís de Gaula*), the Italian epic (especially *Orlando furioso*), and the chivalric tradition as it appears in the *romancero*, the corpus of popular Spanish ballads. The introduction of Cide Hamete Benengeli in part 1, chapter 9 also demands some discussion of Aristotelian poetics and the categories of truth and history, verisimilitude and poetry.

Similarly, I attempt to situate *Don Quixote* within the social, religious, intellectual, and economic climate of Spain at the end of the sixteenth century. To this end, I discuss Erasmianism and its conjunction with the peculiarly Spanish problems of *casta* 'bloodline' and the division of society into Old and New Christians, "clean" and "unclean" people. I also refer to the *Examen de ingenios* of Huarte de San Juan, his theory of personality based on humoral imbalance, and the notion of "existential generativity" that springs from his work. In addition, I feel constrained to deal briefly with the economic infrastructure of Don Quixote's society, its division into *hidalgos* 'nobles' and *pecheros* 'taxpayers' and the practical result of our hero's membership in the former class.

The foregoing contextual material is necessary to the most rudimentary understanding of Cervantes' text. Without *Amadís* and *Orlando*, Don Quixote's artistic creation of an episode in his own life in part 1, chapter 25 is meaningless. Without Huarte de San Juan, students would find it difficult to understand the narrator's report that Don Quixote's brain dried out from too much reading and too little sleep (pt. 1, ch. 1), Don Quixote's own description of his hand and arm in part 1, chapter 43, or the work's title, *El ingenioso hidalgo*. Without Erasmus and the new religiosity, the discussion of sanctity in part 2, chapter 8 makes no sense. And if students fail to understand the economic situation of the small country hidalgo in 1600, they will miss one of the principal environmental pressures that drove our hero to insanity in the first place.

Given the nature of a first course in *Don Quixote* and the inevitable pressures of time, it becomes obvious that any attempt to turn the novel into a psychoanalytic case history is a manifest disservice to the students. Nevertheless, any course in *Don Quixote* must confront two fundamental aspects of the work. The first is the literary principle of verisimilitude enunciated by Aristotle and championed by the sixteenth-century neo-Aristotelian commentators whom Cervantes had read. The other is the simple fact that *Don Quixote* is a book about a madman, a psychotic.

It is convenient to distinguish between two varieties of verisimilitude: circumstantial and psychological. In the first category belong such phenomena as the presence or absence of giants and dragons and a knight's ability to lay waste great numbers of enemies with a single stroke of the sword. The lack of circumstantial verisimilitude is characteristic of the romances of chivalry; indeed, their anti-Aristotelian aesthetics made them the bête noire of sixteenth-century humanists. E. C. Riley (in *Cervantes's Theory of the Novel*) and A. Forcione (in *Cervantes, Aristotle and the Persiles*) have shown that Cervantes was at least willing to accept the existence of a medieval aesthetic in which circumstantial verisimilitude is conspicuous by its absence. Don Quixote's improvised story of the knight who throws himself into the burning lake and descends into a crystalline palace where he is bathed, fed, and otherwise attended by swarms of beautiful women (pt. 1, ch. 50) is presented as a viable alternative to the canon's theoretical discourse on the merits of a poetics of verisimilitude. This story anticipates the "magic realism" of the twentieth-century Spanish-American novel, and if it is lacking in circumstantial verisimilitude, it is certainly not lacking in the other and (for Cervantes) more important variety.

Psychological verisimilitude demands that literary characters act the way real people act, that they formulate projects and react to experience as we ourselves do. This dimension of fictional characters allows us to recognize ourselves in them and to be moved to sorrow and pity by their problems. If, however, our identification with such characters is to be anything but superficial, it is essential that their behavior, like our own, respond simultaneously to conscious motivations and to others that lie below the surface of consciousness. Unconscious concerns can only be brought to light through a process of analysis. Our identification with a character—our recognition of ourselves in a character—is itself a largely unconscious process, but it is an essential one if a literary work is to move us deeply. Even the phrase "to move deeply" expresses an unconscious realization that something is taking place within us, below the level of consciousness. We cannot isolate it or describe it with any degree of accuracy, but we are obliged to acknowledge its presence. This invisible but very real process recalls to mind the unseen realities Plato called "essences" or Hamlet's stricture that there are more things in heaven and earth than are dreamt of in Horatio's natural science.

If students are to progress from a reader's enjoyment to a critic's appreciation, teachers must inform themselves about these unconscious processes that permit authors to create psychically verisimilar characters in which we recognize our own humanity. In this respect, the instructor's familiarity with principles of Freudian psychology can have a decisive effect. Because experience suggests that most undergraduates react negatively to the mention of the name Freud or the term psychoanalysis, it is perhaps advisable to communicate indirectly the theory that enables us to make sense of certain episodes, allowing it to remain implicit in the analysis of the particular characters and their behavior. The instructor's familiarity with the various defenses that the human ego mounts to shield it from an intolerable reality can transform apparently arbitrary and mean-ingless episodes into a coherent structure of behavior and motivation, cause and effect. Phrased in another way, the apparently nonsensical becomes verisimilar within the context of psychoanalytical theory, and a minor episode can provide major insights into a character's personality.

Let us consider for a moment the argument between Don Quixote and Sancho about the animals ridden by the farm girls whom Sancho is attempting to pass off as Dulcinea and her two attendants (pt. 2, ch. 10). Are they riding hackneys (*hacanas*), "cackneys" (*cananeas*), male donkeys (*pollinos*), female donkeys (*pollinas*), or zebras? The spirited debate between the master and his squire is on the surface either trivial or irrelevant. What possible importance can the identification of the young women's mounts possess in comparison with the identification of the girls themselves? This is of course the real issue, but it is so threatening to both men (for different reasons) that neither can afford, psychologically, to bring it up. Yet, because it is so important, it demands to be discussed. Don Quixote and Sancho resolve their impasse by doing what most of us do on occasion; they displace the psychic energy affixed (or cathected) to the girls' identities onto a similar issue of much less importance, where it can be harmlessly discharged. If instructors are attuned to the psychodynamics of the situation and familiar with unconscious processes like displacement, they can offer students a plausible explanation of the "hackney-donkey" debate. They can then show how this debate is relevant to the immediate situation and how it faithfully reproduces actual human behavior. This insight can serve as a point of departure for the discussion of larger issues, such as the maintenance of the myth of Dulcinea and the problems that arise when the responsibility for continually recreating her is transferred from Don Quixote to others. This latter point is particularly important, because it is a major structural characteristic of part 2.

Similarly, Don Quixote's experience in the Cave of Montesinos (pt. 2, ch. 23) yields some of its best fruit if it is discussed within the context suggested by psychoanalysis—as a dream. Like Shakespeare, Cervantes grasped intuitively that a dream is a message not from beyond but from within—a disguised expression of the dreamer's most deep-seated concerns and unresolved intrapsychic conflicts. Don Quixote's own psychic development, his relation to more than one woman in his life, is expressed in his detailed evocation of the postmenopausal Belerma and the farm girl whom Sancho had earlier cast in the role of Dulcinea. The appearance of this young woman also suggests that Don Quixote needs to wrest control of her ongoing creation away from Sancho. Her request for six *reales* and the fact that he can only give her four evoke his impotence with painful clarity and suggest why he brought her into existence in the first place.

The reader unfamiliar with dream interpretation is limited to the most superficial aspects of Don Quixote's experience in the Cave of Montesinos: chivalry, enchantment, and the parody of literary "descents into the underworld." These aspects are present in Cervantes' depiction of the scene, but analysis along Freudian lines enables us to make even more fundamental inferences about Don Quixote's inner life from before the onset of his psychosis in part 1, chapter 1 to his experience of present crisis in the evolution of Dulcinea. The mere fact that readers can be lulled into thinking that Don Quixote had a life before the beginning of the novel is powerful testimony to Cervantes' genius—a genius that also expressed itself in the creation of an astonishingly verisimilar character who dreams a "realistic" dream that meshes so well with what we know about his conscious preoccupations and with what we can infer about their unconscious substructure.

Students accept such analyses without resistance, largely because the analyses point to a coherent inner order and a believable consistency of motivation and behavior in the midst of what appears to be whimsy or arrant nonsense. It should also be pointed out that these episodes are not dependent on Don Quixote's madness as such. All of us dream, and all of us mobilize displacement as a defense. Psychoanalysis allows us to see ourselves—without the taint of madness—in the normal mental processes of characters who act as we do.

We must also deal with the inescapable fact that Don Quixote is crazy. Since the mid-nineteenth century, clinical psychiatrists have been carefully scrutinizing Don Quixote's pathological behavior and relating it to real mental diseases. His malady has been diagnosed by one competent professional as "chronic paranoia or partial systematic delirium of the expansive type, the megalomaniacal form and the philanthropic variety." Since treatment is obviously impossible, literary criticism as practiced by the clinical psychiatrists becomes exclusively a matter of diagnosis. Their labors confirm that Cervantes' understanding of mental illness was centuries ahead of its time and qualifies him as "the Jules Verne of mental pathology" (Bigeard 161), although such observations do not necessarily enhance a student's appreciation of the novel.

Clinical psychiatry offers only a description of Don Quixote's madness; psychoanalysis offers the means to understand how and why he let go his grip on reality in the first place. By explaining his retreat into psychosis as a last, desperate defense against unbearable environmental stress, psychoanalysis provides a framework for the study of Don Quixote's reactions to the people and situations he encounters. It also clarifies the relations he has along his way. After all, the bulk of Cervantes' text is devoted to the evolution of the hero's character and madness from their simultaneous onset in the first chapter to the recovery of sanity and his embrace of death in the final chapter.

In dealing with Don Quixote's madness from a psychoanalytical perspective, I always begin by drawing attention to his situation at the beginning of the book. He is an *hidalgo*, a bachelor, approximately fifty years of age, and he lives in a house dominated by women. His status as an hidalgo effectively prohibits his participation in productive activity; to work would mean the loss of his nobility. His age and his bachelorhood betray the lack of any meaningful relation with a member of the opposite sex. Furthermore, his life is monotonous. He has two suits of clothes, his menu remains the same fifty-two weeks a year, he never travels, he seems to have but two friends, and the only activity open to him is hunting. He apparently does not even have a name that is uniquely his. According to the criteria established by Freud—the ability to love and to work—Don Quixote is, from the very beginning, estranged from mental health. Furthermore, he is succumbing to the identity crisis that Erik Erikson defines as crucial for his age group—the struggle between generativity and stagnation. He has been unable to generate anything, not even a name, and his life is a veritable paradigm of stagnation. In short, Don Quixote is in trouble before readers ever learn anything about his obsessive reading of chivalric romances.

If teachers focus on Don Quixote's mental and social situation at the beginning of the course, students will accept his preoccupation with reading not as a cause but as an effect. In psychoanalytic terms, it is his defense against outside pressures, which he counters by withdrawing into a world of fantasy. What are these pressures? Clearly, the monotony of his humdrum existence figures prominently. Unamuno, Martine Bigeard, and Teresa Aveleyra have also suggested that the existing pressure is rendered even more unbearable by Don Quixote's unconfessed love for Aldonza Lorenzo—a love that finally drives him to seek refuge in books and, ultimately, in psychosis. I myself can no longer accept the "Aldonza hypothesis" as verisimilar, but everything we know about men Don Quixote's age suggests that they have a propensity for falling in love with women much younger than themselves. Thus, the idea that an unconfessed and unconfessable love is lurking in the substructure of the hero's psyche must be taken very seriously. In any case, it is appropriate to point out that Don Quixote does not go crazy because he reads books; he reads books in an effort to keep from going crazy. The inadequacy of this first line of defense is what provokes his final retreat into psychosis, with the assumption of a new identity and a denial of reality.

One of the most characteristic features of Don Quixote's behavior in part 1 is his ambiguous relation to the physical realities around him. He mistakes things; he sees country inns as castles and windmills as giants. This behavior has been perceptively discussed by Américo Castro, from an existential point of view, as the hero's imposition of his inner needs on exterior reality. In the process of creating himself, he must also create an environment appropriate to his needs. Because a knight-errant has no use for inns, he transforms them into appropriate settings for knightly adventures—medieval castles. It is true that Don Quixote imposes his inner needs on reality, but this discussion omits any reference to Don Quixote's madness, to the idea that the imposition of inner needs on external circumstance is an unconscious process, or to the fact that the resultant distortion of reality is a symptom of psychosis. All of us have inner needs, but only psychotics reorganize reality the way Don Quixote does. In short, some knowledge of psychosis and the "extreme" defenses (distortion, delusional projection, denial)—as opposed to the less extreme defenses (repression, displacement, intellectualization) that all of us deploy from time to time—makes Don Quixote's behavior seem plausible and verisimilar.

For years, I allowed students to waste valuable class time in sterile discussions of the question: Is Don Quixote, or is he not, crazy? These sessions were rendered doubly futile because neither I nor the students knew what we were talking about. Having acquired some knowledge of psychic processes—how the mind reacts to environmental stress—we can now lay that argument to rest and use the time for more fruitful discussions. Of course Don Quixote is crazy. His behavior results from motivations that can be identified, and it changes during the course of the novel in response to changing circumstances and developing relationships, such as those he entertains with Dulcinea, with real women like the innkeeper's daughter and Altisidora, or with men like Sancho and Sansón Carrasco.

In addition to rendering Don Quixote's madness verisimilar, this approach removes it from the sphere of moral judgment—the novel is neither a tract against nonconformity nor a romantic glorification of eccentricity as a hallmark of moral superiority. This vexed question is placed into a reasonable context for discussion by applying what we know about psychic processes. Mental illness is neither good nor evil; it is, rather, the aggregate of unconscious defenses, mobilized in a pattern that becomes characteristic and utilized by some individuals to cope with the demands of life. Considering Don Quixote's madness from a psychodynamic point of view, we can communicate to our students certain important and morally neutral facts about him.

First, his madness propels him backward into life. At the most elementary level, the quality of his experience as Don Quixote is unquestionably richer than that of his alienated, monotonous existence as an anonymous hidalgo from La Mancha. Second, and at a deeper level, the profession he chooses allows him to engage for the first time in purposeful, socially useful work. And he can enter into a fulfilling and evolving emotional relationship with another person—not the imaginary Dulcinea, but the very real Sancho Panza. The wonderfully positive human relation between master and squire is the most valuable one that either man has ever experienced. Paradoxically, it is only in madness that Don Quixote achieves the capacity for work and love that Freud regarded as the essence of mental health. Armed with these facts, students can begin to ponder the larger relation between madness and society.

Psychoanalysis allows students to perceive *Don Quixote* as fiction, not as satire, allegory, epistemological treatise, or socioeconomic document. It accomplishes this by revealing the psychic verisimilitude of the characters, their possession of an inner life, and their mobilization of the same unconscious defenses and mental processes that all of us use in attempting to cope with the external world. In addition, psychoanalysis allows us to deal in a productive way with Don Quixote's psychosis: to identify it as a process and to study its evolution and eventual resolution. Finally, a psychoanalytic approach offers a new and relatively dispassionate context for the inevitable classroom discussion of whether Don Quixote is a fool or a hero.

Cervantes' text raises a number of questions, and many of them can only be answered by recourse to psychoanalytic theory. Why does Don Quixote consistently define chivalry in terms of its erotic, rather than its bellicose, aspects? Why is he so fascinated with the story of Lancelot and Guinevere, and why does he pay particular attention to the *dueña* Quintañona? How does his ongoing creation of Dulcinea evolve, and why does he have an imperious need to distance her from Aldonza Lorenzo and from every other real woman in his life? Why does he reveal Dulcinea's real identity to Sancho in part 1, chapter 25? Is it a revelation, or is it the preservation of some deeper secret? How do his relations with real women evolve in parts 1 and 2 of the novel? Why is he so fascinated by Marcela, by Juan Palomeque's daughter, by Dorotea, by Altisidora? What is at stake in his nocturnal encounter with Doña Rodríguez in part 2, chapter 48? Why does he so suddenly recover his sanity when his niece and housekeeper confront him on his return home in part 2, chapter 73?

Such questions indicate the rich possibilities that psychoanalytical theory offers students of Cervantes' masterpiece, but I feel obliged to conclude with one final caveat. It is difficult, but not impossible, for instructors to accept the validity of psychoanalytic theory unless they have themselves been in analysis. It is similarly difficult, but not impossible, to practice psychoanalytic literary criticism without the experience of analysis and at least some special training. This is an area that bears abundant witness to the truth of the old saw about a little knowledge being a dangerous thing, but for those who would like to pursue this path, I recommend Charles Brenner's *Elementary Textbook of Psychoanalysis* and Freud's *Introductory Lectures on Psychoanalysis* for their overall accounts of psychoanalytic theory. Frederick Crews's "Literature and Psychology" and his *Psychoanalysis and Literary Process*, Meredith Skura's recent *Literary Uses of the Psychoanalytic Process*, and Morton Kaplan and Robert Kloss's *The Unspoken Motive*, provide good introductions to the relation between psychoanalysis and literary criticism. For the application of psychoanalytic theory to the analysis of *Don Quixote*, one might profitably consult Teresa Aveleyra's "El erotismo de don Quijote," Martine Bigeard's *La Folie et les fous littéraires en Espagne, 1500–1650*, Helene Deutsch's "Don Quixote and Don Quixotism," Carroll B. Johnson's "A Second Look at Dulcinea's Ass" and *Madness and Lust: A Psychoanalytic Approach to Don Quixote*, Donald Palmer's "Unamuno, Freud and the Case of Alonso Quijano," and John Weiger's *The Individuated Self: Cervantes and the Emergence of the Individual*.

BACKGROUND MATERIALS AND THE TEACHING OF *DON QUIXOTE*

VOICES AND TEXTS IN *DON QUIXOTE*

Elias L. Rivers

Behind Cervantes' major novel we can perceive traditions of language and literature that must have guided his imagination and his pen. Like every other writer, Cervantes cannot function without recalling what he has heard and read; and as we read *Don Quixote*, we realize how Cervantes must have combined in his mind echoes and reflections of two different traditions, one oral and the other written. Sociolinguists in recent years have used the word "diglossia" to characterize the divergent social functions performed by formal written language and by informal oral language within literate communities. The written language, or range of styles, is everywhere more standardized and uniform; the oral language is often radically different from the written language and always displays a wider range of social and affective registers. Modern literacy, at least in most of the world today, is different from medieval diglossia in Europe, where a small specialized minority of clerics read and wrote Latin, a language they learned, not at their mothers' knees, but under a master's rod. Early medieval Europe had a wide range of vernaculars but only one written language, used by church and state as the elite medium of masculine social power. The invention and spread of written literature in the vernaculars, beginning with the poetic exaltation of ladies in twelfth-century Provence, had different results within the different languages and social classes of Europe.

In the Iberian peninsula, the eighth-century Islamic invasion had brought in classical (written) Arabic, greatly weakening Latin literacy, especially in southern Spain. Latin was restored during the twelfth century in northern Spain by crusading clerics from France, but it was accepted only temporarily by the Castilian monarchy, which was using Castilian in administrative documents, law codes, chronicles, and scientific treatises by the middle of the thirteenth century. Castilian, destined to become the national language of Spain, was not regularly used for writing lyric poetry of courtly love until the fifteenth century, but the oral tradition of Castilian ballads (*romances*), which originated with the lyrical fragmentation of longer epic poems, was unusually strong and persistent. Orally composed and transmitted for many decades, Spanish ballads were soon drawing on French and English tails of Charlemagne and King Arthur, as well as on the Spanish legends of Bernardo del Carpio, Fernán González, the Cid, and more recent historical figures. Oral ballads were written down and printed in collections of courtly poetry, most notably in the *Cancionero general* (1511), in inexpensive chapbooks (*pliegos sueltos*), and, by the middle of the sixteenth century, in *romanceros*, or collections of ballads. Since most Spaniards did not read or write, popular ballads were still sung and recited orally, and they were learned by heart at all levels of society.

Prose romances of chivalry (*libros de caballerías*), unlike ballads, belonged primarily to a written tradition. (In most cultures, oral traditions depend heavily on the mnemonic advantages of verse and music; the development of prose as an art form seems to require a written medium.) The Arthurian romance was a literary phenomenon common to all of Europe in the late Middle Ages. By the fourteenth century, many Spaniards were familiar with versions of stories about Merlin, the Grail, Lancelot, and Tristram—stories that combined magic and religion with knightly valor and courtly love. An indigenous Spanish variant developed with *Amadís de Gaula*, rewritten by Garci Rodríguez de Montalvo and published in 1508; this neo-Arthurian romance established the genre in Spain. Though written and sold as printed books, romances of chivalry were read not only privately but also publicly to illiterate audiences. In some cases, public reciters even improvised such texts orally.

The genesis of *Don Quixote* is closely tied to the popularity of chivalric romances and ballads, written prose and oral poetry concerning knights-errant, their adventures, and their devotion to ladies. Rigorous Spanish moralists had often attacked, from a strictly Christian point of view, the self-indulgent habit of reading romances; Cervantes' book made fun of this literature from a burlesque or parodic (as well as from an academic or intellectual) point of view. In the first chapter, the reader of *Don Quixote* meets the protagonist as a reader of romantic fiction. Like the "unoccupied reader" of the prologue, Alonso Quixano is "at leisure" most of the time and hence devotes himself to reading romances of chivalry. Trying to make sense of their involved courtly-love syntax is a strain on his mind. Another source of strain is the suspense of uncompleted action, a feeling of dissatisfaction that pushes the reader toward assuming the role of writer: "many a time he felt the urge to take up his pen and finish it just as the author had promised." Instead, he becomes "so absorbed" in his reading that his brain dries up and he loses his mind (pt. 1, ch. 1; p. 26).[1]

The temporary loss of personal awareness or identity is normal as an integral part of the psychological phenomenon of reading fiction, which involves verbal and imaginative participation in another person's actions and thoughts; this particular reader takes a further step into lasting madness by attempting to act out the narrated adventures. In his first sally, however, Don Quixote's alienation is presented not as that of a reader of romances but as that of a reciter of ballads. When, at his first inn/castle, whores/ damsels help him remove his armor, he recites a ballad fragment concerning the arrival of Lancelot at a castle, inserting his own rhyming name: Lanzarote/Don Quixote. As L. A. Murillo has pointed out in the notes to his edition of the novel and elsewhere, that particular ballad already contained burlesque terms, such as *rocino* 'nag.' Somewhat later (pt. 1, ch. 5), when Don Quixote is flat on his back, he remembers, not a romance of chivalry, but another fragment of the oral tradition, a ballad about Baldwin and the Marquis of Mantua, a "story known by heart by the children, not forgotten by the young men, and lauded and even believed by the old folk, [yet] . . . not a whit truer than the miracles of Mohammed" (pt. 2, ch. 5; p. 44). When his peasant neighbor tells him that he is not Baldwin or anyone else of that sort but an honorable gentleman surnamed Quixana, Don Quixote replies, "I know who I am, . . . and I know that I may be not only those I have named, but all the twelve peers of France." He uses a traditional Jehovah-like formula ("Yo sé quien soy," a common variant of "yo soy quien soy," 'I am the person that I am') to assert an honorable aristocratic identity, the continuity of self that stands behind one's word as a gentleman; but this assertion is completely undercut when Don Quixote adds that he can change his identity at will. The alienating effect of literature, written or oral, is presented as madly and hilariously subversive.

The interplay between oral and written language is essential to the art of Cervantes' novel; the imitation or evocation of voices gives intelligible structure to its text. Don Quixote's first short and abortive sally by himself is canceled by his second and third sallies in the company of his squire Sancho

Panza. Their adventures, which serve as points of reference in time and space, function as mere narrative pretexts for pseudo-oral discourse of various sorts. The dialogue between Don Quixote and Sancho Panza quickly becomes one of the novel's focal points: it is, primarily, a dialogue between a peculiarly intense reader of literature, who talks like a schoolmaster, and an illiterate rustic, who speaks the substandard Spanish of a rich oral culture. These two literary characters provide an ingenious way of organizing a highly complex dialectical text.

The contrasts between Don Quixote and Sancho Panza draw on traditions rooted in oral folklore and, more immediately, on the third chapter of *Lazarillo de Tormes*, the first anonymous picaresque novel, which also drew directly on folklore. The alliance of a tall thin gentleman on a gaunt nag and a short fat peasant on a rotund donkey provokes a laughter suggesting fundamental social and psychological implications within the beholder's mind; a companionship between such antithetical figures seems to be almost mechanically unstable and, perhaps because of this, deeply comic.

Don Quixote is the less traditional of the two figures, combining (to use his own words) arms and letters. Letters—literature about knights—have led him into the anachronistic madness of taking up arms to set the modern world aright. The medieval man of arms had been illiterate; Don Quixote, influenced by the model of the Renaissance courtier, is more literary than military. His basic relation to Sancho is that of master to servant, landowner to peasant. Sancho Panza's name itself reveals a kinship to "Saint Belly," a gluttonous carnival figure, directly opposed to the abstemious Lenten figure of Don Quixote, who represents the repressive authority of spirit over matter. Don Quixote is usually filled with mad faith and generous, self-denying bravery; Sancho, by contrast, is a self-indulgent, greedy, and skeptical coward. This set of antitheses, reinforced by medical theories of the humors, defines the basic physical, psychological, and social stereotypes underlying the dialogue between Quixote and Sancho. The combined social power of literacy and relative wealth would seem to make the former unquestionably dominant, but the latter, representing the subversive and deceptive power of carnival's temporary exchange of social roles, is frequently able to assert himself as superior.

The classical literary tradition of the prose dialogue, from Plato to Castiglione's *Courtier*, had provided textual models for Cervantes' *Galatea* (1585), in which shepherds and nymphs, living in utopian freedom from material pressures, talk to one another endlessly about the joys and problems of love. But the less solemnly intellectual level of the casual conversations between Don Quixote and Sancho Panza are closer in spirit to Erasmus' *Colloquia* and *Adagia*. Sancho's use of proverbs is a burlesque derivative of a Renaissance appreciation for the oral vox populi, and the irony of Erasmus' *Praise of Folly* is reflected in the subtle ambiguities of Cervantes' dialogues between the literary madman and the illiterate fool.

Erasmian irony is also an important element in the two picaresque dialogues that most closely anticipated those of *Don Quixote*. In chapter 3 of *Lazarillo*, the central character is both narrator and protagonist as he records, in a colloquial but written report, his conservations with his third master, a proud but impoverished member of the minor nobility of Old Castile. As a cynical beggar, without his master's excessive self-respect, Lazarillo feels sympathy for the squire's self-imposed hunger and coaxes him to eat humble food without losing face. Cervantes' own "Coloquio de los perros" 'Dogs' Colloquy,' an exemplary novel, is a parody of the picaresque novel; in it, Scipio's commentary on Berganza's autobiographical narrative provokes a running dialogue between the two dogs that serves as a discursive counterpoint to the events being recounted. Within an altogether different narrative framework, the dialogues of Don Quixote and Sancho Panza often constitute a similar commentary on their adventures.

Written dialogue is, of course, a stylization of actual speech: physical gestures and intonation, often essential to oral communication, can be represented in writing only schematically, if at all. But the ideal reader takes into account the context and situation of the imaginary speakers in order to comprehend their disembodied words as meaningful speech. The conversations of Don Quixote and Sancho Panza are often "chemically pure," for they usually converse with one another in social isolation. From the beginning to the end of their relationship, they are engaged in one long, complex dialogue, frequently interrupted by the intrusion of events or people but maintaining a continuity that is partly dependent on reminiscent references to fixed points of frequent allusion, like Sancho's island.

From a pragmatic point of view, courtesy and self-interest seem to be two basic and polar principles that control verbal transactions between individuals. Courtesy includes a wide range of devices, such as proper forms of address, by means of which the "ego" recognizes and confirms the status of his "alter" as a fellow member of a given society; mutual recognition of social status is a precondition for dialogue. The asymmetrical relation between Don Quixote and Sancho is clearly indicated by their respective use of *tú* 'thou' and *vuestra merced* 'your honor.' This distinction establishes ground rules for the appropriateness of certain types of speech acts: Don Quixote can, for example, give commands, whereas Sancho can only make requests. Threats, promises, and bargains are some of the other basic acts that give structure to their more or less cooperative dialogue. There is also a great deal of gratuitous detail in their dialogue, mere "noise" from a narrowly pragmatic point of view; in actual fact, these exchanges serve to refine their relationship, to project socially their self-images and their images of one another.

Don Quixote's literacy and Sancho Panza's illiteracy produce an interweaving of two different types of language. The master's language belongs essentially to the standard literary Spanish developed by Ciceronian humanists and spread by printed books—not only romances but also collections of discursive essays such as those of Antonio de Guevara (1480?–1545). Within this language of Renaissance diction and convoluted syntax, Don Quixote incorporates certain medieval archaisms associated with chivalry, particularly the pronunciation of an initial "f" instead of the more modern aspirated or silent "h" in words such as *ferido* 'wounded,' which is used in place of *herido*. Sancho's substandard pronunciations are also reflected in phonetic spellings, such as *friscal* instead of *fiscal*. Attention is often explicitly drawn to Sancho's uncouth speech by Don Quixote's schoolmasterly corrections, which admonish Sancho to use words like *erutar* 'eruct' instead of *regoldar* 'belch.'

Don Quixote's syntax is typically Ciceronian and hypotactic; Sancho's is simpler, but he soon acquires some of his master's periodicity. Likewise, Quixote's classical written prose has its parallel in Sancho's vast fund of oral proverbs. The number of proverbs in Spanish—many of them translated and adapted from Arabic sayings—has long been regarded as an index of the vitality of Hispanic oral culture, a vitality largely lost in post-Elizabethan English. The paratactic brevity of Sancho's proverbs constitutes a neat contrast to the prolonged hypotaxis of Ciceronian prose. Rhetorical prose is an integral part of Don Quixote's madness—that is, of his mental helplessness in the grips of a style that does his thinking for him—but Sancho's proverbs are sometimes mechanically linked in irrelevant concatenations. On these occasions, purely verbal associations control discourse, regardless of the topic presumably under discussion.

Underlying the structure of the novel as a whole is the voice of the primary narrator in dialogue with the implied reader. In the prologue to part 1, this narrator presents himself physically as seated at his desk "with the paper before me, a pen behind my ear, my elbow on the desk and my cheek in my hand" (pt. 1, prologue, p. 9), trying to write an introduction inviting his reader to read the novel. The formal discursive prose of this prologue soon becomes informal, drifts into a narrative about an anonymous friend dropping in, and then shifts abruptly from indirect to direct discourse—that is, to a dialogue with the friend. The friend's spoken words "so impressed themselves upon [him]" that they become the written words of the prologue itself. The verb used here, *se imprimieron*, inevitably evokes the printing press, that early modern word processor, but it was still the writer's mind and hand that provided the printout, the text of *Don Quixote.*

Cervantes' major novel repeatedly invites its implied reader to be aware of the different types and functions of language, literature, and media: oral ballads and written romances about knights-errant, pastoral and picaresque novels, the possibilities of meaningful dialogue between an illiterate peasant and a literary landowner, the stylistic contrasts between pithy proverbs and Ciceronian eloquence. Within this novelist's macrotext, many different microtexts are juxtaposed and interwoven. Manipulated by these texts, readers repeatedly fall into the writer's traps, but their reading experiences eventually cause them to realize that their dependence on language is not unlike that of Don Quixote, who went mad because he read romances and carried literary texts inside his mind as he charged windmills and armies of sheeps. The writer, the protagonist, and the reader alike inhabit worlds permeated by language and literature, by voices and texts. Teachers and students also live in such worlds, and they need to bring an awareness of this fact to their own readings of Cervantes' masterpiece.

NOTE

[1]All quotations are from *Don Quixote: The Ormsby Translation, Revised,* ed. Joseph R. Jones and Kenneth Douglas. For references to the original Spanish, I have used *El ingenioso hidalgo Don Quijote de la Mancha,* ed. Luis Murillo.

DON QUIXOTE: ARCHETYPAL BAROQUE MAN

Norma L. Hutman

"All the world's a stage and all the men and women merely players," says Jaques in *As You Like It*. He, of course, is the definitive cynic, suffering from a condition likely to be shared by any student who tries to impose order and structure on twenty-five centuries of creative expression in Western literature. But Jaques has a point: as Joseph Campbell observed in a 1967 lecture, occidental civilization is characterized by self-consciousness. We march through the centuries asking "Who am I? What is a human being? How do I relate to society?" We are tortured by problems of free will and individual fate, of immortality, of responsibility and the nature of honor. In our constant preoccupation with identity, we perforce play a role, sometimes assigned and sometimes assumed. We study ourselves in a mirror; we don a mask; we act.

By focusing on this process, the teacher can begin to render intelligible the diversity offered by any survey course in Western literature from the Greeks through the late Renaissance. Starting with the lonely dignity of Achilles, the image of humanity evolves into that expressed during the curtain speech in Webster's *The Duchess of Malfi*, where Delio proclaims over the corpses of princes and cardinals, "These wretched eminent things leave no more trace behind 'em, than should one fall in a frost, and leave his print in snow: As soon as the sun shines, it ever melts, both form and matter" (5.5.114–18). Of course, Western literature did not really plunge headlong from honor to disillusionment, for the era that spawned the nihilism of Jacobean tragedy also produced Cervantes' mad hidalgo, whose lonely dignity matches that of Achilles as he enacts the role according to which the baroque era defined itself.

The baroque eludes easy definition and appears most clearly through the plastic arts, in which the character and conflicts of philosophy and form announce themselves dramatically. Bernini, for example, illustrates the gulf that lies between Renaissance idealism and the dynamic realism of post-Reformation art. Unlike the noble godlike hero sculpted by Michelangelo, Bernini's David is, par excellence, man in action: ugly, vigorous, a kind of prototypical *pícaro*. Action is both his nature and his heroic mode.

Velázquez portrays another, equally dominant baroque concern: the difficulty of distinguishing between reality and illusion. In *Las meninas* the canvas itself is art, yet what it portrays is the creative act. The king and queen are presumably out there, in front of the painting. But what is out there if not the audience, the viewers, what we tend to call the real world? Can our world be the same as that of the monarchs? Are we not separated by centuries and by the distinction between art and reality as well? But if those mirrored in the painting, and thus placed outside it, are not in the same place as the audience, where are they? And where, in effect, are we? No canvas ever proclaimed a philosophy that refuses so resolutely to make absolute distinctions of time, space, and reality.

Rubens, in turn, plays havoc with Renaissance symmetry. His structural principle is not balance but curve. Everything revolves around whirling vortices. Myth and history coexist in the same painting, in the same reality. Nature, humanity, and movement fuse and reject the cool, sharp lines that make Renaissance painting a statement of security, reason, and law.

This recurring shift from repose to action, even to chaos—from reason to paradox and uncertainty, from idealism to realism, from art as order to art as game, jest, and question—flowed logically out of the disorder of the Reformation. The Reformation disrupted Renaissance unity, disintegrating reason, symmetry, and certitudes as surely as it rent the political and religious fabric of European society. The order that shaped Utopia and placed reason above all other human endeavor slid headlong into chaos. For the baroque individual, truth was disorder, an immediately felt loss of structure in reality. In such a world, all constants seemed meaningless. Symmetry became mind's joke, an illusion of balance that yielded Bernini's radical, tortured, mobile forms. Logic became reason's joke, a deception practiced by the mind on itself, and affirmation became will's joke, for human volition found itself mocked by fate. In *Shakespeare's Tragedies*, Clifford Leech describes the generation that inherited the Renaissance ideal and saw it perish in a disillusionment that gave rise to illusionment:

> Standing between a belief in natural order and a growing perception of chaos, between the Renaissance enthusiasm for living and an ever-darkening disillusionment, between the twin poles of Fate and

Chance, of predestination and free will, they went through mental
experiences of a peculiar intensity, knew the darkness and the terror
all the more keenly for the light that still remained in the diminishing
fragment of the heavens.   (44)

When the bottom drops out of reality, what does one put in its place?
Cervantes, uniquely equipped by a history of personal failure and
disillusionment, offers the ultimate radical answer. The mind conjures up a
truth, founded on the slippery basis of art, and makes art, itself an illusion,
yield something more real than that which the senses perceive as real. Don
Quixote embodies in his person the uncertainty, chaos, vision, dream, and
imagination that make art a bulwark against uncertainty. He is in all things a
paradox: funny and noble, mad and wise, blind and visionary, mistaken
and correct, defeated and triumphant. He plays all parts—poet, lunatic,
and lover—in the drama he has concocted. And, paradoxically, we students
and teachers are ennobled by his deeds as we laugh at him.

Moving through the novel, we first perceive Don Quixote the actor. The
part he elects to play at once raises the question of what is real; it also
challenges and mocks reason and offers alternatives to rationality. Gradually, the novel works out the baroque debate that pits action against art,
while reconciling the apparent conflict between them. Don Quixote's fate,
with his final renunciation, incarnates the concept of volition that dominated his age. Finally, the novel itself plays with symmetry, opposing and
transcending it in the juxtaposition of thematic and stylistic elements in
parts 1 and 2. Taken "all in all," *Don Quixote* provides a microcosm of
baroque attitudes and a pattern for the baroque hero.

At the outset, students can easily see that Don Quixote is a consummate
actor, but they should realize as well that his acting does not detract from a
genuine commitment to his sustaining vision. Quixote elects a role, and he
disregards both history and contemporary reality to play it, but he must
also learn the rules by which the game is played. Having tested his
makeshift armor and found it wanting, he is not so foolish as to test it again.
Confronted with the contradictory evidence of the real world, he dismisses
it as enchantment. He has written the play in which he appears, and thus
he can provide (at least in the first part) the stage directions for its
performance.

When students are encouraged to juxtapose Cervantes' game with the
visual paradox central to Velázquez' art, they perceive how the boundary
between art and experience can be erased. Cervantes claims to have found
a manuscript, and his rendering of that discovery becomes the first part of
the novel. Yet, in part 2, the characters divert themselves by discussing the
first part of the novel, the fame of which also inspires the games devised by

the Duke and the Duchess—games that reduce Don Quixote's inspired madness to a casual diversion. If the characters can comment on the novel as art, do they belong to our world—a world in which we too are readers? We are compelled to ask: what separates our world from theirs? And which of the two is really real? The entire notion of fiction is called into question: fiction and its commentary fuse, and the characters in the fictional world step aside to discourse about their own plane of reality.

Don Quixote has lost his hold on distinctions; in fact, he no longer thinks in categories. Likewise, distinctions elude Cervantes' readers. They can no longer step aside and say, "Here fiction begins," just as they cannot step aside from Velázquez' canvas and say, "Here is the frame." This is the baroque world, and it projects beyond its own age, telling us that we do not know with absolute certainty what is real. The madman/dreamer/actor possesses the only available sanity. He knows, he says, who he is and who he can be, if he chooses. He encapsulates the baroque absolute as well as a basic human dilemma in his own capacious madness.

As a madman/wiseman, the Knight of the Mournful Countenance takes on the related baroque problems that set art and action, reason and vision, at odds with each other. For Don Quixote is neither illogical nor unreasonable, except when his vision takes precedence. As a commentator on arms and letters, as Sancho's adviser on governing an island, and as a righter of wrongs, he makes eminent sense; however, it is not his sense but his nonsense that causes others to espouse his cause. Reason has its limits; logic may make converts, but it rarely produces zealots. Unamuno acknowledges this fact when he contends that Don Quixote is most glorious when he inspires others to fight for his cause and to suffer blows on its behalf, when perfectly reasonable people like the curate and the barber affirm that a barber's basin is a helmet. Of course, they are acting out parts, but in so doing they emulate the mad hidalgo. Don Quixote has succeeded in standing the logical world on its head.

In "The Glass Licentiate," Cervantes provides a clue to the merits of perverse reason. If a wise man is mad, he is allowed to be wise. Sanity, like reason, has its limits, defines too much, is subject to laws. But madness writes its own rules, and, within its safe and ample boundaries, wisdom, so dangerous elsewhere, may roam.

Just as dangerous as the mind is the human will. Don Quixote performs two radical acts of will, acts that sustain and cancel each other. He wills himself to be a knight, fabricating as he goes along whatever is necessary to maintain his role, but he declines to test his second helmet: after perceiving that the first fell apart in the testing, he knows how far the will to transform reality can go. Volition will not negate a broadsword, and Don Quixote, for all his rashness, is never rash enough to get himself killed. When his will is subverted by others and breaks down, Quixote accomplishes his other great free act: he liberates himself from the prison of his dream and sets that dream free. He dies without his visionary identity, and the act of renunciation requires a courage that the Knight of the Mournful Countenance himself would have admired. The will to create is matched by the will to renounce. All the great baroque acts of volition involve renunciation: Segismundo renounces his passions; Prospero, his magic; and Don Quixote, his dream. In baroque literatures, no easy and happy ending is possible. Segismundo must rule, Prospero must return to Milan, and Alonso Quijano must die. They renounce because, in a world without certitude, renunciation is the only choice that can be made with certainty.

As actor, arbiter of others' destinies, commentator on reality, adviser, philosopher, and the embodiment of free will (which ultimately becomes the renunciation of will and vision), Don Quixote epitomizes the preoccupations, inconsistencies, problems, and radical solutions of an age. More completely than any other literary figure of his time, Quixote offers answers, many of them painful, in an age of persistent questions. In fact, the *Quixote* itself stands as a commentary on baroque art, embracing a false symmetry that undoes balance and symmetry by means of a circular logic as violent as the ordering principle in any of Rubens' canvases.

Action is the critical structure in part 1, in which Don Quixote rushes headlong through reality. He is a force, a whirlwind, and if he is dashed to earth for his pains he is also, as Unamuno observes, lifted to the stars. He carries others in his wake, converts Sancho, and obliges those who want to bring him home to employ his own devices. But in part 2 he is the object of others' games. The Duke and Duchess stage a play, cast him in a part, and toy with him as though he were a puppet. Ginés de Pasamonte reappears as Maese Pedro. He fits well into the scenario, for the action has become farce. As the object of farce, however, Quixote's divine madness "runs out of steam." Once he had known who he was and what he was doing, but how he can neither see Clavileño fly nor perceive Dulcinea among the country wenches offered to him by Sancho. The idealizing process breaks down, because it has been tampered with. The vast horizon of the creative mind has been reduced to an exercise in illusion. From this trap, Quixote must liberate himself, even though the liberation might cost him his vision. Alonso Quijano's disillusioned last testament, comic and pathetic as it seems, is the price he pays for playing the game seriously with the entirety of his soul.

Don Quixote is too successful in part 1 for the mores of his age. The second part confirms his fame and appears to repeat the pattern of part 1, but its balance is only apparent. Everything is debased; the vision has become someone else's parlor game, and the creative transformation of reality has become a trick that anyone can play. Don Quixote's acquaint-ances are driven to employ his devices in part 1. When we meet these characters again, they have mastered the artist's devices. They excel at technique—the forte of the baroque—but they have lost the motivation of the master. Thus, all symmetry between parts 1 and 2 declines into parody. Even those who, like Sancho, do not intend to harm the knight contribute to his downfall.

This disparity between part 1 and part 2 establishes the paradoxical character of Don Quixote's dual vision: one side of it is conceived in idealism and the other is thrust upon him by fame. On one level, his vitality and active intervention in the real world of part 1 are balanced by the deceptions and final defeat of part 2. But the symmetry, like Hamlet's time, is "out of joint." The entire *Quixote* is dominated by the mad, creative vision of the opening chapters and, in harmony with them, the scene at the inn that brings everyone together to sort out lives and to identify the helmet of Mambrino. People, assorted identities (e.g., Dorothea/Princess Micomicona), objects (the basin/helmut), and motifs (chivalric, picar-esque, Byzantine, pastoral, etc.) unite to witness that the hero has indeed righted wrong and set the world straight "no less for his own greater reknown than in the service of his country." Part 1 is centripetal, although shot through with elements (especially Quixote's enchantment and encaged journey home) that strain the mad unity. In part 2, the knight's fame seems ensured. Art has made him famous; it has cemented his vision in print and in the popular mind.

But part 2 is centrifugal. "Things fall apart; the center cannot hold." The glue of mad faith comes unstuck. Clavileño does not fly, and Don Quixote is repeatedly hoodwinked by actors having fun at his expense. Here moments of triumph (especially Sancho's embracing of the creative vision) are the disparate elements in a rush to defeat. All the constants of the chivalric structure fall away. Finally Dulcinea, conjured up by Sancho, fails. Sansón Carrasco, that epitome of pragmatism, wins as he plays by Don Quixote's rules, but the rules have been subverted.

The baroque solution can be a paradoxically creative one, for it often mocks the art it engenders. The baroque hero reemerges as an artist whose creativity distorts reality, in part because he rejects pattern in existence and in part because he sees a distorted world. The baroque perspective—sometimes excessive, sometimes perverse, sometimes despairing—confirms the creator's vision. If he sees giants where others see windmills, his creative impulse demands equal rights for the giants. Picasso insisted that an object claimed by art loses its right to be what it seems to be in common experience. What is this claim if not the justification for transforming a barber's basin into the helmet of Mambrino?

Baroque art is artifice; it plays with the world. Baroque creation is an eminently self-conscious act, at once autocreation and autocriticism. A consummate actor, Don Quixote remains aware of himself and his enterprise, and in part 2 he becomes a commentator on his own artistic existence. Sancho, in contrast, even at his most imaginative, escapes self-consciousness. He lives in the moment, whereas Don Quixote embraces the moment and its contradiction. He becomes a man of the past, a shaper of his own age, and an archetype in which one can discover the definition of humanity. We and our students all know what "quixotic" means; the vision has outdistanced its creator and belongs to us all.

By juxtaposing adventures, characters, and commentary in the first and second parts of the novel, Cervantes appears to create a symmetrical balance between them, but the great achievements of part 1 descend into defeat, jokes, lies, and renunciation in part 2. Cervantes too is playing a game, mocking symmetry. His structure suits his hero. Following the knight's adventures, he observes a baroque hero creating himself, his goal, and his stratagems. He then watches as they serve to undo him. More entertaining and more effective than the unrelieved pessimism and satire characteristic of much baroque literature, the tone of *Don Quixote* captures the interplay of illusion and disillusionment that is the essence of baroque art. All is not lost, but the word "victory" has been lost from the active vocabulary of the age. *Don Quixote* offers students a portrait of the consummate actor and the definitive visionary. He performs the act of renunciation by means of which the baroque hero acknowledges the limits that are set on all human endeavors. He is a contradiction, yet he aggrandizes imagination and thus transcends his age. Ultimately, he makes the baroque hero meaningful to everyone.

BACKGROUND MATERIAL ON *DON QUIXOTE*

Juan Bautista Avalle-Arce

Bringing background material into the teaching of *Don Quixote* is an easy matter; if there is a problem, it derives more from an embarrassment of riches than from a lack of resources. Yet the teacher of Cervantes' masterpiece must always bear in mind what should be the most obvious fact of all: the *Quixote* is far more than the sum of its parts, far more than the literary and social traditions on which it draws. As the first modern novel, it is also pregnant with all novels to come.

Any introduction to *Don Quixote* should fix the author and the publication of his book in space and time. Cervantes lived from 1547 to 1616. He was from New Castile, and as far as we know, he had no formal schooling. He became a soldier, and at one point he suffered through five years of captivity in Algiers. This sort of biographical background can help students understand Cervantes' objectives in writing *Don Quixote* and the world view embodied in it. For this reason, all teachers of the book ought to consult one of the standard biographies.

The facts of the book's publication are also important and should be introduced early in class discussion, because they suggest relations to other works of the period. For example, the first part of *Don Quixote* appeared shortly after the publication of the second part of Mateo Alemán's *Guzmán de Alfarache*, the most successful of all Spanish picaresque novels. The class might consider why Cervantes never wrote a picaresque novel at the very moment when the genre had reached the height of its popularity. In fact, Cervantes employed novelistic techniques that were just the opposite of those used in *Guzmán*, and a brief outline of any picaresque novel can

127

illustrate this point.[1] The teacher can also discuss the publication of *Don Quixote*, part 2 just one year after the appearance of Avellaneda's spurious continuation of 1614. There are significant differences between this work and the original novel (e.g., Avellaneda's Quixote is no longer in love with Dulcinea), and Cervantes' awareness of these differences exerted a profound influence on what he wrote in the second part of his own novel.

There are important shifts in emphasis between the first and second parts of *Don Quixote*, but even apparently trivial differences offer the instructor an opportunity to discuss important aspects of the text. In the title of the 1605 edition, for example, Don Quixote is identified as an *hidalgo* 'squire,' whereas in 1615 he is a *caballero* 'knight.' One can use this distinction to introduce students to knight-errantry, to the ideals that motivated it, and in particular to the idea of courtly love. These noble concepts and institutions were international in scope, and they provided the historical basis for chivalric literature. Students might well be familiar with the tales of King Arthur and his knights of the Round Table; in any case, some mention of them and other examples of chivalric literature is necessary to establish the context in which Cervantes wrote *Don Quixote*. This material should of course be presented in light of the 1605 prologue, where Cervantes discusses the aims of parody.

The word *ingenioso* appears in the titles of both parts of *Don Quixote*. Although it literally means "ingenious," it also evokes the Renaissance concept of *ingenio*, which relates to the traditional theory of the four humors—blood, cholera, bile, and melancholy.[2] Shakespeare's Hamlet suffers from a superabundance of melancholy, which inevitably results in death. In contrast, Don Quixote is a choleric type, and a consideration of his nature, as defined by classical physiology, serves to explain the progress of his madness as well as the physiognomic and physical traits with which Cervantes endows him.

The preliminary material in the 1605 edition also offers the instructor an opportunity to explain the practice of censorship in Spain and other European countries. The first Spanish censorship law was promulgated in 1502, and Philip II revised it in 1558 to make it even stricter. These laws were largely a response to the spread of Protestantism and the rise of the Inquisition, both of which are important to an understanding of *Don Quixote*, and this might be an appropriate point at which to introduce them to students.

The preliminaries also include the dedication, the prologue, and the laudatory poems. In any study of the dedicatory materials, consider the different roles played in Cervantes' life and works by the Duke of Béjar, to whom the 1605 edition was dedicated, and the Count of Lemos, who was addressed in the 1615 dedicatory epistle. The prologue can be treated within the tradition of Renaissance prologue writing, an special emphasis should be placed on its contents, because a prologue is always really an epilogue: that is, it states the author's artistic conclusions about the finished work. The poems that follow the prologue might serve as a pretext for a brief excursion into history and, of course, the recurrent theme of parody. Amadís de Gaula, putative author of one sonnet, could be discussed at this point for the role he played in Don Quixote's life as well as for his significance in Spanish and European literary history.

In considering the preliminary material to the 1615 edition, one again needs to place special emphasis on the prologue. Avellaneda's apocryphal *Don Quixote* had appeared the previous year, and this prologue was Cervantes' answer to what he regarded as a serious literary crime. Avellaneda stole Cervantes' plans for a continuation as they had been stated in part 1, chapter 52, and this theft forced Cervantes to change his plans beginning with part 2, chapter 59. The absence of preliminary poems in the 1615 edition contravenes the usual literary convention of the period, but it also reflects Cervantes' consciousness that he had mastered a new genre that Avellaneda had understood only in the most superficial terms. The instructor can demonstrate this contrast by having students read Avellaneda's preliminary sonnet; one should also make this point by selectively comparing the contents, narrative techniques, and ideologies of the two books.

In no course have I been able to teach *Don Quixote* in its entirety. Whether the course lasted for a quarter, a semester, or a full year, I found it imperative to be highly selective. For that reason, I will discuss representative episodes to show how background material can be introduced to enhance the students' understanding and appreciation of the novel.

The episode of Grisóstomo and Marcela (pt. 1, chs. 10–14) is one of many pastoral interludes in *Don Quixote*, and instructors may want to consult my *Novela pastoril española* or Renato Poggioli's *The Oaten Flute* for discussion of the pastoral theme in Renaissance literature. In Spain, Jorge de Montemayor's *Diana* (1559) was particularly important, and students should be given the opportunity to reflect on Cervantes' own comments about it in part 1, chapter 6. If there is sufficient time, one can also discuss what Cervantes set out to achieve in his own pastoral novel, *La Galatea* (1585). The pastoral theme at that time was interwoven with the idea of Neoplatonic love, and this interlude provides the opportunity to focus on the Renaissance concept of love. In this episode, however, love is tragic, having brought about the death of Grisóstomo. There are indications that Grisóstomo committed suicide, a theme that reappears in literary works from the *Celestina* to *The Possessed* and *The Myth of Sisyphus*. Suicide can also be discussed within the context of official Catholic doctrine as expressed in the decrees of the Council of Trent (1545–64). Because Philip II decreed that the Tridentine doctrine should become the law of the kingdom, the Catholic Counter-Reformation had a significant impact on literary developments in late sixteenth- and seventeenth-century Spain.

Some comment on baroque thought might be appropriate at this point, and Helmut Hatzfeld's *Estudios sobre el barroco* provides a good introduction to the subject. The teacher might note that, because the epigraph of part 1, chapter 10, is out of place, it seems likely that the Marcela-Grisóstomo episode originally belonged to the cases of love that Cervantes presented in the long Sierra Morena interlude (pt. 1, chs. 23–31). This observation prepares the way for a consideration of Renaissance poetics and its directive principle of "variety in unity," which William J. Kennedy explains so well in his *Rhetorical Norms in Renaissance Literature*. In paying heed to this principle, Cervantes moved the episode from the Sierra Morena to its present place.

"Variety in unity" also seems to explain the presence of two intercalated stories—the "Curioso impertinente" and the "Captive Captain"—in part 1 of the *Quixote*. The literary background for these tales includes the Italian *novella* and its successors in Spain. Walter Pabst's *Novellentheorie und Novellendichtung* provides a good introduction to this subject, and it might be appropriate to remind students that Cervantes stated in his prologue to the *Novelas ejemplares* that he had been the first to write short stories in Spain. The preamble to the "Curioso impertinente" also serves as an excellent point of departure for introducing the concepts of history and fiction in Renaissance poetics. The story of the Captive Captain enables the instructor to discuss the Mediterranean at the time of Philip II, the role of the Turks, the battle of Lepanto, Cervantes' participation in it, pirates, captivity, and related subjects. Fernand Braudel's *The Mediterranean and the Mediterranean World in the Age of Philip II* is a good source of historical information about this period. Because Cervantes mentions himself by name in the "Captive Captain," it would be appropriate to bring in Cervantes' own life at this point and to discuss the problematic relation between autobiography and fiction. The theme of freedom and captivity runs through the whole corpus of Cervantine works and this intercalated story could be a means of introducing it and comparing it to other treatments of captivity from Boethius and Silvio Pellico to modern works like Norman Mailer's *The Executioner's Song*.

Another episode well worth analyzing is that of Quixote's penance in the Sierra Morena (pt. 1, chs. 25–26). He performs this penance for no good reason other than to imitate Amadís de Gaula (Beltenebros). Although this episode necessitates at least a brief return to the chivalric romances, particular attention should be paid to the very pointlessness of Quixote's penance, because his express motivation seems to contradict the cause-effect relation that is at the root of traditional ethics. His action constitutes the first "gratuitous act" in Western literature, and it might well be compared and contrasted with similar acts in *Crime and Punishment, The Caves of the Vatican* and *The Stranger.* Quixote's penance is not a criminal act; rather, it results from the idealistic desire to raise life to the level of art. I have discussed "life as a work of art" in my book *Don Quijote como forma de vida,* and it is a concept that can be exemplified by reference to the lives and aims of Charles V of Spain, Lorenzo the Magnificent of Florence, Francis I of France, and even Henry VIII of England.

In part 2, the Cave of Montesinos episode (chs. 22–23) is the narrative epicenter, as Quixote's penance is in the first part. Everything in part 2 leads to or stems from the cave episode, which presents us with a galaxy of possible interpretations and approaches. For example, Quixote's subterranean descent can be compared with similar adventures undertaken by classical epic heroes; in fact, Quixote and his student-guide might even be regarded as playing the parts of Aeneas and the Cumaean Sibyl, respectively. It is also an original variation on the Arthurian theme of the descent to the nether world. As such, it can be studied with the help of Howard Rollin Patch's *The Other World according to Descriptions in Medieval Literature.* In Spanish literature, Amadís' son descends to hell in Garci Rodríguez de Montalvo's novel *Las sergas de Esplandián* (1510).

Geography should be employed to explain the location and nature of the Ruidera lagoons, the Cave of Montesinos, and the river Guadiana, which appears during the episode in the guise of Durandarte's servant. At this point, reference can be made to Ovid's *Metamorphoses,* which is mentioned by the student-guide and deformed in a fantastic way by Quixote's dream. The instructor can adopt various approaches to the interpretation of dreams, but I prefer those, like Cicero's *Somnium Scipionis* or Calcidius' Platonic *Interpretatio Latina Partis Prioris Timaei Platonici,* that were available to Cervantes. Wayne Shumaker's *The Occult Sciences in the Renaissance* is a good source of information on the practice of dream interpretation at that time. When Don Quixote awakens from his dream, he claims to have been at the bottom of the cave for three days, whereas the student-guide and Sancho maintain that he has only been gone for an hour. These differing perceptions of time can be explained by referring to more modern concepts like Henri Bergson's distinction between *temps* and *durée.*

The subject of Don Quixote's dream is the epic legend of Montesinos, Durandarte, and Belerma. These characters belong to the Carolingian epic cycle but definitely not to the original French version, although one might want to begin a discussion of this material with a brief description of the epic literature that emanated from the court of Charlemagne. Ramón Menéndez Pidal's La Chanson de Roland *y el neotradicionalismo* is an excellent study of this work. The historical disaster of the French army at Roncesvalles took place on 15 August 778, but Montesinos, Durandarte, and Belerma only appeared much later in the Spanish *romancero;* in fact, Durandarte is the Spanish form of Durendal, the sword of Roland in the original *Chanson de Roland.* At this point, it would be appropriate to introduce one of the traditional *romances* 'ballads' that deal with this epic trio and to outline the history of the Spanish *romancero.* Such comments could be amplified to include remarks about the printing of ballads in the sixteenth and seventeenth centuries and a discussion of the *romancero* as oral literature. W. J. Entwistle's *European Balladry* contains a good introduction to the subject.

Dulcinea del Toboso's appearance as the "enchanted" love object in Don Quixote's dream must be understood in the context of the courtly love tradition. The enchantment itself needs to be seen in two dimensions—the history of Dulcinea and the theme of enchanters and enchantment that pervades the novel. In the first dimension, one needs to recall the lies Sancho told about a visit he never made to her (pt. 1, ch. 31) and the "spell" he cast on the peasant woman who he insisted was Dulcinea (pt. 2, chs. 9–10). Note also Merlin's prophecy about the disenchantment of Dulcinea in part 2, chapter 35, the enchanted head in Don Antonio Moreno's house in Barcelona (pt. 2, ch. 62), and the *malum signum* mentioned in part 2, chapter 74. Because Merlin also plays a role in the Cave of Montesinos episode, it might be appropriate to mention the historical Merlin, who is described in R. S. Loomis' *Arthurian Literature in the Middle Ages.* The second dimension of Dulcinea's enchantment involves the role of enchanters and enchantments in chivalric literature, from which Don Quixote originally acquired his belief in them. During his first sally, Quixote daydreams about the fact that someday one enchanter or another will write down the history of his glorious feats. In part 2, chapter 3, Sansón Carrasco brings back to Quixote's village the news that the hidalgo's story has been printed and that he, a university student, has read it. The idea of enchantment thus has literary precedents; it also has the capacity to alter the reality of the objective world. This insight could well serve as a point of departure for considering the role of literature in *Don Quixote.* Such a discussion might begin with a scrutiny of the protagonist's library (pt. 1, ch. 6) and end with a reflection on the implications of the fact that nearly all of the characters in part 2 have read part 1 of the novel.

Don Quixote's stay at the palace of the Duke and Duchess (pt. 2, chs. 36–56) necessitates the introduction of additional background material.

First of all, Quixote and Sancho are no longer in Castille but in Aragon, and they are in contact with genuine Spanish nobility, some of whom led a passive, almost parasitical existence in the Spain of Philip III.[3] The student's understanding of each adventure in this section is also enhanced by recourse to appropriate background materials, but since the Clavileño episode (pt. 2, ch. 41) is both popular and characteristic, I will focus on it. The existence of a flying horse naturally invites comparison with the Pegasus myth, but it must be remembered that Cervantes is working within the chivalric tradition and that analogous incidents (such as those in *Magalona, Clamades,* and *Valentín y Ursón*) might be more relevant. Sancho's colorful description of the journey through the spheres of air and fire to the sphere of the fixed stars should be understood as playing on the medieval concept of the universe as a system of concentric spheres. C. S. Lewis' excellent book *The Discarded Image* helps bring this cosmology into focus.

The Clavileño episode culminates in a cynical bartering with truth on Don Quixote's part. Besides recalling the Cave of Montesinos episode and placing it in a different perspective, Don Quixote's comments at this point reveal the dominant theme of part 2: the slow disintegration and final abdication of the protagonist's willpower, which is the one and only support of his world. This theme comes to a climax when he solemnly declares, "Dadme albricias, buenos señores, de que ya yo no soy don Quijote de la Mancha, sino Alonso Quijano, a quien mis costumbres me dieron renombre de *Bueno*" (pt. 2, ch. 74).[4] This avowal could serve as a prelude to a discussion of will and human ethics, with references to Schopenhauer's *The World as Will and Representation* and to contemporary existentialist thought.

Those who teach *Don Quixote* in the original Spanish should give some consideration to the language. What was the status of the Spanish language around the year 1600? Comments on this topic might begin with the birth of Castilian, a small dialect spoken in the northern mountains of central Spain; it could loosely be described as the Latin spoken by Basque tribes that had never been thoroughly Romanized. But Castilian was only one of the dialects spoken in the Iberian peninsula when the fragmentation of Latin occurred. For political reasons involving the Reconquest, it gained ascendancy over its neighbours, and during the sixteenth century it became the Spanish language. The standard work on the subject is Rafael Lapesa's *Historia de la lengua española*. These matters are important to an understanding of the *Quixote*, because Cervantes was profoundly interested in language, as can be demonstrated by the lively interchange between Don Quixote, Sancho, and the two students before the wedding of

Camacho (pt. 2, ch. 19). Quixote's continuous criticisms of Sancho's language illustrate the same point and offer one way of broaching a controversial subject in Golden Age Spain—the value of proverbs.

Don Quixote drew on all the literary traditions and genres that were available to Cervantes at that time. Drama theory is discussed during Don Quixote's conversation with the canon from Toledo (pt. 1, chs. 47–49), and two dramatic presentations are included in the text of the novel. The first is Maese Pedro's puppet show, which elicits a number of critical comments from the spectators. Each of their points deserves commentary. Even musical history is relevant, and Manuel de Falla's beautiful marionette-opera, *El retablo de Maese Pedro*, could be introduced to illustrate this point. The protagonists also, later, leave the palace of the Duke and Duchess. They encounter a group of gentlefolk who are preparing to stage several pastoral eclogues by Garcilaso and Camões. There are extended commentaries on these poems and on possible approaches to the dramatization of works that were never intended for the theater. This episode could be linked with Don Quixote's pastoral projects after his defeat by the Knight of the White Moon in part 2, chapter 67. Curiously, Don Quixote entertains these projects at the very moment when he returns to the spot where the eclogues were to have been staged. This constellation of circumstances can serve as the occasion for a comparison of the pastoral and the chivalric as well as a discussion of their relation to Don Quixote's fixation with an ideal world.

Poetry and criticism of poetry also abound in the text. The individual poems can be analyzed in the context of Cervantes' other poems and against the background of Spanish and European poetic traditions. There are also many passages of criticism, including Don Quixote's discussion with Don Lorenzo de Miranda after the famous adventure with the lions (pt. 2, ch. 18). Finally, one should not forget that Don Quixote is himself a poet and that examples of his work appear in the novel (e.g., pt. 2, ch. 46).

Yet *Don Quixote* is written in prose, and Cervantes clearly recorded his principal ideas about prose writing. The examination of Don Quixote's library, his discussion with the canon from Toledo about novel writing, and Cervantes' autocriticism in part 2, chapter 3 (when Sansón Carrasco returns to his village with the news that the eccentric squire's adventures have been published) all provide evidence for reconstructing Cervantes' theory of the novel. In point of fact, *Don Quixote* embodies all types of novels known in Golden Age Spain: the chivalric novel, the pastoral novel, the picaresque novel, and so forth. The range of Cervantes' powers of assimilation was extraordinary, and students of *Don Quixote* should become familiar with the literary, social, historical, and philosophical backgrounds on which Cervantes drew. But it must always be remembered that a knowledge of these materials does not constitute a knowledge of *Don Quixote*. Cervantes synthesized his materials in a uniquely creative way, and although the students' understanding and appreciation of his accomplishment can be enhanced by the instructor's ability to demonstrate what Cervantes used and how he used it, commentaries should never become a substitute for the careful reading of the text itself.

NOTES

[1] *Guzmán de Alfarache* could be used, but the anonymous *Lazarillo de Tormes* or Quevedo's *El Buscón* are shorter and would also be appropriate. Reliable discussions of the picaresque genre can be found in Alexander A. Parker, Richard Bjornson, Harry Sieber's *The Picaresque*, and the important essays on the subject in Claudio Guillén's *Literature as System*.

[2] This concept was popularized in Juan Huarte's *Examen de ingenios para las ciencias* (1575), which was subsequently translated into nearly all the major European languages.

[3] A. Domínguez Ortiz' *La sociedad española en el siglo XVII* contains a good overview of Spanish social hierarchies of the period.

[4] "Good news for you good sirs: I am no longer Don Quixote de la Mancha, but Alonso Quixano, whose way of life won for him the name of *Good.*" *Don Quixote: The Ormsby Translation, Revised*, ed. Joseph R. Jones and Kenneth Douglas, 826.

TEACHING NONMAJORS

"QUIXOTIZ Y PANCINO":
DON QUIXOTE AT AN AG AND TECH

Morgan Desmond

Don Quixote has become an essential part of a survey of Western masterpieces in translation that I teach at the State University of New York Agricultural and Technical College at Cobleskill. A two-year institution, Cobleskill has a few liberal arts majors, but most of the students are enrolled in agriculture, business, food service, early childhood education, and laboratory technology. The masterpieces course is one of several three-credit offerings that students may elect as a part of their required six credits in English. Their other three credits will ordinarily be in composition. Many of these students—although not all—view English courses as annoyances or obstacles rather than as opportunities. For this reason, I operate on the assumption that the masterpieces course will be the only college literature course these students will ever take. The objectives of the course are three: to explain what fictional narrative is and how it works, to introduce fundamental ideas about the historical development of Western literature, and to help the students understand and enjoy the specific works under discussion.[1]

The first two objectives strongly color my approach to *Don Quixote:* I present the novel as an illustration of several important characteristics that a fictional narrative may display and as an example of Renaissance and baroque aesthetic principles. I once substituted *Lazarillo de Tormes* for *Don Quixote* in this course, but I soon discovered that I missed both a clear example of fiction that calls attention to itself as fiction and an easily

136

recognized stepping-stone between the objective viewpoint of ancient literature and the subjective preoccupation of modern literature. If the students are already familiar with these concepts, it is much easier to discuss their more abstruse manifestations in modern fiction. In Kafka's *The Trial*, for example, the reality value of fictions within fictions (e.g., Titorelli's account of the nature of the court or the Parable of the Law) is difficult to assess, and the apparently objective external world can be read as a representation of the central character's phenomenal experience.

The course calendar shows five class meetings devoted to *Don Quixote*. Real life seems invariably to require at least one more, but the ideal is always easier to describe. Experience has proved the wisdom of providing the students with some basic information about the novel before they start their reading.[2] For example, I point out to them that *Don Quixote* is fiction, not history, and that the mounted knight was obsolete long before Cervantes' time. In a technical college, these two points require special emphasis. The current fashion in elementary and high schools for "social studies," as opposed to history and geography, has produced a generation lacking even a rudimentary grasp of historical time. Every semester at least one student has Don Quixote "staying at a motel." I also make clear to the students that *Don Quixote* is a parody but more than just parody. In addition, students need to know that part 2 differs from part 1, that the structure of the novel is basically episodic, and that a coherent development lies beneath this episodic structure.

Class coverage begins with a brief account of the fiction that was popular in Cervantes' time (the Byzantine, the pastoral, and particularly the chivalric), the expectations that these works created in their readers, and the consequent possibilities for parody. References to twentieth-century analogues (spy, Western, and romance novels) help to illustrate these points. After an admittedly superficial explanation of the Renaissance spirit of part 1 and the baroque elements in part 2, I move to a consideration of the text itself by reading the second paragraph of the novel, pointing out the suggestions of "jowls," "cheese," and "crank" that lie behind the central character's conjectured surnames as they appear in the original Spanish text. There is an obvious burlesque here that makes clear the distinction between author and narrator (the pompous narrator fails to understand the jokes) and establishes the novel's ironic tone at the outset. If sufficient time remains in the first hour, I also explain reported speech and cite examples from the fifth and seventh paragraphs. This discussion prepares students for a later, more detailed consideration of the opposition between subjective and objective viewpoints.

The second class hour is devoted to levels of fiction. I begin by having the class discuss the relative reality values of various *Sesame Street* characters.

Big Bird is more real than Mr. Snuffle-upagus (a plumed elephantine creature who is probably a figment of Big Bird's imagination) but less real than Mr. Hooper (a conventional human being), who is in turn less real than the nursery school children who participate in the show, since Mr. Hooper is played by an actor working from a script, whereas the children are real children. The students enjoy this discussion, and two points emerge quickly: (1) analysis of reality values can include an account of the observer as well as of the object observed (some student always points out that, for the nursery school children, Big Bird is "real"), and (2) the spectrum of reality values can be expressed as a continuum—a more sophisticated and accurate conception than the unexamined binary "real-unreal" opposition that the students generally begin with. After approximately twenty minutes, there is a ladder of reality on the blackboard: Mr. Snuffle-upagus is at the top, the nursery school children are at the bottom, and other characters are at various points between them. Curiously enough, the order in which these characters are placed is not the same every semester.

The applications of this reality ladder to *Don Quixote* are many and obvious. In my class, I focus first on the (fictional) stages in the evolution of the "Quixote legend" and the intrusions of one stage into another, as occurs when the "Hamete ms." is discovered in part 1, chapter 9, or when the Avellaneda sequel appears in part 2, chapters 59 and 62. I do this because I have found that many students do not understand that every layer in this complex fictional structure is fictional. At this point, I construct another ladder. At the top, I place the actions that Don Quixote "really" performed. In descending order, I list what various "historians" (including Cide Hamete) say he did, what the "translator" says Hamete says Quixote did, what the narrator concludes Quixote did, and, finally, what the reader understands Quixote did. I explain further that characters on one level frequently question the reliability of accounts given by a character on another level. The discussion between Don Quixote and Sancho about the "inaccuracies" in part 1, which they attribute to Cide Hamete (pt. 2, ch. 3), provides a good illustration of this point.

There are other levels of fiction in the novel, and some of them need to be covered explicitly: for example, a gallery of "Dulcineas"—none of them "real"—is woven through the narrative. Of them, Aldonza Lorenzo is the most concrete, yet she never actually enters the narrative, and Don Quixote rejects her for the Dulcinea of his fantasies in a very serious and very comic passage in part 1, chapter 25. Sancho creates two Dulcineas: one out of his attempt to reconcile Aldonza Lorenzo with Don Quixote's fantasy (pt. 1, chs. 30–31) and the other out of a "real" peasant girl and his (momentarily) clear understanding of Don Quixote's madness (pt. 2, ch. 10). From

Sancho's second Dulcinea, Don Quixote constructs the Dulcinea of the Cave of Montesinos (pt. 2, ch. 23). Finally, the Duke and Duchess create a transvestite enchanted Dulcinea whose unfortunate condition preys on the spirits of both central characters for the remainder of the novel (pt. 2, chs. 34–35).

After this discussion, I move to a more theoretical context: a complex reality-value structure is not unique to *Don Quixote*. For example, Odysseus progresses from the fantastic world of the wanderings, which he recounts in the first person (is he a more reliable narrator than Cide Hamete?), to the fairy-tale world of the Phaeacians and from there to the "real" Ithaca. Yet Homer's reasons for employing differing reality values were not the same as Cervantes'. The symmetrical concentric structure of reality levels in *The Odyssey* provides a framework for the hero's ever more firmly grounded selfhood; in contrast, the garbled relations in Don Quixote's world begin to overcome him as his will to uphold an assumed identity deteriorates.

Later in the semester, when we are studying *Crime and Punishment*, I examine the tavern conversation in which Raskolnikov appears to tell Zametov how he hid his ill-gotten gains (pt. 2, ch. 6). Close inspection reveals that Raskolnikov is actually spinning an idealized version of the affair; he is narrating what he would like to think he has done. At this point, I review the concept of levels of fictional reality and lead into a discussion of disjunctions in Raskolnikov's philosophical, fantastic, perceptual, and oneiric "realities"—and of the schism between his consciousness and empirical reality. These comparisons with Homer and Dostoevsky help students to see that Cervantes employs a common fictional technique in a unique way.

Perspectivism is the major subject of the third class hour. I start discussion by asking students to provide a "truth value" for an external object and Don Quixote's perception of it in four selected adventures. For the adventure of the windmills, the students quickly decide that the object is "true" (nondeceptive) and that Don Quixote's perception is false. They also perceive that the Princess Micomicona episode is different; they quickly label the object and the perception false. Usually an insightful member of the class objects, contending that a simple two-value system is inadequate to describe the situation. I agree and point out, if the student hasn't already done so, that the object in this case is two-layered (Dorothea/Micomicona) and that each layer has its own truth value. I then admit that I kept the explanatory system simple only for pedagogical purposes. The attempt to reduce the world of *Don Quixote* to a restricted schema allows the students to discover for themselves its complexity and elusiveness.

The adventure of the Chariot of Death (pt. 2, ch. 11) also presents a two-layered object—a company of actors in costume—and in this instance they are correctly identified as such by Don Quixote. Students usually decide that this episode is a variation on the Micomicona adventure, the object being regarded as false and the perception as true. The adventure of the lions (pt. 2, ch. 17) always provokes enthusiastic discussion, for the lions are not two-layered like Micomicona and the actors, nor are they clearly nondeceptive like the windmills. Rather than insist on an immediate decision in this matter, I express satisfaction with the class's realization that a determination of truth value in this particular perceiver-object relation is no simple task. I then suggest an alternative set of categories: novelistic conventions and conventions established within the framework of characters' and readers' expectations about the behavior of lions in literary and objectively real worlds. The central point in this discussion is that Cervantes manipulates permutations of possible relations between the external world and the characters' assessment of that world. He thereby creates comedy, but he also brings to life a central character who manipulates the reality-perception relation to create and maintain the persona of Don Quixote. To develop this point, I discuss the conversation between Don Quixote and Sancho (pt. 2; ch. 12) in which they conclude that life is like the drama: soldiers, lovers, bishops, and emperors assume costumes and roles just as actors do. In like fashion, Don Quixote has assumed the costume and role of knight-errant.

The realization that the central character creates but ultimately cannot sustain the character Don Quixote leads naturally to the topic of the fourth class hour: the Cave of Montesinos episode and its importance as a turning point in the development and subsequent disintegration of Don Quixote's control of his imagination. Secluded in the cave, Quixote has no windmills and no flocks of sheep on which to base his idiosyncratic perceptions. His imagination begins to fail him, and he becomes vaguely aware that his enterprise is doomed. Because Cervantes based this adventure on the time-honored paradigm of the hero's visit to the underworld, I explain to students the mythological pattern of the dying and rising hero who, having been buried, acquires supernatural characteristics as a result of his contact with subterranean deities and returns to the upper world as a source of renewed life for his community. The groundhog of American folklore (whose exit from the underworld signals the return of spring) provides an excellent example to begin this discussion. I ask the students why the groundhog returns underground if he sees his shadow. The shadow does not frighten him. Rather, it signals absence of the necessary supernatural characteristics.[3] With a few hints, students easily recognize this pattern in its demythologized form in *The Odyssey*. A bit less readily, they also perceive it in the Joseph story of Genesis 37–49. Cervantes, of course, inverts the traditional pattern. Don Quixote hopes to come in contact with the revivifying forces of the supernatural world, but he finds only absurd examples of moribund "enchantment." When he returns from the cave, he is insecure in his understanding of himself and his mission. Later, he must even seek reassurance on these matters from the prophesying ape and the enchanted head. His imaginative powers have been vitiated, and he can no longer maintain coherence among the elements of his fictional world. If time permits, I strengthen this point by contrasting the disorder of the Montesinos episode with Don Quixote's earlier successful creation of a subterranean fantasy (pt. 1, ch. 50). The components of this previous adventure, which correspond to those of the Montesinos episode, are appropriate, ordered, and self-consistent because Don Quixote's imagination has not yet begun to disintegrate.

The underworld motif reemerges later in the course when we discuss infernal themes and imagery in *Frankenstein, Crime and Punishment*, and *The Trial*. Frankenstein's monster's plaint that he bears a hell within himself (ch. 16) applies as well to his creator, to Raskolnikov, and to Joseph K. The students have now seen examples of this motif in ancient, Renaissance, and modern fiction. Whereas ancient literature represents the experience objectively, *Don Quixote* places it within a subjective-objective matrix and the modern novels tend to emphasize its subjective aspects. This generalization helps students understand the historical development of Western literature.

The fifth and final class hour is devoted to a close reading of part 2, chapter 60, a chapter that overflows with Cervantine irony. Here Sancho defines himself by quoting from a *romance*, the character Roque Guinart represents the historical Pero Rocca Guinarda, and Claudia Jeronima's fate contrasts neatly with that of the more "fictional" Basilio and Quiteria (pt. 2, chs. 19–22). I conclude the *Quixote* unit by calling attention to Sancho's statement (as Don Quixote is dying) that acceptance of reality can be the worst sort of madness if it keeps one from living. I also draw attention to Sancho's proposed solution—setting out afresh to become the heroes of a pastoral novel. In essence, Sancho has become Don Quixote, and his transformation is itself a validation of the Quixotic dream.

In conclusion, I would like to anticipate a few questions of a more practical nature. Is *Don Quixote* really appropriate for technical students, particularly two-year technical students? Yes, definitely. The future dairy farmer has the same democratic right to a solid education as the future physician or lawyer. Furthermore, our society desperately needs dairy farmers, computer programmers, and nursery school teachers who understand and appreciate *Don Quixote*. But can these students really handle this material? Yes, if expectations are kept reasonable. They have no serious problems with the reading. Most, when they leave the course, probably cannot evaluate the fictionality of Sancho's enchanted Dulcinea of part 2, chapter 10, as opposed to that of the Dulcinea who appears to Don Quixote in the Cave of Montesinos. Yet most can distinguish the different levels of reality on which Dulcinea, Don Quixote, Alonso Quixano, the narrator, and Miguel Cervantes exist. It is fashionable to design courses around materials that are easily accessible to students. This approach is wrong. The content of literature courses should be significant and challenging. It is the teaching that should be accessible.

What about nuts and bolts? Do the students really do the reading? How are grades assigned? The students do the reading. Timely completion of the reading is a precondition for an acceptable grade in the course, and this policy is enforced by a five-minute, single-question, pass-fail quiz for each work on the syllabus. Typical quizzes require the students to "explain the enchanted head" or to "explain the barber's basin." I expect students to understand the ideas presented in class and to reproduce them, at least in broad outlines, during an essay examination that requires them to compare an element in *Don Quixote* with a similar element in another work on the syllabus. I ask them, for example, to "compare the treatment of idea versus reality in *Don Quixote* and *Frankenstein*" or to "discuss the function of selfhood in *The Odyssey* and *Don Quixote*."

Do the students like reading *Don Quixote*? Most of them enjoy it less than they enjoy any other work on the syllabus, but the minority opinion is vigorous. At any rate, by the time we reach *Don Quixote*, the students are familiar with my cheerful equanimity in the face of complaints that the reading was "hard" or "boring," and they are beginning to understand the implications of my refrain that "You don't have to like frogs to pass anatomy lab."

NOTES

[1]A typical syllabus for this course includes Genesis, *The Odyssey*, *Don Quixote*, Mary Shelley's *Frankenstein*, Dostoevsky's *Crime and Punishment*, and Kafka's *The Trial*.

[2]About fifty chapters are assigned. The choices in part 1 are not critical, although I never include any of the intercalated stories. In part 2, I make certain that the following chapters are included: 1–11, 22, 23, 25, 41, 60, 62–65, 74.

[3]The chapter entitled "The Folk Tale of the Bear's Son" in Rhys Carpenter's *Folk Tale, Fiction, and Saga in the Homeric Epics* helped me in preparing this classroom presentation.

TEACHING *DON QUIXOTE* AS THE STORY OF ONE'S OWN LIFE

James Y. Dayananda

When I teach *Don Quixote* to freshmen and sophomores enrolled in a world literature class at a state college in Pennsylvania, one of my primary objectives is to help them gain insight into themselves and their most deeply felt concerns through an understanding of the fictional universes created by perceptive writers of the past. I do transmit a considerable amount of information about the works under consideration, but even more than that, I want students to recognize the importance of the readings to the conduct of their own lives. In some ways, my approach to *Don Quixote* is a Romantic one that rejects the "hard" interpretations of critics like Anthony Close, P. E. Russell, and Daniel Eisenberg; but I make no apologies for this teaching of Cervantes' masterpiece, because, contrary to them, I believe that a work like *Don Quixote* can grow in significance as successive generations of readers discover new meanings in it. No book should ever be limited to the critical limitations of the age in which it was written, and if we hope to make works like *Don Quixote* come alive for our students, we must convince them that Cervantes was writing about issues of immediate relevance to them. That is precisely what my teaching of the novel is intended to accomplish.

"To be a person is to have a story to tell," says the popular psychological writer Sam Keen; to live is to live the story of one's own life. My teaching is based on Gérard Genette's thesis that the meaning of books is "in front of them and not behind them," that it is already "in us" and waiting to be opened up for us by our contact with "the text." Thus, when I discuss *Don Quixote*, I try to help students find its meanings in their own lives. Through lectures, classroom discussions, and the diaries and journals they are asked to keep, I encourage them to see *Don Quixote* not as a story that occurred long ago and far away but as one taking place here and now in their own lives. I have devised a series of questions, exercises, and suggestions that serve as "entry points" or "launch pads" for classroom discussions and the reflections that students record in their journals. Each question is designed to reveal the relation between *Don Quixote* and the stories being lived by the students themselves. Their own comments clearly indicate that this approach helps them gain a sense of themselves, of others, and of the world around them.

The rationale behind my approach may be stated simply: *Don Quixote* is everyone's story. In many ways it resembles the ongoing stories of the students' own lives. To make them aware of the interpretive possibilities inherent in such a statement, I divide the section of the course devoted to Cervantes' novel into five major topics for discussion: (1) critical and uncritical readers, (2) the identity crisis, (3) role playing, (4) appearance and reality, and (5) idealists versus realists. Each of these topics is treated in two fifty-minute sessions. To study *Don Quixote* in this way enables students to stretch their minds, to discover insights into their own lives, and to seek answers for recurrent questions of universal human concern: What is the appropriate way to read the stories I encounter in books? Who am I really? How can I distinguish between appearance and reality? What roles do I play and why? What is the difference between an idealist and a realist, and how can I determine which stance is appropriate for me?

At the outset, I explain my approach to the students and share my experiences—my own "story"—with them. This openness draws them into a lively discussion, during which I tell them that I don't expect them to read all 830 pages of *Don Quixote* in the recent Jones-Douglas revision of the Ormsby translation. Even W. H. Auden confessed in a 1947 Harvard lecture that he had never "managed to read that novel through to the end." Perhaps few people do. But reading only isolated fragments of great works would hardly be a satisfactory alternative. This difficulty can be overcome by offering students a brief preliminary glimpse of the book's overall structure. In my course, I provide a detailed but schematic outline of the plot, style, and major themes of *Don Quixote*. I then ask the students to look more closely at the work itself. At this stage, the dominant method is not lecture but discussion focusing on a close textual analysis of episodes that have been chosen for their relevance to the five major topics.

The discussion of each topic follows the same pattern: students read the chapters, record their thoughts and feelings in a journal, and then discuss the questions and exercises in class. Sometimes students read their notes aloud, sometimes I give them a few minutes to formulate their ideas, but the real subject of these discussions is *Don Quixote* and its implicit invitation for readers to visit the undiscovered places in themselves.

My first topic revolves around the difference between uncritical and critical readers of fiction; at this time I assign chapters 1, 6, and 7 in part 1 and chapters 2, 3, 4, and 72 in part 2. Alonso Quixano is a bookworm addicted to medieval romances. Like Paolo and Francesca (two other readers of books in Canto 5 of Dante's *Inferno*, which the students have just finished reading in the course), he identifies himself so completely with fictional characters in books that he begins to live his life as he thought they had lived theirs. There are other ways to read books and to profit from them, and this is what I attempt to show my students. For example, one can sympathize with fictional characters while maintaining a critical distance from them. People who read in this way will regard literature not simply as a mirror for self-reflection and self-identification but as a source of self-knowledge based on imaginative identification and critical analysis. At this point in the course, students have already begun to grapple with their own experiences of reading, especially with the sense of confusion that occasionally results when the reality in books becomes momentarily intertwined with the reality of their own daily lives. One student, for example, recorded this comment in her journal:

> Don Quixote reminds me of myself when I was younger. I imagined that I was really Nancy Drew. I would go about solving the same sort of mysteries she would solve. It became an obsession with me. Today, after reading *Don Quixote*, I would read those books differently....I am even reading *Don Quixote* critically, not at all the way Alonso Quixano read books of chivalry.

The second major topic for discussion during the *Don Quixote* section of my course involves Alonso Quixano's identity crisis and the larger underlying questions raised by it. Many people between the ages of thirty-five and fifty pass through an unsettling, disrupting period. It often results in an abrupt career shift or a transformation of one's character. Paul Gauguin, Sigmund Freud, Francisco Goya, Frank Lloyd Wright, and Mahatma Gandhi all passed through such "midlife" crises. So does the fifty-year-old Alonso Quixano. Like countless other individuals who have confronted the same dilemma, he begins to ask himself the questions that we must all ask ourselves at some point in our lives: Who am I? Is this all there is? What significance will the rest of my life have? Alonso Quixano has spent most of his abundant leisure time reading books of chivalry. He is bored. He decides to break with the mundane and oppressive sameness of everyday life by becoming a knight-errant. The road becomes more attractive to him than the study, adventure more attractive than books, and movement more attractive than stasis.

At this point in the course, students are encouraged to reflect on their own identities. Who are they? Are they now the kinds of people they had once dreamed of becoming? What sort of people do they really want to be? Their comments in class and in journals reveal that a reading of *Don Quixote* can enhance their appreciation for the diverse possibilities of life and contribute to a heightened maturity in their own attitudes toward themselves. For example, one student wrote:

> When I am asked "Who are you really?" I am not at all satisfied with the answers I give: a college student with a number, daughter of so and so, a waitress at a restaurant, a member of a sorority, etc. I suspect that under these numerous identities lies one true self of mine whose identity strangely eludes me....I often feel that I am several different selves wrapped up in a single identity. *Don Quixote* has helped me to think clearly about my true self.

The third major topic in my approach to *Don Quixote* requires an extended consideration of Alonso Quixano's role playing; the assignments for this part of the course are part 1, chapters 1, 25, and 26, and part 2, chapters 12 and 74. After rejecting his apparently empty life, Quixano plays the role of Don Quixote during the middle sections of the book, but in the last chapter of part 2 he reverses this process by rejecting his chivalric career in order to assume once again the identity of Alonso Quixano the Good. In a sense, "acting" is his real profession. For a long time he acts the principal role in a vast play, assigning roles to many of the people he meets. As in the magical games of children, he is pretending to be someone he is not. The result is the marvelous enchantment of theater, a make-believe world "ablaze with light and finery," as Don Quixote himself points out:

> Tell me, have you not seen a play acted in which kings, emperors, pontiffs, knights, ladies, and sundry other personages were introduced?...the same things happen in the comedy and life of this world.   (pt. 2, ch. 12; p. 483)

Audiences and readers sometimes confuse actors with their roles, and Don Quixote is a victim of this confusion. In fact, he reminds us of Cary Grant's comment when someone told him, "I would give anything in the world to be Cary Grant." "So would I," replied the famous actor.

In this context, students discuss the several roles they play each day: son or daughter, college student, waiter or waitress, actor or actress in a play, someone else's date. Occasionally they play roles to amuse themselves or their friends or simply to combat the boredom of life. They also tend to protect themselves by wearing masks and concealing their true selves from others. *Don Quixote* helps them to see role playing not only as an escape from the real world but also as a creative response to the harsh limitations of life. Like Paolo and Francesca, who act out the romance of Lancelot and Guinevere, or like Ivan Ilych (the central character of our next text in the course), who plays roles all his life, Alonso Quixano imagines himself as a knight in romances of chivalry. When students become aware of parallels between the roles invented by fictional characters and the roles contrived by themselves and others in the real world, they begin to perceive certain truths about their own behavior. As one student wrote in his journal:

> Don Quixote was a great deal like me. He reminded me of certain times in my life when I pretended to be someone else. Many times my girl friend and I joked about having lots of money. We would talk about our weekend trips to Paris. Just last Christmas she gave me a Cadillac, and I gave her a Piper plane. Sometimes we are so convincing people believe us.

The fourth major topic discussed during my teaching of *Don Quixote* is the age-old theme "appearance and reality" for which the students read chapters 8, 16, 17, 18, 19, 21, 25, 35, and 45 in part 1. According to E. L. Doctorow, "Reality isn't something outside. It is something we compose every moment." Two people participating in the same event necessarily perceive it differently. One might even say that there are as many events as there are people, because all seeing takes place inside a particular person's head, and the inside of each head differs from the inside of every other person's head. In a sense, people choose what they wish to see and ignore what they don't wish to see. Perception itself is a kind of interpretation, for it is "a matter of seeing the present with objects stored from the past," as Richard Gregory writes in *The Intelligent Eye* (36). When confronted with a unique event or constellation of objects, we often don't perceive it, because it does not correspond to our preconceived notions of what is possible. For example, Sancho repeatedly fails to see what Don Quixote sees so clearly. Indeed, Cervantes' masterpiece is based on different ways of perceiving reality, different ways of drawing inferences from the same set of facts. Such a book helps students to understand that appearances are governed by what they expect to see and that, by changing their expectations, they become capable of seeing many things to which they had previously been blind. One student described this insight in these terms:

I once went to a lovely dinner party at which several well-dressed men and women spoke with animation about love, education, tennis, and travel plans. Everyone was having a great time. Everything seemed wonderful. I went home with one of them who told me the unbelievable facts of their lives: one was dying of cancer, one was in a state of suicidal despair, another was on the verge of divorce, and two were having extramarital affairs with the same person. I now think things are seldom what they seem. . . . *Don Quixote* taught me this lesson.

The fifth major topic in my approach to *Don Quixote* involves the perennial conflict between idealists and realists; assignments for this section of the course include chapters 8, 18, and 25 in part 1. Idealism and realism are obviously ambiguous terms, but in general idealists give priority to immaterial constructs, whereas realists accept the primacy of material substance and prefer to deal pragmatically with concrete facts. The idealistic Don Quixote dreams the world as it might be and asks why it cannot be better than it is. The realistic Sancho Panza sees the world as it is and tries to find some way of coping with it. In reality, people are seldom so completely quixotic as Quixote or so completely literal-minded as Sancho: they exist somewhere along a spectrum between these two extremes. Yet Don Quixote and Sancho constantly interact with one another, and at some points in the text they even change places. Cervantes himself seems to defend a synthesis of the two perspectives, tempering an ebullient idealism with down-to-earth common sense, and this is precisely what students do when they begin to comprehend Cervantes' juxtaposition of the two companions and their respective attitudes toward life. Within this context, I encourage students to discuss other pairs of realists and idealists drawn from history, literature, and contemporary life (e.g., Jesus, Columbus, Galileo, Socrates, Nixon, Hitler, holders of nine-to-five jobs). Although the students recognize the need for a balance between idealism and realism, they inevitably develop a genuine admiration for Don Quixote, who usually emerges from our discussions as the archetypal embodiment of humanity's one indestructible quality—the ability to dream.

Like all other masterpieces of world literature, Cervantes' novel can touch today's college students deeply. My approach is designed to help them make meaningful connections between its fictional world and their own real one. In particular, I try to show the students that their stories, like that of Don Quixote, have five major running themes—books they have read, identity crises they have experienced, roles they have played, appearance and reality as they have perceived them, idealists and realists they have encountered. But because these themes are only a small part of the richness and variety in *Don Quixote*, my approach can only serve as a rudimentary introduction to Cervantes' great novel. For that reason, I always encourage my students to become rereaders, returning to *Don Quixote* over and over as the stories of their own lives unfold. Like Scheherazade, they begin to realize that they live as long as they have a story to tell.

APPENDIX

SAMPLE WRITING ASSIGNMENTS

Throughout the class discussions on *Don Quixote*, I ask the students to enter brief notes and paragraphs in their journals. The following questions and suggestions are given to the students as "entry points" or "launch pads" for these writing assignments as well as for the longer autobiographical essays they are asked to write. They are always reminded that they should focus on parallels between *Don Quixote* and the story of their own lives.

1. While I was reading _____ (name of a classic literary work), it struck me that....
2. After reading about _____ (names of characters), I realized that....
3. This character or episode reminds me of _____ (a person I knew) or _____ (an experience I had).
4. I recognize myself in _____ (name of a character).
5. I once experienced an "identity crisis" like....
6. I once experienced a confusion between fantasy and reality while watching _____ (the name of a particular television show) or while reading _____ (the name of a particular book).
7. As I was reading _____ (name of a book), I kept saying to myself, "How true to life, how true to my own experience."
8. Like Don Quixote, I once rationalized my failure to recognize the truth about _____ (a situation).

9. I once mistook _____ (a person or thing) for something or somebody else.
10. I once misread _____ (the name of a book), missed the whole point of it, and misinterpreted its meaning.
11. "I am I, you are you. This is the true me, and these are the roles I play."
12. _____ (the name of a person, character, or historical figure) is one of the idealists (or realists) I know.

GUIDING STUDENT ENCOUNTERS WITH THE INGENIOUS GENTLEMAN OF LA MANCHA

Lewis J. Hutton

Any course dealing with Cervantes' unforgettable *Don Quixote* has an aura of expectancy about it. Whether the text is in Spanish or in an English translation, students enrolled in the course usually look forward to reading the book and few of them are ever disappointed. As for the instructor, the novel continues to retain its contemporaneity, because the dilemmas with which Don Quixote wrestles are the perennial ones we must all face. What makes the responsibility of teaching Cervantes' masterpiece so rewarding is that he himself was writing it at the very moment when nearly all the problems and aspirations of his life and times came into clear focus in a creative vision that he funneled into *Don Quixote*. My approach to the novel attempts to make students feel the power of this synthesizing vision. When I succeed in doing so, the novel acquires a unique and personal significance for them, because this vision undergirds a fictional world where time is transcended and where the seventeenth and twentieth centuries meet.

The imaginative sweep of Cervantes' world view and his uncanny ability to speak powerfully and meaningfully to all sorts of readers originated in his own experiences and in his reactions to them. For that reason, students in my course begin their study of *Don Quixote* by reading an introductory manual and one of the standard biographies, which they discuss in a book review they are asked to write at this early stage in the course. This foundation leads them to focus on two crucial years: 1571 and 1588. The first was important to Cervantes because it was the year of the Battle of

Lepanto, which he later regarded as the most glorious experience of his life. That year also marked the close of his youth, which had been characterized by a springtime mood of renewal and vigor—a period dominated by Emperor Charles V of the Holy Roman Empire and permeated by the iconoclastic thought of Erasmus. In contrast, 1588 was a frustrating year of wasted effort: the Armada proved a considerable drain on Spanish resources and never accomplished its objective. The disillusionment that followed this national debacle converged with an existing sense of frustration in Spanish society and nourished a growing intolerance for all that was new and creative under Philip II and Philip III. As students discuss these periods in Cervantes' life, they begin to see parallels between his experiences and a more universal pattern of human existence: the promise and expectant joys of youth followed by the harsh realities of maturity.

Any biographical study of Cervantes reveals his earnest concern with Spain and its problems. Although relatively little is known about his personal life, it is clear that he was obliged to confront uncertainty and difficulty while attempting to forge an intellectually satisfying attitude toward himself and his world. This struggle may well account for the irony of his later writings, for he did learn to appreciate the comic aspects of what appeared to be tragedies in his own life, to laugh through tears at his own unenviable situation. This attitude is reflected in the title of his major work. Because the name of the principal character in *The Ingenious Gentleman, Don Quixote of La Mancha* has become a household word with many stereotyped connotations, students who are just beginning to read the novel should be encouraged to reflect on the underlying ambivalence of this appellation. Too many readers forget that the author calls his protagonist "The Ingenious Gentleman" in all seriousness. Don Quixote is undoubtedly a man of great worth, as evidenced by his background and by his special abilities, and he should be successful in life. Unfortunately, he is not, because he is "redundant," as the English put it, or "superfluous" in the way so many protagonists in nineteenth-century Russian novels are superfluous. His society is beset by economic and social problems, and it offers him no adequate means of expressing his talents. But, to the dead seriousness of "The Ingenious Gentleman," Cervantes adds the risible "Don Quixote of La Mancha." Just as Cervantes never allows his own problems to overwhelm him, he inevitably gives his readers comic relief before they reach the emotional breaking point.

This combination of the serious and the comic recurs throughout *The Ingenious Gentleman*, and it always provokes a heated discussion in class. Some students even discover that this balanced perspective enables them to perceive reality in a new way. Pursuing the contemporary relevance of this approach to life, I often ask students to invent titles that would have the same import for twentieth-century American readers. Two student efforts stand out: *The Studious Farmer, Sophocles Squash-Head of the Ozarks* and *The Genius, Herbert Figwig of Beaver Falls.*

Because new readers of *Don Quixote* need to understand how books of chivalry function in the novel, I devote the next portion of the course to a discussion of them. Analogies with television soap operas frequently prove convincing to students, who can easily perceive that soap operas and books of chivalry play similar roles in their respective societies. Both view the world in terms of simplistic dichotomy between good and evil, both reinforce idealized stereotypes of human behavior, and both offer their audiences a vicarious escape from the mediocrity of their day-to-day existence. Many of my students are passionately devoted to soap operas; others are outspoken in their denunciation of these "tele-novels," as they are called in modern Spanish. Some students are reserved in their attitudes, possibly because they do not wish to take sides or because they have never seriously reflected on the relation between the "soaps" and the society in which they are living. But whatever their attitudes toward such problems might be, the class discussion launches them into a consideration of Cervantes' problematic. He liked good books of chivalry, but he did not like the way in which most chivalric romances were written, and he wrote *Don Quixote* to end the reign of poorly written books of chivalry. Once the students fully grasp this they often respond favorably to the idea of outlining a soap opera that will put an end to all bad soap operas. In a course dedicated solely to the *Quixote*, several weeks might be spent in discussing the matters outlined thus far, but even in a survey course, where there is less time for preliminary discussion, I have found it useful to approach the book in this way.

Before the students begin to read the text, I draw their attention to the fact that they are about to read the first part of a book that was published in 1605. I mention that there is also a second part that did not appear until 1615, but I refrain from explaining in more detail the relation between the two parts, because I do not want to confuse students at the beginning and possibly diminish their eagerness to plunge into the text. In the 1605 portion of the novel, Cervantes felt the need to express his frustrations with his society and his career. In his *Sentido y forma del* Quijote, the contemporary Spanish critic Joaquín Casalduero argues that Cervantes' purpose was to illustrate the conflict between a "faith" handed down from the past and a contemporary "will" to live in accordance with that "faith" (24). By faith, Casalduero means the values that formed the basis of Spanish society and that Spaniards really believed they still held, even though they frequently chose to behave in ways that did not coincide with these values. According to Casalduero, Cervantes deals not with hypocrisy but rather with the inability of people to understand that what they think they value is not what they actually value, that they are, in essence, "dancing to a different tune." In his confused state, Don Quixote acts in accord with the values most people claim to hold, and his behavior appears to others either as tragic or as comic, thus revealing not merely a flaw in Don Quixote's perception of the world but also a deep-lying contradiction in the social fabric—a contradiction that, incidentally, is not absent from contemporary American society.

In introducing the 1605 and 1615 "books" to the class, teachers should not ignore the appealing prologues. Students appreciate the personal details given there and directed specifically to them as readers. What we have done so far may seem to reflect an overemphasis on preliminary materials, but a detailed introduction is not tiring for students. Rather, it serves to heighten their anticipation. Furthermore, after assimilating information about Cervantes and the romances of chivalry and reading the prologues, they are in a better position to understand what the author is going to unfold before them.

At the very beginning of the first chapter we meet a gentleman of flesh and blood who has no productive activity to occupy his fertile mind. He devotes his time to reading books of chivalry, most of them bad, and this preoccupation catapults him into the unreal world of those books, leaving him utterly confused about himself and about his perceptions of the world around him. At this point, Cervantes has created a magnificent literary personality, but he did not yet know what to do with him. Students enjoy exploring Cervantes' models for these first few chapters, and they can understand why these models failed.

In chapter 6 the book begins in earnest. Cervantes has Don Quixote return home and start out all over again. Sancho Panza is introduced, and with him the full humanity of Spain—indeed, of all the world—is made visible in the delicate but complex relation between "knight" and "squire." As Don Quixote ventures out, his perception of the visible world is confused, but his vision of an inner reality is clear. Sancho leaves home with the power and odor of the earth as his shield, but he remains powerless to grasp the profundity of redemptive spiritual concepts. Repeatedly student readers find themselves caught up in the field of attraction and repulsion that links the fates of these two characters.

Having overcome the problems of chapters 2 through 5 by creating a second major character, Cervantes shows us in the rest of part 1 how the confusion of Don Quixote is alleviated. Society ultimately imprisons the knight in a cage for his bold assertion of perennial values, and Sancho intrudes into the world of the spirit, reducing serious ideals to comedy with his blindness to incorporeal truth. As a means of illustrating growth and change in the two principal characters, I often focus on the adventure of the windmills. How can one do justice to the famous eighth chapter of part 1? This episode has repeatedly been misconstrued by English-speaking readers and critics, and the teacher must find some way of overcoming entrenched preconceptions about it. For example, one semester the students' response to this episode was initially distorted when a local newspaper ran a political cartoon that depicted an elected official as Don Quixote tilting at windmills. In contrast, I had an extremely rewarding experience with this episode when I took a group of American students to Criptana just before twilight; they themselves could see the windmills silhouetted against the sky, towering like monsters over the town and overtopping even the church.

To fully comprehend what they are reading, students should be able to visualize it in concrete terms, and this is difficult because the geography and physical appearance of Spain are not usually familiar to them. The Spanish windmill is neither a Dutch windmill nor an American restaurant windmill along the highway. If students are going to see what Cervantes and Don Quixote saw and not something quite different, they should at least look at slides of Criptana that make clear the relation between the windmills and the town. They should also be aware that the windmills, until 1960, still ground flour to produce bread and that the farmers, who had to carry sacks of grain on their backs up three floors to the grindstone, did not live to be very old. When Cervantes asserted in part 2 that there are various levels of meaning in his writing, he was providing a clue to the interpretation of episodes like this one and inviting readers to look for symbolic significance beneath the surface level of the narrative. Windmills, for example, are like giants who killed the farmers of the region. The confusion of Don Quixote is not only to see giants instead of windmills but also to believe, like Melville's Captain Ahab, that the great problems of humanity lend themselves to simplistic solutions. It might be possible to liberate the farmers from their burdens and give them a longer life by destroying the giants (the windmills), but then the people in the area will die of starvation. Thus, the windmills resist destruction and seek to disguise the qualities that make them similar to giants. Sancho, who cannot see beyond the physical properties of the windmills, believes they are only what they seem to be. For him, the giants of popular folklore belong in a separate category; there is no connection between them and windmills, and to create one is folly. As students begin to grasp what might be at stake on various symbolic levels of meaning, the battle between Don Quixote and the windmills and the conflict between Don Quixote's viewpoint and that of Sancho generally provide the stimulus for spirited discussion in the classroom, almost as spirited as the action itself.

Don Quixote, however, did not remain forever on the heights of Criptana. He did pull himself together, and he did go on to engage a Biscayan in combat. During this battle, Cervantes intrudes himself into the battle and suspends it temporarily. He does this partly to annoy readers of bad chivalric novels and partly to introduce the fictional Muslim narrator Cide Hamete Benengeli. At this point, particular care must be taken to help students understand the significance of the Muslim presence in Spain. For hundreds of years two distinct worlds—the Muslim and the Christian—coexisted on the Iberian peninsula. Eventually elements of both cultures fused into a single world view, and it was this union that enabled Cervantes to write the first modern novel in the Western tradition. For example, there are two words for *to be* in Spanish. They derive from different Latin and Arabic roots and allow for the expression of a distinction that does not exist in English. These words suggest the possibility of two different modes of being, and Cervantes, keenly aware of them both, balanced one against the other. He adopted a Christian understanding of fixed patterns, beginnings and endings, and Creator and creatures, but he mediated them with a Muslim literary experience of character development, an appreciation for unending rhythms and chains of events, and a pantheistic view of the natural world. A lengthy philosophical discussion of Muslim-Christian viewpoints would probably be distracting to students, but they should have some feeling for the Muslim presence in Spain, and it can be evoked for them by projecting slides of Granada or Córdoba, accompanied by the music of Isaac Albéniz and Manuel de Falla.

As the reading of part 1 progresses, students are surprised and then pleased that so many chapters are dedicated to problems experienced by people their own age—the problems of love and marriage. For example, Marcela epitomizes the modern woman who can fulfill her destiny without becoming subservient to a man. Students can identify with her, and when they choose to write papers about the role of women in *Don Quixote*, they tend to admire Cervantes and Don Quixote for their support of her. The Dorotea-Fernando-Luscinda love triangle and the amorous difficulties of other young people in the novel usually provoke further class discussion comparing mores in seventeenth-century Spain and contemporary America. Dorotea is usually praised for her attitudes and achievements; Luscinda is not. Cardenio, who runs off to the woods, is generally considered dumb. No sympathy is ever voiced for Marcela's admirer, Grisóstomo, who commits suicide because she will not marry him. Young people appreciate that such problems are raised by Cervantes, but because they tend to be more direct in their expressions and relationships, they can become impatient with the slower pace of the seventeenth century.

Students who have successfully completed the first part of the novel will have acquired a familiarity with Cervantes' style, and they will have become acquainted wih Don Quixote and Sancho. Yet if readers are to understand part 2 they must learn something about the false *Quixote* by an author who called himself Avellaneda. Much of this material can be explained by the instructor, but it is useful to have students read selections from Avellaneda's apocryphal continuation. For that reason I translate passages from it and make them available to students, who at this time also listen to a tape of representative selections from Dale Wasserman's *Man of La Mancha*. This musical adaptation continues to be popular among students, and they are often familiar with its lyrics. When the story told in *Man of La Mancha* is investigated, however, they recognize similarities between it and Avellaneda's continuation. When this happens, the students tend to become angry. The leading character in the musical they enjoyed is not the "real" Don Quixote who has charmed and dismayed them in Cervantes' novel. This comparison between Avellaneda's continuation and Wasserman's *Man of La Mancha* helps considerably to prepare students for a fuller understanding of Cervantes' 1615 "book."

After the Avellaneda-*Man of La Mancha* interlude, students plunge with renewed zeal into the reading of part 2. At this point, I review the general outline and major themes of part 1 and contrast them with those in part 2, pointing out several significant changes. Some background in baroque art forms and attitudes is helpful here: having transcended his earlier frustrations, Cervantes begins in this part of the novel to recreate a society based on a characteristic set of baroque values and deformations. Students can easily appreciate Cervantes' reaction to Avellaneda's continuation, and they generally come to share it. But baroque attitudes toward death, illusion, paradox, asymmetry, artifice, and psychological realism in artistic representations of the irrational are not so easily understood by today's students, and they should be discussed in class.

The role of Dulcinea also changes in part 2 of the novel. She was elusive for Don Quixote, and she remains so for today's readers. The first time I visited El Toboso, I found myself hopelessly lost until a drunken old man guided me to a monument dedicated to a Spanish educator in America; the inscription informed me that learning had been his "Dulcinea." At that moment, I gave up seeking the landmarks I had come so far to find. Did Dulcinea exist at all, or was she the product of Don Quixote's longing for beauty and truth? Some students are convinced that Don Quixote imagined her. I choose to believe that Sancho unwittingly pointed her out and that she was a person, similar in nature to Marcela, who never realized the potential within her—a potential that Don Quixote knew to be there. As students discuss the rationales behind these opposing views of Dulcinea, they begin to understand the subjectivity of interpretation and the ways in which fictional characters or events are perceived by different readers.

Debates over the true nature of Dulcinea can easily be related to Don Quixote's descent into the Cave of Montesinos. One needs to experience this cave to appreciate the reflective powers it is capable of unleashing. It is still a real adventure to travel there. I had to leave the road, drive across fields, and cross a small stream before reaching the ancient house of an old caretaker. Then, on foot, I accompanied him across other fields and through brambles to the entrance to the cave. He needed to cut away the underbrush so that we could enter. Inside, our only light was the antique carbide lantern he carried. After an hour of careful walking through underground caverns, I had had enough, but I remembered that Don Quixote supposedly fell asleep in this uncanny place, where several rivers of the Iberian peninsula are formed. When I show my photographs to the students, they are greatly interested in the caverns, and they begin to imagine what Don Quixote might have felt when he was there.

In general, students agree with the world view of Cervantes in part 1, but they are confused by part 2. When Cervantes compares young women to monkeys and young men to crocodiles as a means of commenting on the corrupt sexual mores of contemporary youths, his criticism strikes an exposed nerve among students and puts them on guard. They may be somewhat more sympathetic with his assertion that young people are precipitated into such a state of moral degradation by the example of their elders, but they tend to question his suggestion that the only salvation for youth resides in the purity of heart possessed by someone of the older generation. That, however, is precisely what Don Quixote, astride Clavileño, represents. For some students, Cervantes' attitude toward sex resembles Don Quixote's attitude toward the windmills. They refuse to believe that the problem is as disturbing as Cervantes contends, and they cannot accept the paternal role that he gives to the older generation. Yet once again, Cervantes has identified a recurrent human concern—generational conflict—and depicted it in such a way that it provides students with abundant material for debate.

Teaching *Don Quixote* is not always easy. Students complain about the amount of reading, the quizzes, the exams, the term paper, and the periodic requirement that chapters be analyzed. But their encounter with the ingenious Gentleman of La Mancha is invariably regarded as a positive experience. No matter how intensive the course, students never accept the last chapter as an ending. For many of them, the course is the beginning of a lifelong quest for realities that lie behind the facades of social convention, and they frequently develop a sincere desire to remain in touch with their friend Don Quixote. Each time I teach the course, the students help me to see and understand things I did not see and understand before; the successful class on *Don Quixote* always involves a symbiotic relation between myself and the students. I guide them into new areas of experience, and they repay me many times over by intensifying my own joy in the text and by reaffirming my faith in the act of teaching.

PARTICIPANTS IN SURVEY OF *QUIXOTE* INSTRUCTORS

During the preparation of this volume, many scholars and teachers of *Don Quixote* participated in a survey for which they described their approaches to the book and the materials they used in teaching it. The breadth of their experience and their generosity in sharing it have made this volume possible.

John J. Allen
University of Florida

Ricardo Arias
Fordham University

Juan Bautista Avalle-Arce
University of North Carolina

Edward T. Aylward
University of South Carolina

Mac E. Barrick
Shippensburg State College

Geoffrey R. Barrow
Ripon College

Donald W. Bleznick
University of Cincinnati

Benito Brancaforte
University of Wisconsin

Marjorie A. Carper
Spokane Falls Community College

James A. Castañeda
Rice University

James O. Crosby
Florida International University

Richard E. D'Auria
Universidad de Puerto Rico

James Y. Dayananda
Lock Haven University

Morgan Desmond
State University of New York
    Agricultural and Technical
    College, Cobleskill

Peter N. Dunn
Wesleyan University

Daniel Eisenberg
Florida State University

Ruth El Saffar
University of Illinois, Chicago

Patricia N. Fahey
Loyola University

Miguel A. Feal-Deibe
Universidad de Puerto Rico

David Fernández-Morera
Northwestern University

Dominick L. Finello
Rider College

160

Edward H. Friedman
Arizona State University

David L. Garrison
Wright State University

Eunice Joiner Gates
Texas Technical University

Carlos Gijón
Texas A and I University

David Gitlitz
University of Nebraska, Lincoln

Frank Goodwyn
University of Maryland

Cordelia H. Gray
Troy State University

Nancy A. Gutierrez
University of Cincinnati

Monroe Z. Hafter
University of Michigan

Robert L. Hathaway
Colgate University

Norma L. Hutman
Hartwick College

Lewis J. Hutton
University of Rhode Island

Yvonne Jehenson
University of Albuquerque

Carroll B. Johnson
University of California,
  Los Angeles

Harold Jones
University of Houston

Joseph R. Jones
University of Kentucky

Marilyn Scarantino Jones
Lake Erie College

Emilia N. Kelley
Emory University

Ruth Lee Kennedy
University of Arizona

Anne Mills King
Prince George's Community
  College

Astrid Kromayer
Moravian College

Raul A. Laborde
Franklin Pierce College

Donald R. Larson
Ohio State University

Robert T. Levine
North Carolina Agricultural and
  Technical State University

Clayton W. Lewis
University of Oklahoma

Denah Lida
Brandeis University

Theophilus S. Lynch
University of Michigan, Flint

Howard Mancing
University of Missouri

R. L. Moloney
Miami University

Carolyn Morrow
University of Utah

Barbara J. Mortenson
University of San Francisco

Eric W. Naylor
University of the South

Betty Tyree Osiek
Southern Illinois University,
    Edwardsville

James A. Parr
University of Southern California

Helena Percas De Ponseti
Grinnell College

C. Earl Ramsey
University of Arkansas, Little Rock

Michael W. Raymond
Stetson University

Willis G. Regier
University of Nebraska, Lincoln

Arsenio Rey
State University of New York
    College, Geneseo

J. V. Ricapito
Louisiana State University

Elias L. Rivers
State University of New York,
    Stony Brook

Pilar V. Rotella
Saint Xavier College

Enrique Ruiz-Fornells
University of Alabama

Donald E. Schmiedel
University of Nevada, Las Vegas

Dennis L. Seager
Monterey Institute of International
    Studies

Antonia I. Searles
Hope College

Karl-Ludwig Selig
Columbia University

Richard Seybolt
University of Minnesota, Duluth

Renée Sieburth
York University

Armand E. Singer
West Virginia University

Charlotte Stern
Randolph-Macon Woman's College

Jill A. Syverson-Stork
Boston College

Daniel P. Testa
Syracuse University

Pierre L. Ullman
University of Wisconsin, Milwaukee

Vicente Urbistondo
San Francisco State University

Geoffrey M. Voght
Eastern Michigan University

Ruth H. Webber
University of Chicago

Jack Weiner
Northern Illinois University

Celia E. Weller
Whitman College

Howard B. Wescott
State University of New York
    College, Fredonia

Ulrich Wicks
University of Maine, Orono

Robert Wiltenburg
Eastman School of Music

Ann E. Wiltrout
Mississippi State University

Henry Ziomek
University of Georgia

WORKS CITED

EDITIONS, TRANSLATIONS, AND ANTHOLOGIES

The Adventures of Don Quixote. Trans. J. M. Cohen. Baltimore: Penguin, 1950.

Antología de autores españoles. Ed. Antonio Sánchez-Romeralo. New York: Macmillan, 1972. Vol. 1.

Antología general de la literatura española. Ed. Angel Del Río and Amelia A. de Del Rio. New York: Holt, 1960. Vol. 1.

The Best of Spanish Literature in English Translation. Ed. Seymour Resnick and Jeanne Pasmantier. New York: Ungar, 1976.

Don Quijote de la Mancha. Ed. Martín de Riquer. 2 vols. 1944; 1958; rev. Barcelona: Juventud, 1969.

Don Quijote de la Mancha. Illus. Gustave Doré. Madrid: Castilla, 1947.

Don Quijote de la Mancha. Ed. Martín de Riquer. Hispánicos Planeta. Madrid: Cupsa, 1977.

Don Quijote de la Mancha: Edición simplificada para uso escolar y autoestudio. Köbenhavn: Grafisk Forlag, 1972.

Don Quijote de la Mancha: Facsímil de la primera impresión. 2 vols. Palma de Mallorca: Alfaguara, Hispanic Society of America, Papeles de Son Armadans, 1968.

Don Quijote de la Mancha seguido del Quijote de Avellaneda. Ed. Martín de Riquer. Clásicos Planeta. Barcelona: Planeta, 1962.

Don Quixote of La Mancha. Trans. Walter Starkie. New York: Signet, 1964.

Don Quixote of La Mancha. Trans. Walter Starkie. Abridged ed. New York: Mentor, 1957.

Don Quixote: The Ormsby Translation, Revised. Ed. Joseph R. Jones and Kenneth Douglas. Norton Critical Edition. New York: Norton, 1981.

Five Centuries of Spanish Literature: From The Cid *through the Golden Age.* Ed. Linton L. Barrett. 1962; rpt. New York: Dodd, 1967.

El ingenioso hidalgo Don Quijote de la Mancha. Ed. Diego Clemencín. 6 vols. Madrid: Aguado, 1833–39.

El ingenioso hidalgo Don Quijote de la Mancha. Ed. Francisco Rodríguez Marín. 10 vols. Madrid: Atlas, 1947–49.

El ingenioso hidalgo Don Quijote de la Mancha. Ed. Federico de Onís. 2 vols. Bilbao: De Brouwer, 1958.

El ingenioso hidalgo Don Quijote de la Mancha. Colección Austral. 1940; rpt. Madrid: Espasa-Calpe, 1965.

El ingenioso hidalgo Don Quijote de la Mancha. México: Porrua, 1966.

El ingenioso hidalgo Don Quijote de la Mancha. Ed. Francisco Rodríguez Marín. 8 vols. Clásicos Castellanos. 1911–13; rpt. Madrid: Espasa-Calpe, 1967.

El ingenioso hidalgo Don Quijote de la Mancha. Ed. Celina S. de Cortázar and Isaías Lerner. 2 vols. Buenos Aires: Universitaria, 1969.

El ingenioso hidalgo Don Quijote de la Mancha. Ed. John Jay Allen. 2 vols. Madrid: Cátedra, 1977.

El ingenioso hidalgo Don Quijote de la Mancha. Ed. Luis Murillo. 3 vols. Madrid: Castalia, 1978.

El ingenioso hidalgo Don Quijote de la Mancha. Ed. Juan Bautista Avalle-Arce. 2 vols. Madrid: Alhambra, 1979.

The Ingenious Gentleman Don Quixote de la Mancha. Trans. Samuel Putnam. New York: Modern Library, 1949.

Literatura española: Selección. Ed. Diego Marín. New York: Holt, 1968. Vol. 1.

The Norton Anthology of World Masterpieces. Ed. Maynard Mack. 4th ed. New York: Norton, 1979.

The Norton Anthology of World Masterpieces: Fourth Continental Edition. Ed. Maynard Mack. New York: Norton, 1980. Vol. 1.

Obras completas de Miguel de Cervantes Saavedra. Ed. Rodolfo Schevill and Adolfo Bonilla. 18 vols. Madrid: Gráficas Reunidas, 1914–41.

Obras completas (Miguel de Cervantes Saavedra). Ed. Ángel Valbuena Prat. 1942; rpt. Madrid: Aguilar, 1964.

The Portable Cervantes. Ed. and trans. Samuel Putnam. New York: Viking, 1951.

Representative Spanish Authors. Ed. Walter T. Pattison and Donald W. Bleznick. New York: Oxford Univ. Press, 1971. Vol. 1.

SCHOLARLY, CRITICAL, AND FICTIONAL WORKS

Abel, Lionel. *Metatheatre.* New York: Hill & Wang, 1963.

Abellán, José Luis. *Historia crítica del pensamiento español.* Madrid: Espasa-Calpe, 1981.

Agostini de Del Río, Amelia. *Compañero del estudiante del* Quijote. San Juan: Cordillera, 1975.

Alborg, Juan. *Historia de la literatura española.* Madrid: Gredos, 1966.

Allen, John Jay. *Cervantes'* Don Quixote. New York: Monarch, 1975.

———. *Don Quixote: Hero or Fool?* Gainesville: Univ. of Florida Press, 1969.

———. *Don Quixote: Hero or Fool? (Part Two).* Gainesville: Univ. of Florida Press, 1979.

———. *"Traduttori Traditori: Don Quixote* in English." *Crítica Hispánica* 1 (1979): 1–13.

Alonso, Amado. *Materia y forma en poesía.* Madrid: Gredos, 1955.

Alonso Pedraz, Martín. *Enciclopedia del idioma.* Madrid: Aguilar, 1958.

Alter, Robert. *Partial Magic: The Novel as a Self-Conscious Genre.* Berkeley: Univ. of California Press, 1975.

Amadis of Gaul, Books I and II. Trans. Edwin B. Place and Herbert C. Behm. Lexington: Univ. of Kentucky Press, 1974.

Amezcua Gómez, José. *Libros de caballerías hispánicos.* Madrid: Alcalá, 1973.

Arbó, Sebastián Juan. *Cervantes: The Man and His Time.* New York: Vanguard, 1955.

Arnheim, Rudolf. *Art and Visual Perception: A Psychology of the Creative Eye.* 1954; rpt. Berkeley: Univ. of California Press, 1974.

Ars hispaniae: Historia universal del arte hispánico. 22 vols. Madrid: Plus Ultra, 1947–77.

Astrana Marín, Luis. *Vida ejemplar y heroica de Miguel de Cervantes Saavedra.* 7 vols. Madrid: Reus 1948–58.

Aubier, Dominique. *Don Quichotte, prophète d'Israël.* Paris: Laffont, 1966.

Avalle-Arce, Juan Bautista. *Don Quijote como forma de vida.* Madrid: Castalia, 1976.

——. *La novela pastoril española.* Madrid: Occidente, 1959. 2nd ed., 1974.

——. *Nuevos deslindes cervantinos.* Barcelona: Ariel, 1976.

——, and E. C. Riley, eds. *Suma Cervantina.* London: Tamesis, 1973.

Aveleyra, Teresa. "El erotismo de don Quijote." *Nueva Revista de Filología Hispánica* 26 (1977): 468–79.

Avellaneda, Alonso Fernández de. *Don Quixote de la Mancha (Part II); Being the Spurious Continuation of Miguel de Cervantes' Part I.* Trans. Alberta W. Server and John E. Keller. Newark, Del.: Juan de la Cuesta, 1980.

Ayala, Francisco. *Cervantes y Quevedo.* Barcelona: Seix Barral, 1974.

——. *Experiencia e invención.* Madrid: Taurus, 1960.

Babelon, Jean. *Cervantes.* Paris: Nouvelle Revue Critique, 1939.

Bandera, Cesáreo. "Cervantes' *Quijote* and the Critical Illusion." *MLN* 94 (1979): 102–19.

—— . *Mímesis conflictiva: Ficción literaria y violencia en Cervantes y Calderón.* Madrid: Gredos, 1975.

Barbera, Raymond E., ed. *Cervantes: A Critical Trajectory.* Boston: Mirage, 1971.

Bardon, Maurice. *Don Quichotte en France au XVIIe et au XVIIIe siècle, 1605–1815.* 1931; rpt. New York: Franklin, 1971.

Barrett, Linton L. *Barron's Simplified Approach to Cervantes' Don Quixote.* New York: Barron's, 1971.

Barrick, Mac E. "The Form and Function of Folktales in *Don Quijote.*" *Journal of Medieval and Renaissance Studies* 6 (1976): 101–38.

Bataillon, Marcel. *Erasmo y España* (1937). Trans. Antonio Alatorre. Rev. ed. México: Fonde de Cultura Economica, 1966.

Bell, Aubrey. *Cervantes.* 1947; rpt. New York: Crowell-Collier, 1961.

——. *El renacimiento español.* Zaragoza: Ebro, 1944.

Bell, Michael. "The Structure of *Don Quixote.*" *Essays in Criticism* 18 (1968): 241–57.

Bellow, Saul, *The Adventures of Augie March.* New York: Viking, 1953.

Benardete, M. J., and Ángel Flores, eds. *The Anatomy of* Don Quixote. 1932; rpt.

Port Washington, N.Y.: Kennikat, 1969.

Bigeard, Martine. *La Folie et les fous littéraires en Espagne, 1500–1650*. Paris: Centre de Recherches Hispaniques, 1972.

Bjornson, Richard. *The Picaresque Hero in European Fiction*. 1977; rpt. Madison: Univ. of Wisconsin Press, 1979.

Booth, Wayne C. *The Rhetoric of Fiction*. Chicago: Univ. of Chicago Press, 1961.

———. "The Self-Conscious Narrator in Comic Fiction before *Tristram Shandy*." *PMLA* 67 (1952): 163–85.

Borges, Jorge Luis. *Labyrinths: Selected Stories and Other Writings*. Ed. and trans. Donald Yates and James Irby. New York: New Directions, 1964.

Bradford, Charles F. *Índice de las notas de D. Diego Clemencí en su edición de* El ingenioso hidalgo Don Quijote de la Mancha. Madrid: M. Tello, 1885.

Braudel, Fernand. *The Mediterranean and the Mediterranean World in the Age of Philip II*. Trans. Siân Reynolds. 2 vols. New York: Harper, 1972–73.

Brenan, Gerald. *The Literature of the Spanish People*. 1953; rpt. New York: Cambridge Univ. Press, 1976.

Brenner, Charles. *An Elementary Textbook of Psychoanalysis*. Garden City: Anchor-Doubleday, 1957.

Browne, James R. "Cervantes and the Galeotes Episode." *Hispania* 41 (1958): 460–64.

Buendía, Felicidad, ed. *Libros de caballerí españoles: El caballero Difar, Amadís de Gaula, Tirante el blanco*. Madrid: Aguilar, 1954

Byron, William. *Cervantes: A Biography*. New York: Doubleday, 1978.

Caballero, Justo. *Guía-Diccionario del* Quijote. México: España Errante, 1970.

Caillois, Roger. *Man, Play, and Games*. Trans. Meyer Barash. New York: Free, 1961.

Campbell, Joseph. *The Hero with a Thousand Faces*. 1949; rpt. Princeton: Princeton Univ. Press, 1968.

Campos, Juana G., and Ana Barella. *Diccionario de refranes*. Anejos del Boletín de la Real Academia Española, 30. Madrid: Real Academia Española, 1975.

Cárcer y de Sobíes, Enrique de. *Las frases del* Quijote. Barcelona: Subirana, 1916.

Caro Baroja, Julio. *Razas, pueblos y linajes*. Madrid: Revista de Occidente, 1957.

Carpenter, Rhys. *Folk Tale, Fiction and Saga in the Homeric Epics*. Berkeley: Univ. of California Press, 1946.

Casalduero, Joaquín. *Sentido y forma del* Quijote. Madrid: Insula, 1966.

Castro, Américo. *De la edad conflictiva*. Madrid: Taurus, 1961.

———. *Hacia Cervantes*. Rev. ed. Madrid: Taurus, 1967.

———. *An Idea of History: Selected Essays*. Ed. Stephen Gilman and Edmund L. King. Columbus: Ohio State Univ. Press, 1977.

———. *El pensamiento de Cervantes*. 1925; rpt. Madrid: Hernando, 1974.

———. *La realidad histórica de España*. México: Porrúa, 1954.

——. *The Structure of Spanish History.* Trans. Edmund L. King. Princeton: Princeton Univ. Press, 1954.

Catalán Menéndez, Diego. *Siete siglos de romancero.* Madrid: Gredos, 1969.

Cejador y Frauca, Julio. *La lengua de Cervantes.* 2 vols. Madrid: Ratés, 1905–06.

Chambers, Leland H. "Irony in the Final Chapter of the *Quijote.*" *Romanic Review* 61 (1970): 14–22.

Chatelet, François, and G. Marret. *Histoire des idéologies.* 3 vols. Paris: Hachette, 1978.

Chatman, Seymour. *Story and Discourse.* Ithaca: Cornell Univ. Press, 1978.

Church, Margaret. *Don Quixote: Knight of La Mancha.* New York: New York Univ. Press, 1971.

Close, Anthony. "Don Quixote's Love for Dulcinea: A Study in Cervantine Irony." *Bulletin of Hispanic Studies* 50 (1973): 237–55.

——. *The Romantic Approach to* Don Quixote. New York: Cambridge Univ. Press, 1977.

——. "Sancho Panza: Wise Fool." *Modern Language Review* 68 (1973): 344–57.

Combet, Louis. *Cervantes; ou, Les Incertitudes du désir.* Lyon: Presses Universitaires du Lyon, 1980.

Contreras, Juan de. *Historia del arte hispánico.* 5 vols. Barcelona: Salvat, 1931–49.

Cook, Albert S. *The Meaning of Fiction.* Detroit: Wayne State Univ. Press, 1960.

Cooper, J. P., ed. *The Decline of Spain and the Thirty Years War.* Vol. 4 of *The New Cambridge Modern History.* Cambridge: Cambridge Univ. Press, 1971.

Coover, Robert. *Pricksongs and Descants.* New York: Dutton, 1969.

Correas, Gonzalo. *Vocabulario de refranes y frases proverbiales* (1627). Ed. L. Combet. Bordeaux: Institut d'Etudes Ibériques, 1967.

Cortázar, Julio. "La noche boca arriba." In *Final del juego.* México: Presentes, 1956, 45–59. Available in English as "The Night Face Up." In *End of the Game and Other Stories.* Trans. Paul Blackburn. New York: Harper, 1978, 66–76.

Covarrubias, Sebastián de. *Tesoro de la lengua castellana o española* (1611). Ed. Martín de Riquer. Barcelona: Horta, 1943.

Crabb, Daniel M. *Pennant Key-Indexed Study Guide to Cervantes'* Don Quixote. Philadelphia: Educational Research Associates, 1966.

Crews, Frederick. "Literature and Psychology." In *Relations of Literary Study.* Ed. James Thorpe. New York: Modern Language Assn., 1967, 73–87.

——. *Psychoanalysis and Literary Process.* Cambridge, Mass.: Winthrop, 1970.

Crocker, Lester G. "*Don Quijote:* Epic of Frustration." *Romantic Review* 52 (1951): 178–88.

Croll, Morris W. "The Baroque Style in Prose." In his *Style, Rhetoric, and Rhythm.* Princeton: Princeton Univ. Press, 1966, 207–33.

Davies, R. Trevor. *The Golden Century of Spain.* 1937; rpt. New York: St. Martin's, 1970.

———. *Spain in Decline*. 1957; rpt. New York: St. Martin's, 1966.

Defourneau, Marcelin. *Daily Life in Spain of the Golden Age* (1952). Trans. Newton Branch. Stanford: Stanford Univ. Press, 1979.

Del Río, Ángel. *Historia de la literatura española*. 2 vols. New York: Holt, 1963–64.

DeMott, Benjamin. "The Clearer World of Fiction." *Saturday Review*, 19 Oct. 1968, 24–25, 81.

Descouzis, Paul M., *Cervantes a nueva luz*. 2 vols. Madrid: Iberoamericanas, 1966.

Deutsch, Helene. "Don Quixote and Don Quixotism." *Psychoanalytic Quarterly* 6 (1937): 215–22.

Diaz-Plaja, Fernando. *Cervantes: The Life of a Genius*. Trans. Sue M. Soterakos. New York: Scribners, 1970.

———. *La Historia de España en sus documentos*. 4 vols. Madrid: Instituto de Estudios Políticos, 1954–58.

Diaz-Plaja, Guillermo. *En torno a Cervantes*. Pamplona: EUNSA, 1977.

Diccionario de autoridades. 3 vols. 1726; rpt. Madrid: Gredos, 1969.

Domínguez Ortiz, Antonio. *El antiguo régimen: Los reyes católicos y los austrias*. Madrid: Alianza, 1974.

———. *The Golden Age of Spain*. Trans. James Casey. New York: Basic, 1971.

———. *La sociedad española en el siglo XVII*. 2 vols. 1955; rpt. Madrid: C.S.I.C., 1970.

Donoghue, Denis. *Ferocious Alphabets*. Boston: Faber, 1981.

Drake, Dana B. Don Quixote *(1894–1970): A Selective, Annotated Bibliography*. Vol. 1, Chapel Hill: Univ. of North Carolina Press, 1974; vol. 2, Miami: Universal, 1978; vol. 3, New York: Garland, 1980.

Dudley, Edward. "Don Quijote as Magus: The Rhetoric of Interpolation." *Bulletin of Hispanic Studies* 49 (1972): 355–68.

Dunn, Peter. "La cueva de Montesinos por fuera y por dentro: Estructura épica, fisonomía." *MLN* 88 (1973): 190–202.

Durán, Armando. *Estructura y técnicas de la novela sentimental y caballeresca*. Madrid: Gredos, 1973.

Durán, Manuel. *Cervantes*. New York: Twayne, 1974.

———. *La ambigüedad en el* Quijote. Xalapa, Mex.: Universidad Veracruzano, 1960.

Efron, Arthur. *Don Quixote and the Dulcineated World*. Austin: Univ. of Texas Press, 1971.

———. "Perspectivism and the Nature of Fiction: *Don Quixote* and Borges." *Thought* 50 (1975): 148–75.

Eisenberg, Daniel. "*Don Quijote* and the Romances of Chivalry: The Need for a Reexaminaton." *Hispanic Review* 41 (1973): 511–23.

———. *Romances of Chivalry in the Spanish Golden Age*. Newark, Del.: Juan de la Cuesta, 1982.

———, ed. *Espejo de príncipes y caballeros*. Madrid: Espasa-Calpe, 1975.

Eliade, Mircea. *The Sacred and the Profane.* New York: Harcourt, 1959.

Elliot, John H. *Europe Divided.* 1968; rpt. Ithaca: Cornell Univ. Press, 1982.

———. *Imperial Spain.* Rev. ed. New York: New American Library, 1977.

El Saffar, Ruth. *Distance and Control in* Don Quixote: *A Study in Narrative Technique.* Chapel Hill: Univ. of North Carolina Press, 1975.

———. *Novel to Romance: A Study of Cervantes's* Novelas ejemplares. Baltimore: Johns Hopkins Univ. Press, 1974.

Entwistle, William J. *Cervantes.* Oxford: Clarendon, 1940.

———. *European Balladry.* 1939; rpt. Oxford: Clarendon, 1969.

Estades Rodríguez, Damián. *El tesoro mágico de* Don Quijote de la Mancha. Madrid: n.p., 1976.

Fernández Álvarez, Manuel. *La sociedad española en la época del renacimiento.* Madrid: Catédra, 1974.

Fernández Gómez, Carlos. *Vocabulario de Cervantes.* Madrid: Real Academia Española, 1962.

Flores, Ángel, and M. J. Benardete, eds. *Cervantes across the Centuries.* 1947; rpt. New York: Gordian Press, 1969.

Flores, Robert M. "Cervantes at Work: The Writing of *Don Quixote,* Part I." *Journal of Hispanic Philology* 3 (1979): 135–60.

———. *The Compositors of the First and Second Madrid Editions of* Don Quixote, *Part I.* London: Modern Humanities Research Assn., 1975.

Forcione, Alban. *Cervantes, Aristotle, and the* Persiles. Princeton: Princeton Univ. Press, 1970.

Ford, Jeremiah and Ruth Lansing. *Cervantes: A Tentative Bibliography of His Works and of the Biographical and Critical Material Concerning Him.* Cambridge: Harvard Univ. Press, 1931.

Foucault, Michel. *Madness and Civilization: A History of Insanity in the Age of Reason.* Trans. Richard Howard. New York: Vintage, 1973.

———. *The Order of Things: An Archeology of the Human Sciences.* New York: Pantheon, 1970.

Fowles, John. *The French Lieutenant's Woman.* New York: Signet, 1970.

Frank, Bruno. *A Man Called Cervantes.* Trans. H. T. Lowe-Porter. New York: Viking, 1935.

Frazer, James G. *The Golden Bough* (1890). Rev. and abridged ed. New York: Macmillan, 1940.

Frazier, Harriet C. *A Babble of Ancestral Voices: Shakespeare, Cervantes, and Theobald.* Studies in English Literature, 73. The Hague: Mouton, 1974.

Freud, Sigmund. *Introductory Lectures on Psychoanalysis.* 1929; rpt. Harmondsworth, Eng.: Penguin, 1973.

Friedman, Edward H. "Chaos Restored: Authorial Control and Ambiguity in *Lazarillo de Tormes.*" *Crítica Hispánica* 3 (1981): 59–73.

Friedman, Norman. "Forms of the Plot." *Journal of General Education* 8 (1955): 245–53. Rpt. in *Theory of the Novel*. Ed. Philip Stevick. New York: Free, 1967.

Fry, Gloria M. "Symbolic Action in the Episode of the Cave of Montesinos from *Don Quijote*." *Hispania* 48 (1965): 468–74.

Frye, Northrop. "Literary Criticism." In *The Aims and Methods of Scholarship in Modern Languages and Literature*. Ed. James Thorpe. New York: Modern Language Assn., 1970.

Fuentes, Carlos. *Cervantes o la crítica de la lectura*. México: Mortiz, 1976.

Gass, William. *Fiction and the Figures of Life*. New York: Knopf, 1970.

Gella Iturriaga, José. *Flor de refranes cervantinos*. Madrid: De León, 1978.

Genette, Gérard. *Narrative Discourse: An Essay in Method*. Trans. Jane E. Lewin. Ithaca: Cornell Univ. Press, 1980.

Gilbeau, John J. "Some Folk-Motifs in *Don Quixote*." In *Studies in Comparative Literature*. Ed. Waldo F. McNeir. Baton Rouge: Louisiana State Univ. Press, 1962, 69–83.

Gilman, Stephen. *The Spain of Fernando de Rojas*. Princeton: Princeton Univ. Press, 1972.

Girard, René. *Desire, Deceit, and the Novel: Self and Other in Literary Structure*. Trans. Yvonne Freccero. Baltimore: Johns Hopkins Univ. Press, 1965.

———. *Violence and the Sacred*. Baltimore: Johns Hopkins Univ. Press, 1977.

Goggio, Emilio. "The Dual Role of Dulcinea in Cervantes's *Don Quixote de la Mancha*." *Modern Language Quarterly* 13 (1952): 285–91.

Gombrich, Ernst H. *Art and Illusion: A Study in the Psychology of Pictorial Representation*. 1960; rpt. Princeton: Princeton Univ. Press, 1969.

Grant, Michael, and J. Hazel. *Who's Who in Classical Mythology*. London: Weidenfeld & Nicholson, 1973.

Graves, Robert. *Greek Myths*. 2 vols. New York: Penguin, 1955.

Green, Otis. *Spain and the Western Tradition*. 4 vols. Madison: Univ. of Wisconsin Press, 1963–66.

Gregory, Richard. *The Intelligent Eye*. New York: McGraw-Hill, 1970.

Grismer, Raymond L. *Cervantes: A Bibliography*. Vol. 1, New York: Wilson, 1946; vol. 2, Minneapolis: Burgess-Beckwith, 1963.

Guillén, Claudio. *Literature as System: Essays toward the Theory of Literary History*. Princeton: Princeton Univ. Press, 1971.

Hagan, Oskar. *Patterns and Principles of Spanish Art*. Madison: Univ. of Wisconsin Press, 1943.

Hahn, Jürgen. "'El curioso impertinente' and Don Quixote's Symbolic Struggle against *Curiositas*." *Bulletin of Hispanic Studies* 49 (1972): 128–40.

Haley, George. "The Narrator in *Don Quixote*: Maese Pedro's Puppet Show." *MLN* 80 (1965): 145–65.

Hamilton, Earl J. *American Treasure and the Price Revolution in Spain 1501–1650.* 1934; rpt. New York: Octagon, 1970.

Hamilton, Edith. *Mythology.* 1942; rpt. New York: New American Library, 1971.

Hatzfeld, Helmut. *Estudios sobre el barroco.* Madrid: Gredos, 1973.

———. *El* Quijote *como obra de arte del lenguaje* (1927). Madrid: C.S.I.C., 1966.

Hazard, Paul. Don Quichotte: *Étude et analyse.* Paris: Mellotée, 1931.

Historia de la espiritualidad. 4 vols. Barcelona: Flores, 1969.

Hofstadter, Douglas R. *Gödel, Escher, Bach: An Eternal Golden Braid.* New York: Basic, 1979.

Hollander, Robert. "The Cave of Montesinos and the Key of Dreams." *Southern Review* 4 (1968): 756–67.

Hoy, David C. *The Critical Circle: Literature and History in Contemporary Hermeneutics.* Berkeley: Univ. of California Press, 1978.

Huarte de San Juan. *Examen de ingenios para las ciencias.* 1575; rpt. Madrid: Imprenta La Rafa, 1930. Available in English as *The Examination of Men's Wits.* Amsterdam: Theatrum Orbis Terrarum, 1969.

Hughes, Gethin. "The Cave of Montesinos: Don Quixote's Interpretation and Dulcinea's Enchantment." *Bulletin of Hispanic Studies* 54 (1977): 107–13.

Hughes, Patrick, and George Brecht. *Vicious Circles and Infinity: An Anthology of Paradoxes.* Baltimore: Penguin, 1978.

Huizinga, Johan. *Homo Ludens: A Study of the Play Element in Culture.* 1949; rpt. New York: Harper, 1970.

Hurtado y Jiménez de la Serna, Juan, and Ángel González Palencia. *Historia de la literatura española.* 6th ed. Madrid: S.A.E.T.A., 1949.

Immerwahr, Raymond. "Structural Symmetry in the Episodic Narratives of *Don Quixote,* Part I." *Comparative Literature* 10 (1958): 121–35.

Iser, Wolfgang. *The Implied Reader.* Baltimore: Johns Hopkins Univ. Press, 1974.

Iventosch, Herman. "Cervantes and Courtly Love: The Grisóstomo-Marcela Episode of *Don Quixote.*" *PMLA* 89 (1974): 64–76.

Johnson, Carroll B. *Madness and Lust: A Psychoanalytic Approach to Don Quixote.* Berkeley: Univ. of California Press, 1983.

———. "A Second Look at Dulcinea's Ass." *Hispanic Review* 43 (1975): 191–98.

Jones, Harold G. "Grisóstomo and Don Quixote: Death and Imitation." *Revista Canadiense de Estudios Hispánicos* 4 (1979): 85–92.

Jones, R. O. *A Literary History of Spain.* New York: Barnes & Noble, 1971.

Jung, Carl G. *The Archetypes and the Collective Unconscious.* 2nd ed. Princeton: Princeton Univ. Press, 1969.

———. *Man and His Symbols.* Garden City: Doubleday, 1972.

Kagan, Richard L. *Students and Society in Early Modern Spain.* Baltimore: Johns Hopkins Univ. Press, 1974.

Kamen, Henry. *The Iron Century: Social Change in Europe 1550–1660.* New York: Praeger, 1971.

——. *The Spanish Inquisition*. 1966; rpt. New York: New American Library, 1975.

Kaplan, Morton, and Robert Kloss. *The Unspoken Motive: A Guide to Psychoanalytic Literary Criticism*. New York: Free, 1973.

Kennedy, William J. *Rhetorical Norms in Renaissance Literature*. New Haven: Yale Univ. Press, 1978.

Kenniston, Hayward. *Syntax of Castilian Prose: The Sixteenth Century*. Chicago: Univ. of Chicago Press, 1937.

Ker, William P. "*Don Quixote*." In his *Collected Essays*. London: Macmillan, 1925, 2: 28–44.

Kermode, Frank. *The Sense of an Ending*. New York: Oxford Univ. Press, 1966.

Knowles, David. *The Evolution of Medieval Thought*. New York: Collier, 1962.

Koenigsberger, Helmut G., and George L. Mosse. *Europe in the Sixteenth Century*. London: Longmans, 1968.

Krauss, Werner. *Miguel de Cervantes: Leben und Werk*. Berlin: Luchterhand, 1966.

Krutch, Joseph Wood. "Miguel de Cervantes." In his *Five Masters*. New York: Cape, 1930, 61–105.

Kubler, George A., and Martin Soria. *Art and Architecture in Spain and Portugal and Their American Dominions, 1500–1800*. Baltimore: Penguin, 1959.

Lapesa, Rafael. *Historia de la lengua española*. Rev. ed. Madrid: Escelicer, 1959.

Leech, Clifford. *Shakespeare's Tragedies, and Other Studies in Seventeenth-Century Drama*. New York: Oxford Univ. Press, 1950.

Lees-Milne, James. *Baroque in Spain and Portugal, and Its Antecedents*. London: Batsford, 1960.

Leonard, Irving A. *Books of the Brave*. 1949; rpt. New York: Gordian, 1964.

Levin, Harry. *The Gates of Horn: A Study of Five French Realists*. New York: Oxford Univ. Press, 1963.

Lewis, Clive S. *The Discarded Image*. 1964; rpt. New York: Cambridge Univ. Press, 1971.

Locke, Frederick W. "El Sabio Encantador, the Author of *Don Quixote*." *Symposium* 23 (1969): 46–61.

Lollis, Cesare de. *Cervantes reazionario*. Firenze: Sansoni, 1947.

Loomis, Roger S. *Arthurian Literature in the Middle Ages*. Oxford: Clarendon, 1959.

——, and Laura H. Loomis, eds. *Medieval Romances*. New York: Random, 1956.

Lukács, Gyorgy. *The Theory of the Novel* (1920). Trans. Anna Bostock. Cambridge: MIT Press, 1971.

Lynch, John. *Spain under the Hapsburgs*. 2 vols. 2nd ed. New York: New York Univ. Press, 1981.

Mackey, Mary. "Rhetoric and Characterization in *Don Quixote*." *Hispanic Review* 42 (1974): 51–66.

Madariaga, Salvador de. Don Quixote: *An Introductory Essay in Psychology* (1926). Trans. Salvador de Madariaga and Constance de Madariaga. Rev. ed. London: Oxford Univ. Press, 1961.

——. *Spain* (1930). London: Cape, 1972.

Mades, Leonard. *The Armor and the Brocade: A Study of* Don Quijote *and* The Courtier. New York: Las Americas, 1968.

Maeztu, Ramiro de. "Don Quijote o el amor" (1926). In *Don Quijote o el amor, ensayos en simpatía*. Madrid: Anaya, 1969.

Malraux, André. *Les Noyers de l'Altenburg*. Paris: Gallimard, 1948.

Mancing, Howard. *The Chivalric World of* Don Quixote: *Style, Structure and Narrative Technique*. Columbia: Univ. of Missouri Press, 1982.

——. "The Comic Function of Chivalric Names in *Don Quijote*." *Names* 21 (1973): 200–25.

Mandel, Oscar. "The Function of the Norm in *Don Quixote*." *Modern Philology* 55 (1958): 154–63.

Maravall, José Antonio. *Estado moderno y mentalidad social*. Madrid: Revista de Occidente, 1972.

——. *Estudios de historia del pensamiento español*. 2 vols. Madrid: Cultura Hispánica, 1973–75.

——. *Las factores de la idea del progreso en el renacimiento*. Madrid: Real Academia de la Historia, 1963.

——. *Utopía y contrautopía en el* Quijote. Santiago de Compostela: Pico Sacro, 1976.

Marín, Diego, and Ángel Del Río. *Breve historia de la literatura española*. New York: Holt, 1966.

Márquez Villanueva, Francisco. *Fuentes literarias cervantinas*. Madrid: Gredos, 1973.

——. *Personajes y temas del* Quijote. Madrid: Taurus, 1975.

Martínez Bonati, Félix. "Cervantes y las regiones de la imaginación." *Dispositio* 2 (1977): 28–53.

——. "El *Quijote*: Juego y significación." *Dispositio* 3 (1978): 315–36.

——. "La unidad del *Quijote*." *Dispositio* 2 (1977): 118–39.

Martínez Kleiser, Luis. *Refranero general ideológico español*. Madrid: Real Academia Española, 1953.

Martínez Ruiz, José [Azorín, pseud.] *La ruta de Don Quijote*. 1905; rpt. Buenos Aires: Losada, 1970.

McGaha, Michael D., ed. *Cervantes and the Renaissance*. Easton, Pa.: Juan de la Cuesta, 1980.

McGrady, Donald. "The *Sospiros* of Sancho's Donkey." *MLN* 88 (1973): 335–37.

McKendrick, Malveena. *Cervantes*. Boston: Little, Brown, 1980.

Mendelhoff, Henry. "The Maritornes Episode: A Cervantine Bedroom Farce." *Romance Notes* 16 (1975): 753–59.

Menéndez Pidal, Ramón. "Un aspecto en la elaboración del *Quijote*" (1920). In his *De Cervantes y de Lope de Vega*. Buenos Aires: Espasa-Calpe, 1948.

———. *La Chanson de Roland y el neotradicionalismo*. Madrid: Espasa-Calpe, 1959.

———. *Romancero hispánico*. 2 vols. Madrid: Espasa-Calpe, 1953.

Menéndez y Pelayo, Marcelino. *Orígines de la novela*. 3 vols. 1905; rpt. Buenos Aires: Espasa-Calpe, 1946.

Molho, Maurice. *Cervantes: Raíces folklóricas*. Madrid: Gredos, 1976.

Monas, Sidney. "The Lion in the Cage: The Quixote of Reality." *Massachusetts Review* 1 (1959): 156–75.

Mondadori, Arnoldo, ed. *Cervantes: His Life, His Times, His Works*. Trans. Salvator Attanasio and selections by Thomas G. Bergin. New York: American Heritage, 1970.

Montaigne, Miguel de. "Of Cannibals." In *The Complete Works of Montaigne*. Trans. Donald M. Frame. London: Hamilton, n.d.

Morales Oliver, Luis. *Sinopsis de* Don Quijote. Madrid: Fundación Universitaria Española, 1977.

Morón Arroyo, Ciriaco. *Nuevas meditaciones del* Quijote. Madrid: Gredos, 1976.

Murillo, Luis A. *The Golden Dial: Temporal Configurations in* Don Quijote. Oxford: Dolphin, 1975.

Navarro y Ledesma, Francisco. *Cervantes, the Man and the Genius* (1919). Trans. Don Bliss and Gabriela Bliss. New York: Charterhouse, 1973.

Nelson, Lowry, ed. *Cervantes: A Collection of Critical Essays*. Englewood Cliffs, N.J.: Prentice-Hall, 1969.

Nepaulsingh, Colbert I. "Cervantes, *Don Quijote*: The Unity of Action." *Revista Canadiense de Estudios Hispánicos* 2 (1978): 239–57.

Oelschläger, Victor. "Sancho's Zest for Quest." *Hispania* 35 (1952): 18–24.

Orozco Díaz, Emilio. *Manierismo y barroco*. Salamanca: Anaya, 1970.

Ortega y Gasset, José. *Meditations on Quixote* (1914). Trans. Evelyn Rugg and Diego Marín. New York: Norton, 1961.

Osterc, Ludovik. *El pensamiento social y político del* Quijote. México: Andrea, 1963.

Pabst, Walter. *Novellentheorie und Novellendichtung: Zur Geschichte Ihrer Antinomie in den romanischen Literaturen*. 1953; rpt. Heidelberg: Winter, 1967.

Palmer, Donald D. "Unamuno, Freud and the Case of Alonso Quijano." *Hispania* 54 (1971): 243–49.

Parker, Alexander A. *Literature and the Delinquent: The Picaresque Novel in Spain and Europe 1599–1753*. Edinburgh: Edinburgh Univ. Press, 1967.

Patch, Howard R. *The Other World according to Descriptions in Medieval Literature*. 1950; rpt. New York: Octagon, 1970.

Payne, Stanley. *A History of Spain and Portugal.* Madison: Univ. of Wisconsin Press, 1973.

Percas de Ponseti, Helena. *Cervantes y su concepto del arte.* 2 vols. Madrid: Gredos, 1975.

Pfandl, Ludwig. *Cultura y costumbres del pueblo español de los siglos XVI y XVII.* 1929; rpt. Barcelona: Araluce, 1959.

Pico della Mirandola, Giovanni. "On the Dignity of Man." In his *On the Dignity of Man.* Trans. Charles G. Wallis. Indianapolis: Bobbs-Merrill, 1965.

Pike, Ruth. *Aristocrats and Traders: Sevillian Society in the Sixteenth Century.* Ithaca: Cornell Univ. Press, 1972.

Pinta Llorente, Miguel de la. *La Inquisición española y los problemas de la cultura y de la intolerancia.* 2 vols. Madrid: Cultura Hispánica, 1953–58.

Poggioli, Renato. *The Oaten Flute: Essays on Pastoral Poetry and the Pastoral Ideal.* Cambridge: Harvard Univ. Press, 1975.

Predmore, Richard. *Cervantes.* London: Thames & Hudson; New York: Dodd, 1973.

——. *An Index to* Don Quijote: *Including Proper Names and Notable Matters.* New Brunswick: Rutgers Univ. Press, 1938.

——. *The World of Don Quixote.* Cambridge: Harvard Univ. Press, 1967.

Read, Malcolm K. "Man against Language: A Linguistic Perspective on the Theme of Alienation in the *Libro de buen amor.*" *MLN* 96 (1981): 237–60.

Reed, Walter. *An Exemplary History of the Novel: The Quixotic versus the Picaresque.* Chicago: Univ. of Chicago Press, 1981.

Riley, E. C. *Cervantes's Theory of the Novel.* Oxford: Clarendon, 1962.

——. "Metamorphosis, Myth and Dream in the Cave of Montesinos." In *Essays on Narrative Fiction in the Iberian Peninsula in Honour of Frank Pierce.* Ed. Robert B. Tate. Oxford: Dolphin, 1982, 105–19.

——. "Symbolism in *Don Quixote,* Part II, Chapter 73." *Journal of Hispanic Philology* 3 (1979): 161–74.

——. "Three Versions of *Don Quixote.*" *Modern Language Review* 68 (1973): 807–19.

——. "Who's Who in *Don Quixote?* or, An Approach to the Problem of Identity." *MLN* 81 (1961): 113–30.

Riquer, Martín de. *Aproximación al* Quijote. 1960; rpt. Barcelona: Teide, 1970.

——. *Caballeros andantes españoles.* Colección Austral 1397. Madrid: Espasa-Calpe, 1967.

Rius, Leopoldo. *Bibliografía crítica de las obras de Miguel de Cervantes Saavedra.* 1895–1904; rpt. New York: Franklin, 1970.

Rivers, Elias L. "On the Prefatory Pages of *Don Quijote.*" *MLN* 75 (1960): 214–21.

——. "Talking and Writing in *Don Quixote.*" *Thought* 51 (1976): 296–305.

Robert, Marthe. *The Old and the New: From Quixote to Kafka.* Trans. Carol Crossman. Berkeley: Univ. of California Press, 1977.

———. *Roman des origines et origines du roman.* Paris: Grasset, 1972. Available in English as *Origins of the Novel.* Trans. Sacha Rabinowitz. Bloomington: Indiana Univ. Press, 1980.

Rodríguez Marín, Francisco. *Más de 21,000 refranes castellanos no contenidos en la copiosa colección del Maestro G. Correas.* Madrid: Tip. de la *Revista de Archivos, Bibliotecas y Museos,* 1926, with supplements in 1930, 1936, 1941.

Rosales, Luis. *Cervantes y la libertad.* Madrid: Valera, 1960.

Rosen, Gerald. *The Carmen Miranda Memorial Flagpole.* New York: Avon, 1979.

Rosenblat, Ángel. *La lengua del* Quijote. Madrid: Gredos, 1971.

Roy, Gregor, and Ralph A. Ronald. *Monarch Notes on Cervantes'* Don Quixote. New York: Simon, 1965.

Ruiz-Fornells, Enrique. *Las concordancias de* El ingenioso hidalgo Don Quijote de la Mancha. Madrid: Cultura Hispánica, 1976–80. Vols. 1 and 2.

Rumeau de Armas, Antonio. *Historia de la censura literaria gubernativa en España.* Madrid: Aguilar, 1940.

Russell, Bertrand. "Descartes." In his *A History of Western Philosophy.* New York: Simon, 1945, 557–68.

Russell, Peter E. "*Don Quixote* as a Funny Book." *Modern Language Review* 64 (1969): 312–26.

Salinas, Pedro. *Reality and the Poet in Spanish Poetry.* Trans. Edith Helman. Baltimore: Johns Hopkins Univ. Press, 1966.

Sbarbi y Osuna, José M. *El refranero general español.* 10 vols. Madrid: Fuentenebro, 1874–78.

Schevill, Rodolfo. *Cervantes* (1919). Rpt. New York: Ungar, 1966.

Schklovsky, Viktor. "Comment est fait Don Quichotte." In his *Sur la théorie de la prose* (1929). Trans. Guy Verret. Lausanne: Age d'Homme, 1973.

Scholes, Robert, and Robert Kellogg. *The Nature of Narrative.* New York: Oxford Univ. Press, 1966.

Schopenhauer, Arthur. *The World as Will and Representation* (1819). Trans. E. F. J. Payne. 2 vols. New York: Dover, 1969.

Schutz, Alfred. "*Don Quixote* and the Problem of Reality." In his *Collected Papers.* The Hague: Nijhoff, 1964, 2: 135–58.

Selig, Karl-Ludwig. "The Battle of the Sheep (*Don Quixote* I, xviii)." *Revista Hispanica Moderna* 38 (1974–75): 73–77.

Serrano Plaja, Arturo. "*Magic*" Realism in Cervantes: Don Quixote as Seen through Tom Sawyer and The Idiot. Trans. Robert Rudder. Berkeley: Univ. of California Press, 1970.

Shumaker, Wayne. *The Occult Sciences in the Renaissance.* 1972; rpt. Berkeley: Univ. of California Press, 1979.

Sieber, Harry. "On Juan Huarte de San Juan and Anselmo's *locura* in 'El curioso impertinente.'" *Révista Hispánica Moderna* 36 (1970): 1–8.

———. *The Picaresque.* Critical Idiom Series. London: Methuen, 1977.

Siles Artés, José. *El arte de la novela pastoril*. Valencia: Albatros, 1972.

Simón Díaz, José. *Bibliografía de la literatura hispánica*. Madrid: C.S.I.C., 1970, 8: 3–442.

Sinnigen, John. "Themes and Structures in the 'Bodas de Camacho.'" *MLN* 84 (1969): 157–70.

Skura, Meredith A. *Literary Uses of the Psychoanalytic Process*. New Haven: Yale Univ. Press, 1981.

Smith, Bradley. *Spain: A History in Art*. New York: Simon, 1966.

Smullyan, Raymond. *What Is the Name of This Book?* Englewood Cliffs, N.J.: Prentice-Hall, 1978.

Sobré, J. M. "Don Quixote, the Hero Upside-Down." *Hispanic Review* 44 (1976): 127–41.

Solana, Marcial. *Historia de la filosofía española*. 3 vols. Madrid: Real Academia de Ciencias Exactas, Físicas y Naturales, 1941.

Soons, C. Alan. "Cide Hamete Benengeli: His Significance for *Don Quixote*." *Modern Language Review* 54 (1959): 351–57.

Spitzer, Leo. "Linguistic Perspectivism in the *Don Quijote*." In his *Linguistics and Literary History*. Princeton: Princeton Univ. Press, 1948.

Stagg, Geoffrey. "El sabio Cide Hamete Benengeli." *Bulletin of Hispanic Studies* 33 (1956): 218–25.

Sterne, Laurence. *The Life and Opinions of Tristram Shandy*. Ed. Ian Watt. Boston: Houghton, 1965.

Stevick, Philip. *Theory of the Novel*. New York: Free, 1967.

Sturman, Marianne. *Cliffs Notes on Cervantes' Don Quixote*. Lincoln, Neb.: Cliffs Notes, 1964.

Suñé Benages, Juan. *Fraseología de Cervantes*. Barcelona: Lux, 1929.

Sypher, Wylie. *Four Stages of Renaissance Style: Transformations in Art and Literature, 1400–1700*. New York: Doubleday, 1955.

Tatlock, Robert T., et al. *Spanish Art: An Introductory Review of Architecture, Painting, Sculpture, Textiles, Ceramics, Woodwork, Metalwork*. London: Burlington Magazine, 1927.

Terrero, José. "Las rutas de las tres salidas de Don Quijote de la Mancha." *Anales Cervantinos* 8 (1959–60): 1–49.

Thomas, Henry. *Spanish and Portuguese Romances of Chivalry*. Cambridge: Cambridge Univ. Press, 1920.

Thompson, I. A. *War and Government in Habsburg Spain*. London: Athlone, 1976.

Thorburn, David. "Fiction and Imagination in *Don Quixote*." *Partisan Review* 42 (1975): 431–43.

Todorov, Tsvetan. *Grammaire du Décaméron*. The Hague: Mouton, 1969.

Togeby, Knud. *La estructura del Quijote*. Publicaciones de la Universidad de Sevilla, 56. Trans. Antonio Rodríguez Almodóvar. Seville: Univ. de Seville, 1977.

Torbert, Eugene C. *Cervantes' Place-Names: A Lexicon*. Metuchen, N.J.: Scarecrow, 1978.

Torrente Ballester, Gonzalo. *El* Quijote *como juego*. Madrid: Guadarrama, 1975.

Trend, John B. *The Civilization of Spain*. 1944; rpt. New York: Oxford Univ. Press, 1967.

Trilling, Lionel. *Beyond Culture*. New York: Viking, 1955.

————. "Manners, Morals, and the Novel." In his *The Liberal Imagination: Essays on Literature and Society*. 1950; rpt. New York: Doubleday, 1957, 199–215.

Tripp, Edward. *Crowell's Handbook of Classical Mythology*. New York: Crowell, 1970.

Turkevich, Ludmilla B. *Cervantes in Russia*. Princeton: Princeton Univ. Press, 1950.

Ubieto Arteta, Antonio, et al. *Introducción a la historia de España*. 12th ed. Barcelona: Teide, 1979.

Unamuno y Jugo, Miguel de. *Our Lord Don Quixote: The Life of Don Quixote and Sancho, with Related Essays* (1905). Trans. Anthony Kerrigan. Princeton: Princeton Univ. Press, 1976.

Van Doren, Mark. *Don Quixote's Profession*. New York: Columbia Univ. Press, 1958.

Van Ghent, Dorothy. "On *Don Quixote*." In her *The English Novel*. 1953; rpt. New York: Harper, 1961, 9–19.

Varo, Carlos. *Génesis y evolución del* Quijote. Madrid: Alcalá, 1968.

Vásquez de Prada, Valentín. 3 vols. *Historia económica y social de España*. Madrid: Cajas de Ahorros, 1973.

Vilanova Andreu, Antonio. *Erasmo y Cervantes*. Publications of the Instituto Miguel de Cervantes de Filología Hispánica, vol. 10. Barcelona: C.S.I.C., 1949.

Vilar, Pierre. *Spain: A Brief History*. Trans. Brian Tate. 2nd ed. New York: Pergamon, 1977.

Wardropper, Bruce. "The Pertinence of 'El curioso impertinente.'" *PMLA* 62 (1957): 587–600.

Warnke, Frank. *Versions of the Baroque: European Literature in the Seventeenth Century*. New Haven: Yale Univ. Press, 1972.

Wasserman, Dale. *Man of La Mancha*. 1966; rpt. New York: Dell, 1969.

Watt, Ian. *The Rise of the Novel*. Berkeley: Univ. of California Press, 1962.

Weiger, John G. *The Individuated Self: Cervantes and the Emergence of the Individual*. Athens: Ohio Univ. Press, 1979.

Wellek, René. "The Concept of Baroque in Literary Scholarship." In his *Concepts of Criticism*. New Haven: Yale Univ. Press, 1963, 69–127.

Welsh, Alexander. *Reflections on the Hero as Quixote*. Princeton: Princeton Univ. Press, 1981.

Wernham, R. B., ed. *Counter-Reformation and Price Revolution 1559–1610*. Vol. 3 of *The New Cambridge Modern History*. Cambridge: Cambridge Univ. Press, 1968.

White, Hayden. "The Historical Text as Literary Artifact." In his *Tropics of Discourse*. Baltimore: Johns Hopkins Univ. Press, 1978, 81–100.

——. *Metahistory*. Baltimore: Johns Hopkins Univ. Press, 1973.

Williamson, Edwin. "The Conflict between Author and Protagonist in Quevedo's *Buscón*." *Journal of Hispanic Philology* 2 (1977): 45–60.

Willis, Raymond S. *The Phantom Chapters of the* Quijote. New York: Hispanic Institute, 1953.

——. "Sancho Panza: Prototype for the Modern Novel." *Hispanic Review* 37 (1969): 207–27.

ICONOGRAPHY, SLIDES, AND FILMS

The Adventures of Don Quixote. British Broadcasting Corporation, 1972. Color videotape.

Ashbee, Henry S. *An Iconography of* Don Quixote, *1605–1895*. London: Bibliographical Society, 1895.

Don Quijote de la Mancha. Barcelona: Ancora, 1956. Filmstrips, sound tapes, and guidebook. Available from Gessler Publishing, New York.

Don Quijote de la Mancha. Gerona, Spain: Audifilm, 1972. Slides and sound cassettes.

Don Quijote de la Mancha. Madrid: Radio Nacional de España, 1974. Filmstrips and sound cassettes. Available from Regents Publishing, New York, and Gessler Publishing, New York.

Don Quijote de la Mancha by Miguel de Cervantes Saavedra. Madrid: C.I.F.E.S.A., 1962. Filmstrips, sound cassettes, and study manuals. Distributed by Educational Audio-Visual, Pleasantville, N.Y.

Don Quixote. Great Classics of Literature. Chicago: Encyclopaedia Britannica, 1959. Filmstrip.

Galbaldon, Roberto, dir. *Don Quijote cabalga de nuevo*. Also released as *Un Quijote sin mancha*. With Cantinflas. Madrid: Filmoteca Nacional de España, 1972. Scenario published as *Don Quijote cabalga de nuevo*. Madrid: Fragua, 1973.

Gil, Rafael, dir. *Don Quijote de la Mancha*. With Rafael Rivellas. Mount Vernon, N.Y.: Macmillan Films, 1948. English subtitles.

Givanel y Mas, Joan. *Historia gráfica de Cervantes y del* Quijote. Madrid: Plus-Ultra, 1946.

Goicoechea Arrondo, Eusebio. *La Mancha, tierra de Don Quijote*. Madrid: 1978. Slides. Distributed by Fernando Ortiz, New York.

Heinrich, Manuel. *Iconografia de las ediciones del* Quijote *de Miguel de Cervantes Saavedra*. Barcelona: Heinrich y Cía., 1905.

Helpmann, Robert, dir. *Don Quixote*. Film of the ballet *Don Quixote*. With Rudolf Nureyev. New York: Walter Reade, 1973. Four excerpts (Basilio, Market

Place in Barcelona, Camacho's Wedding, and A Tavern Celebration). Also available from Univ. of Illinois, Urbana.

Herreros, Enrique. *Principales aventuras de Don Quijote.* 1964; rpt. Madrid: Nacional, 1974.

Hiller, Arthur, dir. *Man of La Mancha.* With Peter O'Toole and Sophia Loren. United Artists, 1972. Also available from Modern Sound Pictures, Omaha, Neb.

Kozintsev, Grigori, dir. *Don Quixote.* With Nikolai Cherkssov. Mount Vernon, N.Y.: Macmillan Films, 1957.

La Mancha, tierras de Don Quijote. Barcelona: Ancora, n.d. Slides. Distributed by Continental Book, New York.

Pabst, G. W., dir. *Don Quixote.* With Fyodor Chaliapin. Dover-Foxcroft, Me.: Classic Film Museum, 1932. English subtitles.

Roger-Marx, Claude. *Don Quichotte de Cervantes par cinquante artistes du XVIIe siècle à nos jours.* Paris: Peintures du Livre, 1968.

Sánchez, Alberto. *Literatura española en imágenes.* Madrid: Muralla, 1973. Slides.

RECORDINGS

Albeniz, Isaac. *Iberia.* With Aldo Ciccolini (piano). Seraphim SIB 6091. Also available with Alicia de Larrocha on London CSA 2235. The orchestral suite is available on Angel DS 37878, Nonesuch 71189, and London STS-15374.

——. *Suite Espanola.* With José Iturbi (guitar) and G. Granados y Campiña (piano). Angel S-35628. Also available on London 6581.

Alonso, Amado. *Don Quijote.* West Medford, Mass.: Vocarium Records, 1956.

Canas, Juan. *Don Quijote de la Mancha.* Barcelona: Juventud, 1971. Sound cassettes. Distributed by National Library Service, Washington, D.C.

Don Quixote as a Funny Book. Toronto: CBC Learning Systems, 1975. Cassette. Only available in Canada.

Don Quixote of La Mancha. Great Moments in Literature. North Hollywood, Cal.: DAK Industries, 1977. Cassette. Excerpts in English and discussion.

Falla, Manuel de. *El retablo de Maese Pedro.* London Sinfonica. Argo ARG-921PSI. Musical Heritage Society MH1746.

Florit, Eugenio. *Lectura de* Don Quixote. SMC Pro Arte SMC-1031. Reading of four episodes. Distributed by the Spanish Music Center, New York.

Giamatti, A. Bartlett. *Don Quixote.* Deland, Fla.: Everett/Edwards, 1973. Cassette.

Gómez, Fernando Fernán, and Agustín González. *Diálogos de Don Quijote y Sancho.* Madrid: Aguilar, 1966. Available from Continental Book, New York (AG30).

Lightfoot, Gordon. *Don Quixote.* Reprise MS2056, 1972.

Massenet, Jules E. M. *Don Quichotte.* Orchestre de la Suisse Romande. London

13134. Also available as a cassette and in a two-record set from Everest Records, Los Angeles.

Miguel de Cervantes y su tiempo. Grandes Figuras de la Historia. Madrid: Dial Discos, 1979. Cassette. Distributed by the Ministry of Culture, Madrid.

The Pleasures of Cervantes (Vocal and Instrumental Music of Spain of the 15th, 16th, and 17th Centuries). Nonesuch H71116.

Rodríguez, Jorge Juan. *Don Quijote de la Mancha.* Pleasantville, N.Y.: Educational Audio Visual, 1958. Folkways FL9930. Readings of excerpts. An English version read by Lester G. Crocker (FL9866) is also available.

Starkie, Walter. *Don Quixote.* Mentor Records 12-A1. Starkie reads from his own translation.

Strauss, Richard. *Don Quixote.* Cond. Fritz Reiner, Chicago Symphony Orchestra. RCA AGL 1-3367. Other recordings of Strauss's *Don Quixote* are available on Philips (Concertgebouw Orchestra, cond. Bernard Haitink; 9500.40), Odyssey (Cleveland Orchestra, cond. George Szell; Y-32224), Columbia (New York Philharmonic, cond. Leonard Bernstein; MG-33707), Angel (Berlin Philharmonic, cond. Herbert von Karajan; RL-32106), Deutsche Grammaphon (Berlin Philharmonic, cond. Herbert von Karajan; 2535-195), and Seraphim (Dresden State Orchestra, cond. Rudolf Kempe; S-60363).

Telemann, Georg Philipp. *Don Quixote Suite.* Academy of St. Martin-in-the-Fields Orchestra. Argo ZRG-836. Also available on Decca and London.

Varios, Don Quijote de la Mancha. Madrid: Discos CBS, 1979. Cassette.

Wasserman, Dale. *Man of La Mancha.* Original Broadway cast. MCA 2018.

INDEX

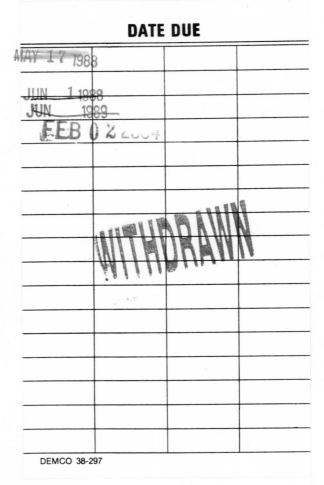